Studies in Social Policy and Welfare XXV

PUBLIC HOUSING AND PRIVATE PROPERTY

1970–1984

Studies in Social Policy and Welfare

PUBLIC HOUSING AND PRIVATE PROPERTY

1970–1984

Stephanie Cooper

Gower

Published by

Gower Publishing Company Limited
Gower House, Croft Road
Aldershot, Hants GU11 3HR, England

Gower Publishing Company
Old Post Road, Brookfield
Vermont 05036, U.S.A.

Printed and bound in Great Britain at The University Press, Cambridge

British Library Cataloguing in Publication Data

Cooper, Stephanie
   Public housing and private property: 1970–1984.
   — (Studies in social policy and welfare; 25)
   1. Housing policy — Great Britain — History —
   20th century
   I. Title   II. Series
   363.5'56'0941   HD7333.A3

Contents

Tables and Figure

Tables

Figure

Preface

Coincidentally the period covered by this book spans my working life in housing. Although it was not my intention when I started writing to change occupation, this change of direction presented an opportunity to think about public housing more objectively. After 14 years' close involvement in housing, as a manager and lecturer, I had a personal commitment to the public sector that even years of exposure to its shortcomings had not shaken.

In the course of researching this study, which was first prepared as a PhD thesis for London University, I have had occasion to recall some of the events of the seventies and have clear recollections of the determination with which the Clay Cross Councillors fought the Housing Finance Act 1972. As the campaign against the abolition of the GLC shows, things are much more sophisticated now; I doubt that back in 1972 anyone would have thought of bringing in Boase Massimi Pollitt or indeed considered it necessary to do so, so sure were they of the rightness of their cause and of the support of their constituents. While many of us greeted the 1972 legislation with a degree of (youthful?) incredulity we are no longer surprised even at the handouts for housing association tenants who buy under the 1984 Housing and Building Control Act. This may in part be due to a profound sense of disappointment that the opportunity for reforming housing finance was lost in the seventies; however, I remain optimistic and hope for a measure of fairness in the eighties.

I owe an enormous debt of gratitude to Professor Della Nevitt who has advised and encouraged me throughout and from whose friendship and scholarship I have greatly benefited; and to my husband, Jeff, who has helped in more ways than it is possible to say and has put up with my almost single-minded determination to complete this project during the past five years. I would also like to thank Helen Abbott who has typed several manuscripts with great patience and efficiency. Finally, the responsibility for any errors, omissions and vagaries of interpretation of data which I may have made remain mine alone.

Stephanie Cooper   *Marylebone, January 1985*

Abbreviations

ADP	Approved Development Programme
BA	Base amount
CIPFA	Chartered Institute of Public Finance and Accountancy
DHSS	Department of Health and Social Security
DOE	Department of the Environment
EEC	European Economic Community
FIS	Family income supplement
GDP	Gross Domestic Product
GLC	Greater London Council
GNI	General needs index
GRE	Grant Related Expenditure
GRF	Grant redemption fund
HAG	Housing association grant
HCD	Housing cost differential
HCY	Housing cost yardstick
HIP	Housing investment programme
HPR	Housing Policy Review
HRA	Housing Revenue Account
IMF	International Monetary Fund
LCD	Local contribution differential
MHLG	Ministry of Housing and Local Government
MIRAS	Mortgage interest relief at source
NALGO	National and Local Government Officers' Association
NEC	National Executive Committee, Labour Party
NIT	Negative Income Tax
PESC	Public Expenditure Survey Committee
PSBR	Public Sector Borrowing Requirement
RDG	Revenue deficit grant
RFC	Rate fund contribution
RSG	Rate Support Grant
SDP	Social Democratic Party

1 Perspectives on Public Housing

Irrespective of whether George Orwell's account of life in *Nineteen Eighty-Four* was modelled on totalitarian regimes of the 1940s or whether it was his vision of the future it is not only a compelling story of a society where the state keeps a check on every action, word or thought and of one individual's revolt against its rules, but it raises questions about freedom and choice, justice and fairness and individuals' rights and collective provision that are of universal concern. These issues have been at the centre of debates about public policy in Britain and other countries throughout the post-war period but have an added significance at times of economic recession. When Orwell published his book, just a few years after the end of the war, the Labour government were pledging themselves to provide public rented housing for all, to ensure that accommodation was allocated according to need and not ability to pay. Despite the economic crisis which forced them to abandon their ambitious building programme they kept faith with their socialist principles and with the Keynesian belief that full employment and economic growth could be achieved without inflation.

Fundamental questions about social values and social priorities are raised during periods of economic recession when it is no longer possible to go on spending on new projects without cutting back elsewhere: an experience consistent with Anthony Crosland's view that the capacity of a welfare state is limited by the government's ability to sustain economic growth. From 1970 onwards governments endeavoured to come to terms with recession and low rates of economic growth. In tackling these problems successive governments raised questions about public housing policy and in particular the division of housing costs between the individual and the state, the provision of public housing and the power of municipal landlords and instituted piecemeal reforms which inadvertently as well as consciously redistributed housing assistance and residential property and contributed to the restructuring of the welfare state.

In *Nineteen Eighty-Four* Winston Smith worked in the Records

Department of the Ministry of Truth, rewriting history. On one occasion in the course of adjusting the Ministry of Plenty's figures he reflected that his work 'was not even forgery. It was merely the substitution of one piece of nonsense for another. Most of the material that you were dealing with had no connexion with anything in the real world, not even the kind of connexion that is contained in a direct lie. Statistics were just as much a fantasy in their original version as in their rectified version' (Orwell 1954: 36). Those who have read the Government's Public Expenditure Plans published between 1970 and 1984 might be forgiven for coming to the same conclusion. It is difficult to discern either intentions or outcome: constant prices which facilitate comparison between one year and another because they allow for inflation were replaced by cash figures; capital and current expenditure were included in the same programme although this resulted in double counting; tax concessions were excluded although they were undeniably a form of public spending; some items like housing benefits were transferred from one account to another, others like option mortgages disappeared without trace. Even the geographical areas covered were subject to change; whereas figures were once provided for Great Britain, in later years there were separate tables for England, Scotland and Wales. Figures which appeared as firm plans were later written down until this became too frequent an occurrence and a decision was taken to provide no detailed breakdown of expenditure for future years.

Public Expenditure Plans

Governments throughout the seventies and eighties have been preoccupied with controlling the level of public expenditure and apart from two brief periods there has been a surprising consistency in their approach. The adoption of monetarist economic strategies brought housing spending under close scrutiny and it became a prime target for cuts, particularly after 1979. Housing's share of public expenditure has been falling since 1975/6 (apart from an increase during 1979/80) and over the period between 1970/1 and 1983/4 collapsed from 8 per cent to just over 2 per cent (Tables 1.1 and 1.2).

Although the Heath government achieved their planned reductions of housing expenditure in 1971/2 and 1972/3, spending subsequently increased so that during their period in office, housing's share of public expenditure rose marginally from 8.0 to 8.5 per cent. After only 18 months in office rising unemployment and rising earnings led the government to abandon their monetarist approach to the control of inflation in favour of a more interventionist strategy. They introduced a statutory incomes policy and tried spending their way out of the recession by boosting expenditure by local authorities and nationalised industries. Although initially rises in expenditure on the housing programme were not as substantial as elsewhere, when cuts were subsequently imposed in December 1973 as a result of a balance of payments crisis and the conditions imposed in return for an International Monetary Fund (IMF) loan, housing was the only major programme to be specifically exempt (Lansley and Fiegehen 1974; Craven 1975).

After 1974 this option no longer existed. The new Labour government had to face rising inflation and a worsening economic crisis with an unprecedented balance of payments deficit, increasing oil prices, the three-day week and a pay dispute in the National Health Service (Wilson 1979). They had committed themselves to devote more of the nation's resources to housing than at any time in the past: house price inflation followed by the collapse of private housing in 1973 had convinced Labour that further building by local authorities was required but in addition they had to allow for the costs of rent control. The rent freeze was an important element in the government's plan for controlling inflation and an integral part of the social contract made with the unions. However, while housing's share of public expenditure rose to 10.2 per cent in 1974/75, after one year it fell to 8.9 per cent and was below 8 per cent in 1978/79. Although Labour managed to avoid a major disruption to the social services, cuts were made in virtually all social programmes, including housing, between 1975 and 1979 in an attempt to reverse the worsening economic position and meet the conditions attached to another IMF loan in 1976. Even so Labour was unable to revive the flagging economy; economic growth was still slow, unemployment high and inflation only slightly lower than when they took office (Coates 1980). Nevertheless Chancellor Denis Healey's budgets were less deflationary in 1977 and 1978 and this accounts for the slight increase in housing's share of expenditure during the first year of the Conservative administration through meeting commitments entered into earlier.

Under the Conservative governments of 1979 and 1983 housing declined from a major to a minor service. *The Government's Expenditure Plans 1980–81 to 1983–84* (Cmnd 7841, 1980) provided for housing to bear 75 per cent of the planned reductions in public expenditure, resulting in a 48 per cent reduction or a fall from £5,372 million in 1979/80 to £2,790 million by 1983/4, as it was felt that any shortfall in production would be met by the private sector. As public expenditure on housing fell in line with these plans housing's share was reduced from 5.8 per cent in 1979/80 to 2.3 per cent in 1983/4 (although the sharp fall in 1983/4 is partly attributable to the costs of housing benefit being transferred to the social security programme). These cuts were sustained while public expenditure's share of GDP increased from 40 to 43 per cent (Parliamentary Debates (Commons) 1984, vol. 64, col. 446).

Table 1.1 Composition of public expenditure by programme 1970/1 to 1978/9 (United Kingdom)

	£ million at 1974 survey prices (percentages)				£ million at 1979 survey prices (percentages)				
	1970/1	1971/2	1972/3	1973/4	1974/5	1975/6	1976/7	1977/8	1978/9
Defence	3 683 (12.9)	3 747 (12.81)	3 652 (11.88)	3 604 (11.17)	7 462 (10.62)	7 830 (11.00)	7 721 (11.26)	7 550 (11.51)	7 502 (10.85)
Overseas services	464 (1.62)	499 (1.71)	600 (1.95)	653 (2.02)	1 314 (1.87)	1 127 (1.58)	1 345 (1.96)	1 836 (2.80)	1 962 (2.84)
Commerce and industry	4 198 (14.67)	4 120 (14.09)	4 245 (13.81)	4 643 (14.39)	8 884 (12.64)	8 036 (11.29)	5 651 (8.24)	3 303 (5.03)	4 793 (6.93)
Transport	1 409 (4.93)	1 370 (4.68)	1 449 (4.71)	1 577 (4.89)	3 820 (5.44)	3 913 (5.50)	3 505 (5.11)	3 022 (4.61)	2 975 (4.30)
Housing	2 297 (8.03)	1 994 (6.82)	2 047 (6.66)	2 740 (8.49)	7 154 (10.18)	6 299 (8.85)	6 262 (9.13)	5 519 (8.41)	5 256 (7.60)
Other environmental services	1 344 (4.70)	1 368 (4.68)	1 458 (4.74)	1 522 (4.72)	3 541 (5.04)	3 702 (5.20)	3 343 (4.87)	3 262 (4.97)	3 330 (4.81)
Law, order and protective services	852 (2.98)	918 (3.14)	948 (3.08)	1 017 (3.15)	2 172 (3.09)	2 311 (3.25)	2 352 (3.43)	2 285 (3.48)	2 329 (3.37)
Education, libraries, science and arts	3 862 (13.50)	4 136 (14.14)	4 427 (14.40)	4 459 (13.82)	9 584 (13.64)	9 757 (13.71)	9 722 (14.17)	9 363 (14.27)	9 516 (13.76)
Health and personal social services	3 236 (11.31)	3 365 (11.50)	3 588 (11.67)	3 787 (11.74)	8 328 (11.85)	8 620 (12.11)	8 716 (12.71)	8 777 (13.38)	9 023 (13.05)
Social security	5 747 (20.09)	6 121 (20.93)	6 470 (21.04)	6 460 (20.02)	14 172 (20.17)	15 378 (21.61)	15 838 (23.09)	16 655 (25.38)	18 266 (26.41)
Common and other public services	852 (2.98)	914 (3.12)	1 078 (3.51)	953 (2.95)	1 918 (2.73)	2 138 (3.00)	2 066 (3.01)	1 997 (3.04)	1 980 (2.86)
Northern Ireland	663 (2.32)	698 (2.39)	784 (2.55)	846 (2.62)	1 925 (2.74)	2 056 (2.89)	2 064 (3.01)	2 054 (3.13)	2 233 (3.23)
TOTAL[1]	28 607 (100)	29 250 (100)	30 746 (100)	32 261 (100)	70 274 (100)	71 167 (100)	68 585 (100)	65 523 (100)	69 165 (100)

[1] Percentages may not total 100 due to rounding.

Sources: Table 3.1 *Public Expenditure to 1978–79*, Cmnd 5879, 1975; Table 1.6, *The Government's Expenditure Plans 1980–81 to 1983–84*, Cmnd 7841, 1980.

Table 1.2 Composition of public expenditure by programme 1978/9 to 1983/4 (United Kingdom)

£ million at outturn prices (percentages)

	1978/9	1979/80	1980/1	1981/2	1982/3	1983/4 (estimated)
Defence	7 497 (11.40)	9 228 (11.84)	11 173 (12.01)	12 605 (12.05)	14 408 (12.65)	15 716 (12.91)
Overseas services	1 845 (2.81)	2 076 (2.66)	1 621 (1.74)	1 685 (1.61)	2 164 (1.90)	2 294 (1.88)
Commerce and industry	4 803 (7.30)	5 014 (6.43)	6 494 (6.98)	8 153 (7.79)	7 652 (6.72)	8 167 (6.71)
Transport	2 672 (4.06)	3 278 (4.21)	4 000 (4.30)	4 277 (4.09)	4 395 (3.86)	4 560 (3.75)
Housing	3 571 (5.43)	4 520 (5.80)	4 461 (4.80)	3 128 (2.99)	2 640 (2.32)	2 760 (2.27)
Other environmental services	2 222 (3.38)	2 640 (3.39)	3 071 (3.30)	3 108 (2.97)	3 554 (3.12)	3 787 (3.11)
Law, order and protective services	2 034 (3.09)	2 577 (3.31)	3 160 (3.40)	3 731 (3.57)	4 174 (3.67)	4 681 (3.85)
Education, libraries, science and arts	8 094 (12.31)	9 346 (11.99)	11 376 (12.23)	12 365 (11.82)	13 298 (11.68)	13 980 (11.48)
Health and personal social services	7 425 (11.29)	8 899 (11.42)	11 362 (12.21)	12 724 (12.16)	13 817 (12.13)	14 688 (12.07)
Social security	16 437 (25.00)	19 417 (24.92)	23 429 (25.18)	28 567 (27.31)	32 445 (28.49)	35 324 (29.02)
Common and other public services	1 819 (2.77)	2 165 (2.78)	2 513 (2.70)	2 992 (2.86)	3 191 (2.80)	2 616 (2.15)
Scotland	3 713 (5.65)	4 547 (5.84)	5 359 (5.76)	5 830 (5.57)	6 242 (5.48)	6 767 (5.56)
Wales	1 489 (2.26)	1 769 (2.27)	2 112 (2.27)	2 218 (2.12)	2 386 (2.10)	2 587 (2.13)
Northern Ireland	2 132 (3.24)	2 446 (3.14)	2 899 (3.12)	3 215 (3.07)	3 500 (3.07)	3 799 (3.12)
TOTAL[1]	65 753 (100)	77 922 (100)	93 030 (100)	104 598 (100)	113 866 (100)	121 726 (100)

[1] Percentages may not total 100 due to rounding.

Source: Table 1.3, *The Government's Expenditure Plans 1984–85 to 1986–87*, Cmnd 9143, 1984.

The reduction in housing expenditure has to be seen as part of cuts in public expenditure which the Thatcher government claimed were necessary if resources were to be diverted to productive areas of the economy and inflation brought under control. Moreover like the preceding Labour government they were also concerned with rising levels of local authority expenditure; central government was committed to a large share of local spending and to the extent that they had to arrange deficit financing rather than meet this out of taxation it could affect the Public Sector Borrowing Requirement and was therefore regarded as a legitimate target for cuts.

Throughout the period 1970–1984 housing expenditure was limited by the extent to which other areas of government spending were given priority or could be controlled, as well as by the level of economic growth. Yet despite their harsh remedies the Conservatives presided over a period in which there was little economic growth. The Conservatives chose to halt the growth in total expenditure while providing additional resources for defence and law and order but in the event there were additional unplanned increases in these areas because of both world developments and domestic events such as the Falklands War in 1982 and the 1984–85 Miners' Strike. Labour had also found how difficult it was to cut defence (Wilson 1979).

Within the social budgets housing had benefited during the late sixties at the expense of health and education but in the seventies and eighties preference was given to these programmes and to social security whose budgetary outturn proved increasingly difficult to predict. Demographic trends necessitated additional expenditure on pensions and supplementary benefits and there were further unplanned increases in spending as a consequence of rising unemployment and higher rents after 1974/5. A decade later reductions in housing expenditure planned for 1984/5 were directly attributable to increases in these payments.

One of the reasons housing made a good target for cuts in expenditure was its large capital component. Capital expenditure could be cut more quickly and less visibly than equivalent reductions in current expenditure because it did not have an easily identifiable impact on a particular group, there were time lags before any reduction in housing supply was felt. In addition there was the advantage of savings on future debt charges and subsidies (Glennerster 1981). However, as Chapters 4 and 5 demonstrate, the control of housing expenditure has resulted in reductions in both Exchequer and rate fund subsidies as well as investment. The reduction in subsidies has been paralleled by an increase in rents for public sector tenants which has led to their increasing dependence upon means-tested benefits and to additional growth in the social security payments. Although the rationale behind the use of means tests is the restriction of public expenditure, in this case, as Chapter 4 shows, the outcome is a surprising one.

Welfare and Property
Despite differences in ideology a broad consensus was reached in the years after the Second World War on the form and degree of state intervention necessary in a welfare state. Although there is no general agreement on what constitutes a welfare state Thoenes (1966: 125) has defined it as 'a form of society characterised by a system of democratic, government-sponsored welfare placed on a new footing and offering a guarantee of collective social care to its citizens, concurrently with the maintenance of a capitalist system of production'. Marshall (1981) has put it more succinctly as 'democratic-welfare-capitalism' and has described the way a consensus was reached between the conflicting values of collectivism and individualism through the democratic political process. Whether or not this process is regarded as productive or as Titmuss (1968; 1973), Robson (1976) and George and Wilding (1976) suggest as destructive, nonetheless there developed an institutional framework designed to promote welfare.

The concept of welfare originally encapsulated in the post-war welfare state is but one idea of welfare (Pinker 1979), one in which inequalities of income and other goods were tolerated but tempered by the belief that all citizens were entitled to equal respect and by an aspiration for social justice that had much in common with Rawl's (1972) notion of justice as fairness. State intervention to regulate the free market was therefore justified by the aim of improving equity, equalising opportunities and meeting the needs of minorities. Neither was this to be achieved at the cost of the loss of freedom and self-determination because these were values that were built into the framework of the welfare state alongside those of altruism and mutual aid which it was believed would be promoted by universal social services.

In the same way as there are different ideas of welfare associated with free market economies, welfare societies and socialist states so there are different systems of property through which societies seek to realise the purposes of their members, or some of the purposes of some of their members. This is why 'Property is controversial . . . because it subserves some more general purposes of a whole society, or the dominant classes of a society, and these purposes change over time: as they change, controversy springs up about what the institution of property is doing and what it ought to be doing' (Macpherson 1978: 11).

Property rights are legal rights created by the state to give an individual an enforceable claim to some use or benefit of something (and sometimes, but not always, to its disposal). As this enforceability depends upon a society's belief that it is morally right any institution of property requires a justifying theory and at different times property has been justified as a natural right or by the social or economic functions it performed (Phillips 1979). Because property is a right to use or to benefit from something and it is not the thing itself 'a property right is a relation not between an owner and a thing, but between the owner and other individuals in reference to things' (Cohen 1978: 159). The right is always exercised against one or more individuals and to the extent that a person can exclude others from things necessary to life the law confers a power that can be used to influence their behaviour. One of the attributes of property is therefore the power it gives the owner over things and over people (Denman 1978).

Systems of property can range from individualised private ownership to those based on common property where in contrast to the concept of exclusive possession each individual is guaranteed not to be excluded from the use or benefit of something. In practice it is questionable whether a society could function without some form of private property in the basic necessities of life such as food, shelter, clothing and household goods and in personal possessions like jewellery or hand-tools and most societies therefore have property systems which combine private property with common property in, say, public parks or streets. Many societies also have state property, which is a form of private property as it 'does not give the individual citizen a direct right to use, nor a right not to be excluded from, the assets held by the state acting as a corporation' (Macpherson 1978: 5), in railways, industrial undertakings like coal or shipbuilding or in public housing. While all forms of property require moral justification some like property in the means of production (land or capital) may require more justification than others (Tawney 1978).

Market societies require conditions where the full and free exchange of all things, including income and wealth, takes place independent of the intervention of a political authority, hence the development of systems of private property with exclusive possession and the full rights of ownership, including disposal. In welfare states and socialist societies there would be a greater propensity for common property and state ownership and for the state to curtail private property rights so that the distribution of things did not reflect purely market criteria. There would be no necessity for individuals to hold the full rights of owner-ship because the state would be undertaking the work of allocation, but a more forceful argument for such state intervention would be the desire to rectify possible injustices that would arise as a system of un-restrained private property intensifies existing social and economic inequalities. Thus in Britain public landlords have been used to provide tenants with opportunity to use and occupy dwellings but they have had no control over their disposal and have had to rely on administrative arrangements for access, transfers and exchanges. Neither have they been able to benefit from any increase in the value of the dwelling (except through historic cost finance) or pass on such profits to succeeding generations.

Direct provision of services is not a necessary condition for a welfare state although this has been a characteristic of the British model in education, health care and housing. An alternative or complementary approach is to guarantee a right to income through benefits or tax concessions. While such rights are still essentially private property as they can only be enjoyed by individuals for their exclusive benefit, they represent a new kind of property in that they are not in material things and provide an individual right not to be excluded. Such rights which have been described as the 'new property' by Macpherson (1978) and Cohen (1978) and as 'citizenship property' by Saunders (1984) would be most fully developed in socialist societies as a right not to be excluded from the use or benefit of the achievements of the whole society and which would take either or both of two forms:

(a) an equal right of access to the accumulated means of labour, i.e., the accumulated capital of society and its natural resources (with a consequent right to an income from one's work on them); or
(b) a right to an income from the whole produce of the society, an income related not to work but what is needed for a fully human life. (Macpherson 1978: 206)

The kind of social relations created by systems of property where all have a right not to be excluded could be seen as a unifying force in society whereas exclusive possession would be divisive. After all the residential property right is the basis of the individual's power to assert and protect himself against his fellow men (and the state) through isolating himself by converting his home into his castle (Marshall 1981).

Property systems therefore not only arise to meet a society's needs but develop and adjust as social and economic circumstances change. In this way the system of property can be said to reflect societal values. However, property rights can also be created because of the belief that they form the basis of the kind of social relations that are needed for the ideal society. The relationship between property rights and human behaviour is more fully explored in Chapter 6 but it will suffice to say at this stage that systems of private property can be justified because by providing the maximum opportunities for the exercise of individual freedom they create the values necessary for the functioning of capitalism. However, any system of property which maximises individual freedom will place limits on the achievement of equality in the same way as an egalitarian distribution can only be achieved at the cost of certain basic freedoms. These conflicts between freedom and equality had been resolved within the consensus of the post-war welfare state but as that consensus began to break down so the differences between the two basic ideologies in the British political system — capitalism and socialism — began to be felt.

Public Housing and Party Politics

The place of public housing, the division between state provision and individual rights in residential property and the development of new forms of assistance towards housing costs forms the subject-matter of this book. The political development of these policies in the 1970s and 1980s is set in an historical and administrative context where the level of home ownership and the cost of housing support are of particular importance. However, in choosing possible policy options governments select not only politically appropriate policies – especially those that will win votes in marginal constituencies – but ones that are administratively feasible. The choices are therefore constrained by the agencies available to implement the proposals: local authorities, housing associations or central government departments and the rapport between them. The relationship between central and local government is of special interest: already by 1970 centralist tendencies were in evidence, setting the scene for the battle for the control of local housing policy.

Although it is fashionable to present housing policies as an adjunct of economic policies and the level of public expenditure as a product of macroeconomic necessities, economic policies are selected on the same basis of political judgement as, for example, building or selling council houses. Economic crises may force change but they do not dictate its form, there is always a choice (Ball 1983). It is, however, pertinent that both Labour and Conservative administrations have perceived the crisis as one of the level of public expenditure and have not seriously considered solutions where tax revenues are increased.

With no assurance of economic growth, rising costs as a result of high interest rates and inflation and increasing competition for funds from more 'productive' areas of the economy, the possibility of continuing with the welfare policies of the sixties was seriously questioned. As there was little prospect of growth in national output social expenditure could only be sustained by more onerous taxation and if people were willing to give up individual improvements in living standards. The choice for the electorate would therefore be between lower take-home pay plus a 'social wage' or a higher income and complete discretion over its spending. Yet the very act of questioning the desirability of public rather than private provision and whether the state need cater for everyone or just those who could not cope in the market place presented a challenge to the consensus upon which the post-war welfare state had been built and to the belief that there was a need for collective social provision. There was no simple answer to these questions; what it would be possible to achieve depended in part on the universality and popularity of the service under threat and whereas it was difficult to dismantle the education and health services because of their broad-based appeal, state housing was neither popular nor the 'normal' form of provision.

The lower priority accorded to welfare objectives is largely but not entirely attributable to the economic liberalism of Conservative governments, and in particular those of Margaret Thatcher which were much more radical than that of Edward Heath, whose faith in monetarist solutions was shaken by his experience of office (Judge 1982; Walker 1982). Mrs Thatcher committed her Party to rolling back the frontiers of the state and leading the economy and society towards the free market (Layton-Henry 1980). They rejected the contention that 'the state can and should do everything' (Conservative Party 1983) in the belief that 'The role of the state can sensibly be reduced where it has taken over what private initiative can better achieve; and where it has been reducing incentives, increasing bureaucracy and distorting markets' (Sir Geoffrey Howe quoted in *Guardian*, 27 March 1980). Nevertheless when challenged they refuted the charge that they wished to dismantle the welfare state by stressing that 'Conservatives believe. . . strongly in the duty of Government to help those who are least able to help themselves' (Conservative Party 1983) and accepted that the state would have to retain responsibility, for example, for the sick, the elderly and the disabled.

The Conservatives' belief in the property-owning democracy in its widest sense justified the reduction in state holdings and the sale of council houses, new town development corporation assets and British Telecom, British Petroleum, Cable and Wireless, Jaguar and other company shares but the return to the market was also an essential part of their economic strategy. Economic recovery was deemed to be dependent upon restoring incentives to work and ensuring larger rewards for success and hence upon cuts in taxation. This was one reason for curtailing public expenditure but it was also argued that welfare spending was in itself a major contributor to inflation: being financed from taxation it added to the cost of living and was therefore inflationary. The alternative to cutting expenditure would be to borrow heavily but this would also be inflationary and would affect the prospects for growth and employment. Increased government competition for funds would push up interest rates and reduce industrial investment. The monetarist approach was therefore to rely on the private sector for economic growth through the control of the money supply, interest rates and the Public Sector Borrowing Requirement (PSBR). Government expenditure plans reflected this philosophy and substantial reductions were made in the planned expenditure on housing in the belief that private investment would make good the losses and allow housing requirements to be met. So great was the 1979 Conservative government's distaste for public decision-making that they refused to produce any assessment of housing requirements or of the likely response of public and private sectors despite pressure from the Environment Committee to do so (HC 714 1980; Cmnd 8105 1980).

The Conservatives consistently presented their housing programmes in ideological terms but as Chapters 4 and 6 show there were inconsistencies evident in the application of their principles.

Labour's ambitious plans for rectifying inequalities in power, income and wealth in favour of working people and their families were sacrificed in less than two years after taking office to the exigencies of economic problems and to ensure they did not further alienate an electorate already pressed by inflation and heavy taxation. They had entered government in 1974 with a radical, left-wing programme comprising: increased expenditure on public services, investment in industry, more public ownership including an enlarged house-building and municipalisation programme, controls on rents and the price of food and consumer goods, wage restraint, industrial democracy, better social welfare payments and more progressive taxation. However, it was not easy to bring inflation, unemployment and economic stagnation under control nor manage the EEC negotiations, devolution and the Northern Ireland and Rhodesian affairs while pursuing social justice for all (Wilson 1979). The government's belief in the three central socialist values — equality, freedom and fellowship — and its faith in Keynesian economic management appeared to be finally shaken by the financial crisis of 1976 (Wright 1981) and thereafter economic and social policies were made subservient to the Treasury's monetarism.

During the war and the early post-war period 'Fundamental thinking about the role of government in housing, and the relationship between housing and other government activities such as income maintenance, town planning and population dispersal policies were conspicuous by their absence' (Nevitt and Rhodes 1972: 213). In contrast to health, education and social security there had been no reappraisal of housing policy and the 1945 Labour government simply followed previous practice. This was to ensure that individuals were adequately accommodated at a price they could afford by subsidising direct provision by local authorities and housing associations from the Exchequer and the rate fund and pooling rents. These arrangements had been made in 1919 at a time when renting was the normal form of tenure. Local authorities were the state's principal instrument for this transfer to the propertyless classes as housing associations operated on a very small scale and almost entirely in London and other major urban areas (Tarn 1973; Gauldie 1974). Public housing therefore developed alongside the private market and not as an alternative to it as with education and health care and initially the state's role in housing provision was seen to be a short-term expedient while post-war shortages lasted and until such time as the market could re-establish itself. In the circumstances it was not surprising that the tenancies were modelled on the private sector, that public landlords were given the same kind of property rights as private landlords and public tenants a weekly tenancy.

Possibly because of the 'temporary' nature of the problem and because previous attempts to house the poor had relied on shortening the term of the tenancy or applying subsidies from the rates or gifts from benefactors no consideration was given to a general redistribution of income so that people could afford housing (Murie 1983). It was only later when it became evident that council and housing association rents were too high for those not in skilled manual occupations or regular employment that rebates of rent were legalised by the 1930 Housing Act. This allowed for some redistribution of the general need subsidies and for rents to rise without those in need paying any more. Although encouraged to do so, councils were not obliged to make use of these powers or to include tenants in receipt of supplementary benefit in any rebate scheme.

The financing of public housing evolved in a haphazard fashion: with fixed rate subsidies available to any authority, building accommodation assistance was over-generous for some areas and inadequate for others. Furthermore under Labour's Housing Subsidies Act 1967 the total cost of assistance was considerable and likely to escalate because of a 'flaw' in the subsidy design. The subsidy was based on building costs and interest rates at the time of construction and like previous subsidies, once determined, remained unaltered in money terms and was paid for 60 years. To avoid an open-ended commitment by the Exchequer building costs reckonable for subsidy were limited by a housing cost yardstick (HCY) but there was no similar arrangement for capping interest rates. As a result with the introduction of the new system the average basic annual subsidy rose from about £24 per dwelling to £67 per dwelling. As interest rates rose so the subsidy bill would increase making a 'staggering addition to the nation's tax burden' (Cmnd 4728 1971, para. 6(v)). Upon investigation the system was felt to be running away with itself and 'incapable of taking account of changing social, financial, and administrative circumstances' (HC 473 1969, para. 146), and as a result tenants were regarded as cosseted while home owners were struggling to make ends meet. Yet in subsidising interest rates the government provided similar assistance to that given to home owners. Although this was not acknowledged by the Ministry of Housing and Local Government or the Treasury, or even by the Labour Party, tax relief on mortgage interest without liability for Schedule A tax was a subsidy. If Labour had recognised this there would have been an opportunity to equalise assistance between the tenures and by providing help for tenants through tax legislation they could have made it much more difficult for the Conservatives to withdraw the subsidy. Subsidies paid to housing associations were equally illogical. There was very little difference between charitable, non-charitable, cost rent and co-ownership associations and yet there were different systems of financial support resulting in different rent structures (DOE 1971).

It was widely believed that over-generous subsidies allowed local authorities to charge unrealistically low rents. Yet despite the high level of subsidy overall there was no guarantee that the poor would receive adequate assistance. Local authorities had complete discretion over subsidies and many continued to pool them. If a case could be made for greater equality in the treatment of poor tenants there was the precedent for governments to intervene, for while local authorities had traditionally enjoyed the discretion to determine their own rents Labour's use of rents as an element in their counter-inflation policy in the sixties had committed councils who wished to increase rents to submit their proposals to the Ministry for approval.

At a time when renting was the dominant tenure it seemed logical not only to model public housing on private practice but to tax owner-occupiers as if they were private landlords. Hence they were assessed on an imputed rental income and allowed to offset expenditure such as mortgage interest against this liability. It was only as home ownership spread in the 1950s and tax thresholds fell that tax relief became an important element in housing finance (Donnison and Ungerson 1982); but its importance increased when the tax on imputed rental income was abolished as part of tax reforms in 1963. The valuations upon which the tax was based had not been revised since 1936 and so the real burden of this Schedule A tax had fallen to very low levels. The loss of income was therefore a relatively small price to pay for avoiding the political consequences of restoring the yield of the tax in real terms (Nevitt 1966). This change, which appeared to be a minor one at the time, became of greater significance when Labour in 1967 paid option mortgage subsidy equivalent to tax relief at the standard rate to house-buyers who had incomes too low to claim the full value of the relief in the ordinary way and exempted loans used for acquisition and improvement of dwellings when abolishing tax relief on interest in 1969. Despite the growing amount of assistance provided for home owners most of the dissatisfaction felt about public finance for housing was with the public sector. The public did not accept that tax relief on mortgage interest payments was a subsidy, despite its importance in re-distributing income, although they recognised the 'bargain' offered by owner-occupation. This was one of the reasons why Labour was committed to making it available to marginal groups.

The post-war Labour government's plans to relieve the housing shortage relied on local authorities; even though the need for central control over scarce resources justified the use of public agencies and extending the wartime practice of licensing, the Party favoured council building because it ensured allocation on the basis of need. However, by the mid-1950s the Conservatives, who had been in office since 1951, felt that the private market was capable of providing for general needs and only recognised a wider role for public housing in times of crisis, such as the early 1960s. During this period the Conservative Party developed into the party of owner-occupation and yet, practically, did very little to promote their preferred tenure apart from freeing private builders from the restrictions of licensing in 1954 and making available funds for loans for house purchase under the House Purchase and Housing Act 1959.

In contrast the 1964–70 Labour governments took several positive steps to increase home ownership including the introduction of option mortgage subsidy, exemption of owner-occupied homes from capital gains tax and the enfranchisement of long leaseholders. Granting to long leaseholders a right to acquire the freehold or an extension of their lease was the most radical redistribution of residential property since the property legislation of the 1920s and was more revolutionary than either rent restriction or requisitioning during the War and immediate post-war years. The 1967 Leasehold Reform Act was to become an important precedent for the state's altering the established form of property relations so that they catered for current needs but the reform was prompted by political pressure precipitated by the falling-in of leases in Labour strongholds in South Wales (Karslake 1967; McDonald 1969). After 13 years out of office Labour had recognised that their political future depended on becoming 'the party of *all* the housing classes and thereby [able to] isolate the Conservative enemy with its evident contempt for the tenant "class"' (Merrett 1982: 35).

This was Labour's way out of their dilemma. There was a widespread desire for home ownership and as Labour's traditional supporters became richer so more of them could afford to buy their own home. In Britain, in common with other countries, there has been a propensity to increase spending on housing as personal incomes have increased and incomes had been growing in real terms during the fifties and sixties as a result of both rising real wages in periods of economic growth and an increased number of dual-earner households. Labour, while assessing it was politically feasible to recognise home ownership as the natural form of tenure, tried to be even-handed. This provided their justification for a further programme of public housebuilding for 1965–70 while acknowledging the building for owner-occupation as 'normal' and as reflecting 'a long-term social advance which should gradually pervade every region' (Cmnd 2838 1965).

When local councils were first empowered to build it was not envisaged that they should hold the land in perpetuity. The Artisans' and Labourers' Dwelling Improvement Act 1875 and the Housing of the Working Classes Act 1890, for example, ruled that council-built dwellings should be sold within ten years of their completion and this obligation to resell was not removed until the 1909 Housing and Town

Planning Act. By the time the 1936 Housing Act consolidated previous legislation councils were merely empowered to sell and all disposals required ministerial permission. These consents were not automatic and in the years immediately following the Second World War Labour refused such sales.

The Conservatives assumed that a property-owning democracy would evolve without intervention and did little to actively encourage council house sales (Murie 1975). They did, however, relax Labour's restrictions and issued a general consent whose only proviso was that the Ministry should be notified on completion. These consents were generally revised on changes of government if and when it was felt a change of policy was warranted. Hence the guidance issued by the Conservatives in 1960 was not withdrawn or revised by Labour until 1967 when a circular (MHLG Circular 24/67) was issued to dissuade local authorities from selling in areas where there was still an unsatisfied demand for accommodation to rent. However, authorities only remained free to sell until the following year when a quota of a quarter of one per cent of the housing stock was imposed on sales in a number of designated districts, largely in the major conurbations (MHLG Circular 42/68). The government was forced to adopt this stance when faced with councils which were implementing policies inconsistent with their views. After their defeat in the 1964 General Election and as part of a strategy to regain power nationally Conservative Central Office encouraged local councils to adhere to Party policy (Dale 1984) and accordingly those which were Conservative controlled cut back on housebuilding to a greater extent than national policy proposals and promoted council house sales. This was one of the reasons why central government was prepared subsequently to pursue a more cavalier approach towards local government autonomy and raised the possibility of sanctions and even of positive controls where local authorities refused to co-operate. For similar reasons, while both Labour and Conservative parties accepted the case for local government reform they hesitated at uncompromising solutions which strengthened the powers and the financial base of local government.

Detailed examination will be provided of a number of interrelated issues that were raised during the 1960s (although people may have been unaware of their possible consequences) and resolved, to greater or lesser extent, over the period 1970 to 1984. The escalating subsidy bill raised the question of how housing costs should be divided between the individual and the state and of the extent to which society as a whole should subsidise housing. The form this assistance should take was a related issue. The lack of an objective basis for rent fixing and the need for greater equality in the treatment of poor tenants would be sufficient justification for the reform of rents, rebates and subsidies in the public sector. However, in addition to deciding between general building subsidies and those tailored to individuals' needs and between forms of universal assistance and means testing there were wider questions to be answered about whether support should be tenure specific or housing assistance integrated with general provision made for income maintenance or the tax system. Whichever solution were adopted some consideration would have to be given to balancing financial equity between the tenures. The reform of the housing finance system is examined in Chapters 2, 3 and 4 and although isolated for the purpose of academic analysis should not be seen as divorced from the wider issue of the distribution of residential property evaluated in Chapters 5 and 6. Part of the justification for the disposal of public housing was its public expenditure implications and the prospects for raising revenue from council house sales. The second part of the book therefore examines the case for private property, the changing balance between the public and private sectors of housing and the political and social repercussions of the restructuring of residential property.

Neither the provision of public housing nor its financing can be considered without raising the question of the relationship between the state and public landlords. During the 1960s public landlords still enjoyed considerable autonomy over investment, sales and the charges they made for housing. Nevertheless, by the beginning of the seventies the seeds of many of the great controversies of the 1970–84 period had been planted and upon their outcome depended the future of local authority and housing association housing. In 1970 there were no serious contenders to local authorities as providers of social housing but governments could look to the countries of western Europe and to their traditions of co-operative, condominium, housing association, employer and trades union involvement in housing provision. The distinction between central and local government relations and local authorities' role as landlord would become increasingly difficult to sustain. By 1970 there were already signs of government's housing policies being integrated with their wider political objectives. The battle for power between central and local government which pervades the book is paralleled by the consideration of the fiscal and political power attributed to the individual in the property-owning democracy.

By the end of the sixties it was evident that public housing could hardly be allowed to continue in its current form. While there were, of course, other important housing issues – homelessness, obsolescence and improvement, the role of the private rented sector, building society practices and regional and local variations in housing provision – it is not possible to cover them adequately in a book of this nature, nor is it necessary for there are a number of excellent studies of these aspects of British housing policy. Even if the necessity for reform of public housing had not been recognised the seventies would have witnessed a break with the past for this decade must surely represent the most significant period of change since the inception of the post-war welfare state: a time when 'the protracted crisis of the mixed economy and the apparent failure of Keynesian economics to put things right has spelled the end of the golden age of western affluence as well as of the welfare state' (Mishra 1984: 161).

Along with other welfare states in the industrialised West the British welfare state is in disarray. In place of the 'Butskellite' consensus, or what Mishra (1984) describes as the synthesis of capitalist and socialist values of social democracy or centre-Left, there are the more extreme positions of the neo-conservatives and neo-Marxists with the spirit of pre-welfare state capitalism in the ascendancy (Marshall 1981). The role of the state in housing has therefore been reassessed during a period in which the welfare state came to be regarded as a barrier to economic recovery, where governments deliberately chose to meet the gap between the resources necessary to finance public expenditure and the revenue actually raised by cutting back on social services and on public housing in particular and when there was a general loss of confidence in state intervention and its desirability was seriously questioned. As foreshadowed earlier in this chapter housing bore the brunt of public expenditure cuts during the eighties and the question of the state's ability to manage was at the centre of the debate about tenant dissatisfaction and the inefficiency of council landlords. In deciding whether or not there would be a future for public housing the future of the welfare state would be called into question.

2 Rent Fixing and Local Freedom

The level of local authority rents was called into question not only because of the rising subsidy bill but also because of the 1966–70 Labour government's use of rents as a counter-inflation measure. The process of controlling rent increases had revealed the startling lack of uniformity in rents between areas and led to demands for more objective measures of rent fixing (Cmnd 3604 1968).

It was evident that a wide range of interpretations had been placed upon the duty to charge 'reasonable rents' and to review them from time to time. The practice of pooling both income and expenditure meant that rent levels were dependent upon the past history of building and provision and that subsidies were used to keep rents down generally rather than to benefit the poorer tenants. Several proposals for a uniform basis for rent fixing had been made including an attempt, albeit unsuccessful, to agree upon a common approach to rent determination within the London area (Nevitt and Rhodes 1972). The National Board for Prices and Incomes (Cmnd 3604 1968) had considered 'fair rents', historic cost rents and replacement cost rents for the public sector and while their examination had been cursory it could form the basis for decision-making by an incoming government.

The Conservative government came to power in 1970 confident in asserting the merits of free enterprise and of reducing the role of the state in all areas of policy (Lansley and Fiegehen 1974). In housing their primary objective was to restore some sanity to housing finance by which was meant raising rents and reducing the subsidy bill. It was felt that rents had been 'too low for too long' and 'the sooner we get realism into the rents of local authorities, the better' (Goudie 1972: 2). However, their strategy for controlling housing expenditure also included cuts in investment on new building and improvement work and increasing receipts from council house sales (Klein *et al.* 1974).

Labour had left council tenants in a very vulnerable position. There did not appear to be any legitimate reason why council rents should be controlled or why tenants should not pay higher rents, especially in those authorities which had persistently kept rent levels down despite mounting deficits on their Housing Revenue Accounts (HRA). Nevertheless the government's proposals in the White Paper 'Fair Deal for Housing' were justified on grounds of equity:

> These reforms are based on the principle of fairness. They will establish a fair balance between owner occupiers and tenants and parity of treatment for council tenants and private tenants. They will do justice between landlord and tenant. They will have due regard to the reasonable claims of the citizen as a taxpayer and as a ratepayer, without placing on either the inflationary burden of unnecessary taxes. (Cmnd 4728 1971: para. 86)

Little was said about the position of the home owner in relation to the tenant or about the level of assistance enjoyed by those in this tenure and there were no suggestions for change. Instead the problems of lack of fairness were seen as mainly existing in the rented sector and here equity would be achieved by:

    (i)   fair rents for all unfurnished tenants who can afford them;
    (ii) a rent rebate or allowance for those who cannot;
    (iii) the concentration of Exchequer subsidies on authorities with the worst housing problems. (Cmnd 4728 1971: para. 20)

This would result in the two main sectors of the market for rented housing being governed by one common equitable principle — fair rents for all.

Fair Rents

The White Paper was followed by the Housing Finance Act 1972 after 'the longest Committee Stage fight in history . . . an unprecedent 57 sittings, including seven which lasted all through the night' (Sklair 1975: 253). Predominantly a financial measure, its proposals were hung on the new system for the determination of public sector rents. While in the past local authorities had fixed 'reasonable rents' at levels dictated by the amount necessary to balance the HRA and subject to the non-profit rule; in the future the position would be reversed. Tenants would pay 'fair rents' and subsidies and rate fund contributions would only be payable if it were necessary to balance the account. Under the Act authorities were placed under a duty to charge 'fair rents' for all HRA dwellings. For the first time rents were not to be related to the costs of providing, managing and maintaining council houses.

The principles to be applied in determining a 'fair rent' were to be similar to those used in the private sector under the Rent Act 1968 and related to the age, character, locality and state of repair of the dwelling. The fact that the dwelling was vested in a public body was to be disregarded as was scarcity of dwellings in the area. The Opposition had unsuccessfully tried to amend the Bill so that regard had to be paid to the authority's duty to meet social needs, what it considered to be a reasonable rent and to the effect of increases in rent on the economy and the general market in housing but 'having chosen the term "fair" for the artificial rents to be determined for the private sector, the Labour Party had some difficulty in denying its relevance to the public sector: their clothes had been stolen' (Cullingworth 1979: 56). The Act not only laid down the basis for rent fixing but specified the procedures to be followed. The authority was allowed six months from the date of the Act coming into force in July 1972 to fix 'provisional fair rents' and publish them to its tenants. The tenants had two months in which to make representations and the authority a further two months in which to consider these and to prepare its proposals for submission to a Rent Scrutiny Board. These Boards, established by the Act, had their members selected from the Rent Assessment Panels which already existed to form the Rent Assessment Committees that dealt with appeals in the private sector and from the additional members appointed by the Secretary of State, the majority of whom were valuers or in the legal profession.

The role of the Rent Scrutiny Boards would be to determine the rents and in so doing to achieve comparability between different authorities. To this end they had the authority to approve or disapprove rents and in the latter case could substitute their own figures for those of the authority. If this happened the authority, but not the tenant, would have the right to make observations, but the final decision rested with the Board. The procedure thus differed from that used for the private sector where both landlord and tenant were entitled to make representations to the Rent Officer and both enjoyed a right of appeal and to be heard by the Rent Assessment Committee. There was no right of appeal for either party in the public sector and the tenants had no right even to be heard, except by the landlord, who was not entitled to make the decision. The Rent Scrutiny Boards, unlike the Rent Assessment Committees, did not follow a judicial procedure and hear both sides fully but were rather administrative and executive bodies under no obligation to pay regard to any representations made to them.

In coming to its decision on fair rents the Board did not have to fix rents for individual dwellings but could determine the rents for a block of dwellings or dwellings of a similar kind. This, like the other procedures, differed from the approach used in the private sector and was evidently designed to speed up the process. Fixing each rent for in excess of five and a half million dwellings would have been both time-consuming and costly, necessitating the appointment of thousands of Rent Officers. Furthermore if both landlord and tenant had a right to be heard by a Rent Assessment Committee the whole process would have been further drawn out as hearings involving representatives of both parties would inevitably result in delays. Under the established procedures once the rent was fixed by the Rent Scrutiny Board it became the 'fair rent' for the dwelling until it was reviewed after three years.

The result was an increase in central government powers, through its executive agents the Rent Scrutiny Boards, at the expense of the local authorities who lost their longstanding responsibility for fixing their own rents. 'This removal of a highly prized political responsibility would have caused anger at any time, but as a prelude to legislation on local government reorganization (the aim of which was to strengthen local government and reduce central control), it seemed particularly obnoxious' (Cullingworth 1979: 55). Authorities' experience of rent fixing was the justification for their role in determining 'provisional fair rents', nevertheless it was thought necessary to give them guidance on how to set about the task. Ministers advised them to consider gross values, the costs of provision, the general level of earnings in the area and the rents of comparable dwellings in the private sector. It was also written into the Act that consideration should be given to the return it would be reasonable to expect on a dwelling as an investment to ensure that rents for local authority dwellings were arrived at by the same methods as were used for assessing fair rents in the private sector, which meant relying on comparables.

The idea of setting public sector rents according to levels prevailing in the private sector was not a new one as prior to 1949 local authorities had been required to fix rents in the light of what was generally paid for working-class housing in the area but with an increasing proportion of council housing this yardstick became almost impossible (Parker 1967). The government refused to accept that such a problem existed despite the fact that the Francis Committee (Cmnd 4609 1971) had shown that of some 1.2 million regulated tenancies at the end of 1969 only 165,900 (under 14 per cent) had been the subject of applications to register and there was no information as to the proportion that had rents fixed by the Rent Officer or were recorded as rents which the tenant had accepted. Furthermore by the end of 1970 only 18,000 post-1919 dwellings had been registered and as most local authority dwellings had been purpose-built since 1919 comparables would be difficult to find (Goudie 1972).

The definition of fair rent in the 1972 Act followed that established for the private sector and was therefore to be a market rent where the effect of scarcity had been disregarded. It had proved in practice to be extremely difficult to fix this type of rent. The Francis Committee (Cmnd 4609 1971) had found it was difficult to isolate the effects of scarcity and that Rent Officers and Rent Assessment Committees were using their judgement as to the balance of supply and demand in the locality and indeed on the area they considered to be the 'locality'. The result was rents that in all probability reflected market value.

There were no objective criteria that could be used to determine a fair rent; it was part of a system that had been devised to provide a reasonable rent for private landlords so that they would maintain the property while offering a degree of protection for the tenants. There would be naturally an element of profit but the Rent Officer and Rent Assessment Committees were there to arbitrate between the parties (Nevitt 1971). The government failed to explain the logic of fixing public rents according to the levels prevailing in the market or indeed the reason why the comparison was to be made with artificially arbitrated rents. Little thought appears to have been given to the question of exactly what the public sector tenant should be expected to pay for: the historic cost of his own accommodation, pooled historic costs, the current costs of replacement or whatever. Neither was it clear the extent to which he should be responsible for expenditure that might be more properly charged to the rates — such as the provision of estate roads, street lighting and some sewerage disposal systems — although the costs of some community services were to be excluded from the HRA. Without a rigorous attempt to define exactly what costs the council tenant should be liable for it appeared that: 'The council tenant is expected to pay for the elimination of the errors of his grandfather, his own present needs and the construction of buildings which will meet the needs of his grandson' (Nevitt 1971: 20).

In the event the council tenant, as Chapter 4 shows, would be responsible for these costs and more besides; the cost of rent rebates and rent allowances were made a first charge upon the HRA and only if tenants could not meet these costs in full would ratepayers and taxpayers make a contribution. Rents had to reach a level sufficient to finance income maintenance. It was claimed that the new basis for rent determination would produce a fairer system yet no explanation was given as to why it might be considered fair to shift some of the burden of income maintenance onto public tenants when 'These welfare payments were arguably a national responsibility which ought to be borne by the taxpayer or ratepayer at large' (Cullingworth 1979: 57). It was evidently the Conservatives' view that the public sector should be self-financing on a local basis and that wherever possible the rented sector as a whole should also cover its housing costs locally regardless of the differences in wealth between one part of the country and another and one tenure and another.

Although the government declared itself to be 'a great deal in the dark as to what fair rent levels council houses will command' (Beirne 1977: 148) it was evident that rents would increase. The average rent determined by Rent Assessment Committees for private rented accommodation was almost exactly twice the average council rent and

Frank Allaun had leaked confidential Department of the Environment estimates which suggested that rents would double; although the estimates produced by the Minister, Julian Amery, in response suggested a 50 per cent increase (Goudie 1972; Beirne 1977). After the initial increase rents would continue to rise in line with market trends. The result would be higher rents which exceeded the unit costs of supplying the dwelling by two or three times (Nevitt 1971). It is thus difficult to escape the conclusion that the government selected the 'fair rent' approach rather than say historic cost or replacement cost methods of rent fixing because of the potential for profit, regardless of the fact that the 1968 Report of the Prices and Incomes Board recommended using historic costs in the short term and replacement costs in the long term (Cmnd 3604 1968). Where this relationship was unlikely to hold true the fair rent system was not adopted. In Scotland private rents were so low that if used as a basis for comparison it was likely that rent reductions rather than rent increases would result so, instead of 'fair rents', legislation required Scottish authorities to charge rents which would cover costs.

As it was evident that substantial increases would be necessary, provision was made for local authorities to begin the progression towards fair rents before the rents were determined and even before the Act reached the statute book. Annual rent increases of £26 per dwelling were to be made until the fair rent level was reached; this was to include the financial year 1972/3 and necessitated an increase of £1 per week after the Act came into force, unless the authority staggered the increase and raised its rents by 50p per week in April and again in October. The only exception to this was where the council could convince the Secretary of State that increases of this order would take 2 or more per cent of its dwellings substantially above the fair rent level, when a lower rate of increase could be agreed. This concession, known variously as the 'Newcastle amendment' or the 'Birmingham salient' after two of the first authorities to be allowed to increase their rents by less than the specified amount, was exploited by Conservative-controlled councils during the local elections to increase their chances of being returned to office and by Labour councils who negotiated on this point in return for agreeing to implement the Act. Birmingham Corporation announced a rent rise of 35p per week instead of £1 just before the local elections in May 1972. In the event the rents were increased by 55p per week (Sklair 1975). However, even where increases were in line with statutory guidelines they were insufficient to keep pace with rising costs and inflation; the government therefore failed to achieve their objective of creating surpluses on most local authorities' housing accounts.

The Clay Cross Chimera

With the loss of freedom to fix their own rents local authorities felt very strongly that one of their last remaining powers was being eroded, if not totally destroyed, so that it was not surprising they opposed the legislation. Fair rents and the compulsory rent increases in the progression towards them were the main issues but the tightening of the rein of control was felt throughout the subsidy system. With Labour controlling most of the major cities and therefore most of the country's housing stock, the government was clearly aware that the Act could founder in the face of concerted opposition. They had anticipated such confrontation and provided themselves with the means for dealing with authorities which were unwilling to collaborate.

Under the Act two sanctions could be used should an authority fail to comply with any of its requirements but before they could be used the Secretary of State had to make formal inquiries to establish if the council was in default and warn the authority of his intention to place a default order on it. If such an order were made it would specify the steps to be taken to remedy the default and a time limit for compliance. Failing this a Housing Commissioner could be appointed to take over the operation of the housing service, with all expenses falling on the local authority, or housing subsidies could be withheld or both. Should a Housing Commissioner be appointed, both officers and members would be under a duty to assist him and could be fined if found guilty of failing to do so.

As the Bill was passing through its final stages, representatives of those councils which had declared their intention not to implement the Act met in Sheffield to discuss tactics. At this time, June 1972, there were over 70 authorities defying the government but their number had reduced to just over 40 in October and by November there were only about a dozen holding out. Sklair (1975) divides these authorities into three groups — those who never implemented (Clay Cross and Bedwas and Machen), those who held out into 1973 (including Conisborough, Merthyr Tydfil, Biggleswade and Camden) and those who implemented after October 1972 but before January 1973. In the face of such opposition to the Act the government selected carefully from the measures at its disposal. Some authorities — Halstead and Eccles, for example — gave way under pressure of default orders while others that refused to comply — Bedwas and Machen and Merthyr Tydfil — were quickly taken over by a Housing Commissioner. A Commissioner was appointed in December 1972 for Bedwas and Machen and in March 1973 for Merthyr. Authorities like Camden were brought into line by the threat of withdrawal of subsidies, which if carried out would have effectively paralysed slum clearance and building programmes.

None of these measures seemed likely to deter Clay Cross Council; they had even requested the appointment of a Housing Commissioner stating that this was the only way that the Act would be implemented in their area. Yet the government chose not to do so, no doubt because of the nature of the area and its councillors. The council was unusually militant with a very determined and united leadership and already had a reputation for obstinacy over its defiance of the government in 1971 over the issue of free school milk (Skinner and Langdon 1974) and its longstanding policy of keeping rents low had resulted in threats of surcharge and warnings from both the District Auditor and ministers that rent increases were necessary (Mitchell 1974). The population consisted largely of council tenants and the Labour council, all of whom were council tenants, had been elected on a mandate which included a promise to keep rents down.

From the day of publication of the White Paper the council had openly declared its intention not to implement the Act and no rent increases were made in either April or October 1972. However, rather than appointing a Housing Commissioner as he had done in similar circumstances elsewhere, the Secretary of State decided to hold the councillors personally responsible for the loss of rent income and ordered an extraordinary audit of the accounts under Section 228 Local Government Act 1933. This approach had been used before to prevent local authorities increasing the pay of manual workers (Parris 1975) and to control local government's 'generosity' in the allocation of unemployment benefits in the 1930s (Minns 1974) and so there was no question but that the District Auditor would have to surcharge the councillors to the extent of the loss to the rate fund caused by not increasing rents. However, the 1933 Act not only made provision for surcharging but provided that any councillor who became liable to a surcharge of £500 or more would be automatically discharged from holding public office for five years. When each councillor was held responsible for £635 the claim against them was met by appeals to the High Court and a local rent and rates strike which lasted six weeks and achieved more than 80 per cent support (Skinner and Langdon 1974). Meanwhile the government threatened the withdrawal of £20,000 housing subsidy but the council retaliated by retaining £20,000 of repayment due to the Public Works Loans Board.

The appeal in the High Court was heard in July 1973 and as expected the appeal was dismissed and the councillors disbarred from office. However, they continued their fight by taking action against the Secretary of State and the District Auditor and by December 1973 they were back in court. In the interim the Environment Secretary, Geoffrey Rippon, decided to appoint William Skillington, a retired civil servant, as Housing Commissioner in October 1973. The council were unwilling to co-operate and refused him even a room in their offices. He was thus forced to establish himself in offices in Chesterfield and engage his own staff of rent collectors. After some delay the Commissioner notified the tenants that the increased rent would be due from the beginning of January 1974 but before he could collect the council had ordered their own collectors out onto the streets and had taken the old rent.

During this period the legal battle finally came to a head; the case against the Environment Secretary and the District Auditor had been lost but the councillors had been given leave to appeal and this was heard in January 1974 before Lord Denning, the Master of the Rolls, Mr Justice Lawton and Lord Justice Orr. When the appeal was dismissed the councillors began to lose heart; they had been debarred from office and so were forced to stand down to allow elections to be held for a new council (Mitchell 1974). Meanwhile the Housing Commissioner continued to press for the extra rent. In February 1974 he announced that the £1 increase would now be collectable from 11 March 1974 with no arrears but, before he could do so, there was a change of government and events in Clay Cross had taken a further unexpected turn. The newly elected council took the same stance as their predecessors but with the added hope of finding some support from the new Labour government. This was not forthcoming and so when the Housing Commissioner ordered council staff to collect the higher rent, under threat of fines, and it seemed likely that they would do so, the council suspended them. In turn, this led to a strike by NALGO officers and in this chaotic state Clay Cross passed out of existence as part of the process of local government reorganisation, to be replaced by North Derbyshire District Council. So long as Clay Cross Urban District Council existed the new rents were not collected.

A number of questions arise as a result of the Clay Cross incident. Firstly, why did the government delay so long before sending in the Housing Commissioner? It may have been because they expected the councillors to agree to implement with the threat of surcharge hanging over them and by delaying any action they hoped that the problem would simply go away. Certainly they chose their methods of enforcement carefully and had even induced some Labour councils to implement with concessions over the amount of rent rise (Sklair 1975). Secondly, why did the Housing Commissioner not take a stronger line? Powers were available in the 1972 Act which would have allowed him to take over all the council's housing functions and action could have been taken against officers and councillors for non-co-operation. Only at the end did he threaten the officers with fines and apparently never contemplated using powers to have the councillors imprisoned: 'Mr Skillington himself admitted that he could have been rougher, and that if he thought that it would have helped in any way he could have jailed the councillors' (Skinner and Langdon 1974: 79). The Housing Commissioner's performance was so ineffectual and insignificant that one must assume that he was acting thus under the Department of the Environment's instructions: 'The Department obviously reached a decision of policy in the light of the Industrial Relations Act contempt cases, and based no doubt on political considerations that it would not utilise its legal powers to have the defaulting councillors imprisoned' (Street quoted in Sklair 1975: 289). This may have been the case or alternatively the use of a Housing Commissioner ill-advised. A sole official with limited support may have been an inadequate solution in a situation in which both council and tenants were united against him. Furthermore, if it is correct to surmise that the commissioner was restrained by the Department of the Environment this could have been due to the government's equivocal attitude to local authority discretion. Although they were willing to impose rent increases upon local authorities and deprive them of their control of rent fixing they held back when faced by the prospect of a forced take-over of local government functions. Even in Clay Cross the government appeared to prefer the road of negotiation and concession.

Clay Cross was a special case because council and tenants were united in their opposition to the Act. Although Sklair (1975) details a plethora of marches, rallies, demonstrations, strikes and rent and rate strikes throughout the country they quickly died away once councils began to co-operate with the government. There were even cases of Labour councils who took legal action against tenants withholding rent. Perhaps the opposition would have been more resolute had the Labour leadership directed the campaign but they were reluctant to do so because it had been evident from the outset that some Labour councils would implement, as several had even increased their rents by the optional 50p in April 1972 before the Bill became law.

The party hierarchy clearly considered non-implementation to be a totally misconceived way of opposing the Act and this was discouraged in no uncertain terms (Sklair 1975). The evidence that resistance to the Act was crumbling as early as July 1972 confirmed Harold Wilson's opinion that the risks for the Labour Party of advising all-out opposition far outweighed the risks of counselling opposition within the law. Accordingly Anthony Crosland, Shadow Environment Secretary, advised local authorities to obey the law but to apply for lower levels of rent increases using the Birmingham salient. In any case, the party leadership could not simply order councillors to break the law and it would be a dangerous precedent as a future Labour government would expect local authorities to implement what they might regard as unacceptable policies. This approach was maintained by the 1974 Labour government who, when approached by the Clay Cross councillors, refused to meet their request to withdraw the Housing Commissioner.

Although this problem was resolved by local government reorganisation, after which Clay Cross ceased to exist, the issues of the surcharges imposed by the District Auditor and the disbarment from political office remained. Support for the Clay Cross councillors had been consistently stronger amongst the rank and file of the party than the leadership and it was because of this base of support that Conference had passed a resolution in 1973 placing upon any future Labour government the responsibility of removing all penalties — financial and otherwise — from the Clay Cross Eleven (Skinner and Langdon 1974). The government was therefore faced with two issues, the unpaid surcharge and the ban on holding political office. Any Act indemnifying the rebel councillors would contravene all constitutional practice and could have adversely affected Labour's standing in the country. Yet the issue could not be ignored because when the District Auditor had ordered the former councillors to pay the outstanding surcharge in March 1974, the councillors appealed to the National Executive Committee (NEC) of the Labour Party who asked the government to take action. This placed the Cabinet in an embarrassing position; either they would have had to pass retrospective legislation or face very grave charges of disloyalty towards party members and risk the emnity of the militant left. The Cabinet's decision was to refuse to accept responsibility on the grounds that such commitment as there was lay not with the government but with the Party Conference and the NEC. It was not their intention to deal with either the surcharge or the disqualification from office with an election in the offing; although Labour had formed a government they were in a minority and so it was evident from the outset that there would be an early General Election.

A special Party Conference to discuss the situation was arranged for June 1974, by which time the District Auditor was threatening court action to recover the debt. The Conference demanded that the Labour government should honour its pledges but before it was able to do so the matter was settled outside Parliament because the District Auditor obtained a judgement against the former councillors in the High Court in August 1974. The former councillors were never able to meet these payments and as they were all council tenants did not run the risk of losing their homes and had little in the way of personal assets that could be sold to meet the debt which was dissolved through their bankruptcy.

Once safely back in office Labour introduced a Bill to absolve the Clay Cross councillors — and their equivalents elsewhere — from the consequences of defying the Housing Finance Act 1972. The Housing Finance (Special Provisions) Act 1975 did not relieve the councillors of the amount already surcharged but from any amount for which they might be surcharged subsequently and it did remit the disqualification of those already surcharged. In this way the government avoided a break with constitutional precedent by not making unlawful acts lawful and by not granting a pardon. In effect the Act represented a form of amnesty (Beloff and Plender 1975). The Conservatives were not so forgiving. The bitterness generated by the implementation of the Housing Finance Act was to have a lasting influence on the Party and its future housing programmes. Their indulgent attitude to local government autonomy had been eroded and they would be prepared to compel compliance on council house sales when this became pre-eminent amongst the Party's housing policies as the prospects for profitability in the public sector diminished.

The Return to Reasonable Rents
Only in relation to the future of the 1972 Act was there a measure of agreement within the Labour Party. Being fair to public sector tenants meant ending the obligation to charge fair rents and the possibility of making a profit on the HRA. The Manifesto (Labour Party 1974a) re-affirmed that the Housing Finance Act would be repealed and local authorities' powers to fix rents restored. It was therefore important to the Party that it should reward its supporters and honour its election pledges and, in particular, to halt the rise in rent levels. It had already been agreed as part of the Social Contract with the unions in 1973 that rents would be frozen as an element in a package of price controls in return for wage constraint. Therefore one of the first actions of the new government was to freeze all residential rents. The freeze, initially to last from 1 April 1974 until 31 December 1974, was later extended until 31 March 1975.

Although it was evident by 1974 that rent increases had not been sufficient to keep pace with rising costs and inflation, that authorities had not made profits on their HRAs and that fair rents in the private sector had been increasing at 7 per cent per annum, 'a good deal lower probably than many of us supposed' (Parliamentary Debates (Commons) 1974, vol. 881, col. 911), Labour went ahead with its planned repeal. It was a political obligation more than a rational decision and the spirit in which it was undertaken was aptly summed up by Anthony Crosland, Secretary of State for the Environment, in his rationale for the legislation: 'With this short Bill the Government aim to cut the throat of the Tory Housing Finance Act at a stroke' (Parliamentary Debates (Commons) 1974, vol. 881, col. 904).

There were three main issues to be resolved in relation to council house rents: how the rents should be fixed, the level of the rents and the degree to which these should be determined by the local authorities. The government saw the Act as dealing primarily with the procedure for rent fixing. It swept away 'fair rents', the Rent Scrutiny Boards and the system of compulsory annual rent increases and replaced them with the mechanisms that had existed before the 1972 Act. Local authorities' powers to fix reasonable rents were restored. The concept of 'reasonable rent' had not been statutorily defined although there was a good deal of case law on the subject to the effect that authorities in fixing their rents should strike a reasonable balance between tenants and ratepayers, avoiding setting rents so low that an unreasonable burden was laid on ratepayers. In practice this had amounted to setting rents based on pooled historic costs and it was likely that this approach to rent fixing would be re-adopted as the Act prevented any profit from being made on the HRA. However, pooling rents in this manner had proved unacceptable in the past and laid the government open once again to charges that rents would be low in some districts and high in others and that tenants would be paying different rents for similar dwellings. Furthermore this was a system they had acknowledged as unacceptable in the past. Richard Crossman stated on one occasion of the pre-1972 position that the legislation:

> has led to the existence of a cosseted and privileged class in our society – the council house tenant. These people are jealous of their privileged position – because a council house is a prize hard to come by. Councils must use their powers. They are not limited to charging just an economic rent. Charge the rich man £1,000 a year rent – that will sort the problem out. (Parliamentary Debates (Commons) 1974, Standing Committee A, col. 122)

The government's answer was to reject the idea that rents of similar properties should be the same across the country and to embrace the notion of local housing markets where rents could be fixed according to local needs. It was explained in the House that this would, for example, enable an authority to take local wage levels into account and that this was 'one of the most important reasons why a local authority, in conjunction with central Government subsidies, should be allowed to assess its own level of rents, without the imposition of a doctrinaire basis from Whitehall' (Parliamentary Debates (Commons) 1974, vol. 881, col. 1001). The argument, of course, was untenable, the use of pooled historic costs was one of the reasons why rents were not adjusted to local needs, with rent levels often being high in inner city areas with characteristically low wage levels. Despite the difficulties the government offered some justification for the restoration of a system that earlier investigations on their behalf had suggested was in need of reform: pooled historic costs had the merit of placing council tenants on a similar footing to owner-occupiers who paid on the basis of historic costs and local authorities were in a 'better position to fix rents than an elusive, transitory, appointed board remote from the electors, a board that did not even remain in existence afterwards to see the consequences of its decisions' (Parliamentary Debates (Lords) 1975, vol. 356, col. 320).

Although it seemed likely that there would be more variation in rents, the government did not make a statement as to the effect of a return to reasonable rents upon rent levels generally or whether reasonable rents would be higher or lower than 'fair rents'. They offered no definition of reasonable rents on the grounds that this was unnecessary. The local authorities could decide what was reasonable and there was plenty of guidance: the term 'reasonable rents' had been hallowed by case law over two generations of housing administration. However, it was clear that there would be no reduction in rents and although they would inevitably rise there was 'no reason why average rents should rise anywhere near £1 a week under the subsidy arrangements under this Bill' (Parliamentary Debates (Commons) 1974, Standing Committee A, col. 194).

As rent control was an integral part of the government's programme to counter inflation a provision was made in the Housing Rents and Subsidies Act 1975 for the Secretary of State to control future rent rises by order. The power could not be used to limit individual authorities' rent increases as it could only be applied to classes of authority or types of dwellings. However, to reassure local authorities of their intentions it was made clear that the government would only consider using this measure if a significant number of increases were unduly large or frequent and that they hoped it would not be necessary to make use of it. Yet its existence alongside the reintroduced non-profit rule suggested that the increase in local democracy as a result of the Act would be fairly limited and it was evidently intended that the threat of statutory action would be sufficient to remind local authorities of the need 'to ensure that rent increases are no higher than is necessary' (Parliamentary Debates (Commons) 1974, Standing Committee A, col. 135).

Whatever the scale of the increases in future years, in individual cases they would be limited by the rule that authorities should not budget for a surplus on the HRA. They would, however, be allowed to have a working balance. This was to allow authorities to even out rent increases and expenditure on repairs and maintenance and to plan for unexpected events (like rising costs) but it was to be 'no larger than is reasonably necessary having regard to all the circumstances' (Section 1(3) Housing Rents and Subsidies Act 1975). Yet in the absence of any guidance it was not at all clear at what point a working balance would become a profit. The Minister attempted to clarify the position – without actually succeeding in doing so: 'Once the authority begins to budget for a surplus larger than a reasonable working balance, it has begun to make such a profit' (Parliamentary Debates (Commons) 1975, vol. 887, col. 180). It was felt that authorities knew from their own experience what a reasonable working balance was and that it was not for the government 'to spell out these points in legislation. They are part of the management of housing estates which local authorities have been concerned with for over half a century' (Parliamentary Debates (Commons) 1975, vol. 887, col. 188). From the Act therefore it was not clear what would happen to local authority rents as it dealt only with procedures for rent fixing and not policy guidelines. Such guidelines might have been expected to emerge from the recently instituted Housing Finance Review.

In November 1974 as steps were being taken to dismantle the Housing Finance Act the Environment Secretary, Anthony Crosland, announced the government's intention to undertake a 'searching and far-reaching inquiry into housing finance' (Parliamentary Debates (Commons) 1974, vol. 881, col. 914). The fundamental questions to be resolved were the extent to which society as a whole should subsidise housing and how this subsidy should be distributed among individuals and tenure groups. But in the meantime there was only an indication that some limit might be placed on rent increases. While authorities were not to be allowed to have too high a rent increase nothing would be done if it were too low: 'the mirror-image of the situation under the Conservative Government' (Craven 1975: 113).

The new legislation left authorities free to review both their rents and methods of valuation but it is unlikely that many took this opportunity. Because the 1972 exercise would have been a costly one, at least for the short term there would be the temptation to retain the fair rents or provisional fair rents (as many of the rents were never actually approved by the Rent Scrutiny Boards). Webster (1979) subsequently examined the practices of three local authorities, Manchester, North Tyneside and Slough, and while two of them did review their rents in 1976 they used data gathered for the fair rents exercise.

It had been the intention of the preceding Conservative administration not only to increase local authority rents but also to standardise both rent levels and the process for their review and increase. Rents would be reviewed at least every three years and until fair rents were reached there would be compulsory annual increases. The 1975 Act provided for decisions regarding rents to be taken at local level and allowed complete discretion over the size and regularity of rent increases. In fixing rents for specific dwellings authorities were again able to decide on the distribution of subsidy, although few authorities appreciated that they were doing so (Webster 1979). In the absence of any specific decision to do otherwise subsidy would benefit all tenants regardless of their income (Craven 1975).

Profits from Public Housing
Once more Labour left council tenants as 'lambs for the slaughter', their rent policies had allowed rents to fall relative to costs so that the low proportion of outgoings met by rents could not fail to generate anger amongst right-wing politicians. However, there was equal concern from those on the left who recognised the claims of other services, particularly education and health, to scarce resources. Nor did there

appear to be any legitimate reasons for such a state of affairs, it was not argued that council tenants could not afford to pay higher rents or explained why they were paying rents that did not always cover management and maintenance expenses nor why rents should be allowed to fall in relation to earnings. In just three years from 1972/3 the proportion of costs met by rents had fallen from about 70 to 45 per cent, a fall sufficiently severe to suggest the need for urgent action and the replacement of the temporary system by something more permanent. This is not to suggest that rents did not rise under Labour because as Chapter 4 shows, their policies actually encouraged councils to increase rents partly because the previous restrictions were removed and partly because the whole benefit would accrue to the local community, there was no longer a possibility of 'profits' being diverted to the Exchequer (Hepworth 1975). Rents also rose as a consequence of local government reorganisation which removed many of the 'inefficient' councils like Clay Cross. Inevitably the merging of two or three authorities would have resulted in improved management as it would have required some reappraisal of rent policy and management and maintenance procedures. In the process some of the lowest rents would have been increased to align them with others in the new district council.

The Conservatives had learnt two lessons from 1972, they would ensure that rent increases were large enough to meet rising costs and inflation and choose indirect rather than direct controls over local authority housing. Apart from the repeal of the non-profit rule in the Housing Act 1980 the system for fixing rents was left intact and they relied on the subsidy and rate support systems to achieve their ends. Chapter 4 provides details of the mechanisms used to induce local authorities to raise rents, rather than rate fund contributions, to compensate for loss of assistance. With no objective ceiling for rents increases could go on indefinitely and ironically 'the former bitterly opposed "fair rents" might have given council tenants a greater degree of protection against rent increases than the current "reasonable" rents!' (Yates 1982: 212). In practice the approach was less successful: the pressure to raise rents lessened as authorities lost all entitlement to subsidy and their HRAs went into surplus, unforeseen anomalies which resulted in Conservative-controlled councils being penalised forced the government to set lower guidelines for rent increases and 'irresponsible' authorities tried to transfer their burdens to the national taxpayer by putting all rents up and telling tenants to claim from the national housing benefit scheme.

3 Rent Rebates to Housing Benefits

By the late 1960s it was widely accepted that there were problems with both income tax and the social security system and a lack of co-ordination between them. The income tax system was considered to be too complicated and too costly both in its administration and in the burdens it placed upon employers while the social security system was criticised for its failure to relieve poverty. There had been no comprehensive review of the social security system since the Beveridge Report of 1942 despite evidence of structural problems and the continual erosion of the value of benefits with accelerating inflation which necessitated almost annual adjustments to the levels of contributions and benefits. The Beveridge Scheme catered primarily for situations in which earnings were interrupted and made inadequate provision for the long-term sick and disabled and young unemployed who were unable to earn anything in the first place, nor had the scheme kept pace with changes in family structure so that new groups, like one-parent families, were not provided for (Harris 1979). This resulted in over-reliance on means-tested benefits and associated problems of inadequate take-up.

The overlapping of benefits and personal taxation resulted in a 'poverty trap' and very high marginal rates of taxation and this, together with the decision to shift the balance between family allowances and tax allowances in favour of the former in 1968, revealed the extent to which taxes and benefits were bound up together and the anomalies inherent in these two forms of welfare. Not only were large sums annually remitted by the Exchequer through the tax system in respect of dependent children, mortgage interest and life insurance premiums but such allowances were of little or no benefit to the poorest families and increased in value with the recipient's income because the value of the allowance was related to the rate at which tax would otherwise have been payable. This injustice was exposed by the Child Poverty Action Group and others in the poverty lobby.

The cost of social security also led to pressure for a radical review of welfare from the Right, partly inspired by the Negative Income Tax (NIT) movement in the United States. NIT was thought to have advantages over other forms of selective provision for income maintenance for not only did it ensure efficient use of resources but also avoided stigmatising the poor. In theory NIT could have replaced the existing income tax and social security systems removing the necessity for means-tested benefits and allowing the provision of all goods and services, including housing, through the market mechanism. However, such schemes were extremely difficult to design and even their most avid proponents failed to work them out and to present them in operational detail (Townsend 1972).

In the post-war period the amount of housing subsidy had been determined according to the cost of providing new housing and what it was felt tenants could be expected to pay. How this subsidy was used was left to local authorities' discretion: some pooled the subsidy to reduce rent levels generally while others set differential rents or granted rebates to tenants on lower incomes. Although rebate schemes had been explicitly sanctioned by the Housing Act 1930 local authorities made little use of them until the 1950s when, in preference to extending the rate subsidy, they raised rents to meet rising costs (Parker 1967). These schemes differed greatly in both the form they took and in their generosity; many failing to relieve hardship because the amount of assistance was inadequate or did not reach the poorest families.

It had been the 1966—70 Labour government's view that: 'Subsidies should not be used wholly or even mainly to keep general rent levels low. Help for those who most need it can be given only if the subsidies are in large part used to provide rebates for tenants whose means are small' (Cmnd 2838 1965, para. 41) and that poor tenants should be treated the same everywhere (MHLG Circular 46/67). But, although it had been suggested to the Housing Minister, Richard Crossman, that the government introduce a mandatory rebate scheme he chose not to do so and pushed instead for rate rebates (Crossman 1975). Rate rebates would be more popular with the electorate and would not involve the detailed interference in local affairs that would be necessary with rebates of rent. Before a statutory rent rebate scheme could be introduced the variation between local authority rents would have to be reduced and the basis upon which rents were determined rationalised. Labour therefore missed the opportunity to introduce a comprehensive and equitable rent rebate scheme, relying instead on an advisory circular (MHLG Circular 46/67).

It was generally accepted that whatever the extent of the tax and social security reforms separate provision would have to be made for assistance with housing costs (Barker 1971; Townsend 1972). Labour's model scheme could have formed the basis of a statutory rebate scheme for tenants in both public and private sectors (Cmnd 3604 1968) but there was no consensus that this was the best way to proceed. There was some support for the introduction of a universal housing allowance extending to tenants and home owners although its advocates recognised that devising a rational scheme would necessitate the reintroduction of the unpopular Schedule A tax (Gray 1968; Nevitt 1968a, 1968b; Greve 1969).

A National Rebate Scheme
The Conservatives had indicated their support for NIT in the 1970 election manifesto (Conservative Party 1970) but their immediate priorities on gaining office were to deal with the problems of poor families by introducing two new means-tested benefits, family income supplement (FIS) and rent rebates and allowances. As discussed in Chapter 2, the government's ability to raise rents and hence reduce the level of Exchequer subsidy depended on their ability to protect poor tenants from the full impact of the increases. In the longer term it was their intention to introduce a tax-credit scheme to cover the employed, national insurance beneficiaries and occupational pensioners with incomes above a specified level. Those below this 'poverty line', considered to be a small minority of about ten per cent, would be assisted by supplementary benefit, FIS (introduced in 1971 for low-income wage earners) and other means-tested benefits. Apart from home owners not in receipt of supplementary benefit, who would continue to receive tax relief on mortgage interest payments, there would be separate assistance towards housing costs 'since it is not part of the normal administration of income tax to take into account rent and rates and other special needs nor to respond immediately to changes in these factors' (Cmnd 5116 1972, para. 1). The government's view was that there should be unification not of the more general kinds of housing subsidies but of those means-tested subsidies available to the poor.

Means testing was retained as the most efficient mechanism to direct state aid to the poor while administrative considerations played no small part in the decision to provide under the Housing Finance Act 1972 a separate system of rent rebates and allowances (for housing association and private sector tenants) through the local authorities. By 1972 75 per cent of local authorities in England were operating some kind of rebate scheme (Legg and Brion 1976). Their previous experience and their knowledge of the local housing market which would enable them to judge, for example, the reasonableness of private rents or whether accommodation was over-occupied, made the decision about administrative arrangements relatively easy to resolve.

Nevertheless the introduction of a national rebate scheme posed a number of administrative problems including decisions on methods of checking income, the timetable for the introduction of the scheme and time periods for reapplication and revision of rebate and how to ensure an adequate rate of take-up (given the evidence of low take-up rates for other means-tested benefits, often despite extensive publicity campaigns). However, there were also problems of a more fundamental nature and in particular the relationship between rebates and rent levels and whether tenants should be liable for a minimum rent. It would be inappropriate to design a rebate scheme where the majority of tenants were entitled to rebate because any increase in rent would be minimised and the administrative costs would be high. A decision also had to be made about the eligibility of tenants who were in receipt of supplementary benefit, especially as an increasing proportion of these were council tenants: 43 per cent by 1965 against 21 per cent in 1954 (Parker 1967). Where authorities operated their own rebate scheme they generally excluded such tenants as, without any hardship to the tenants, they could increase their rent income. They received the rent in full and tenants were reimbursed by the Supplementary Benefits Commission. It was questionable whether councils should be allowed to maximise their rent incomes at the expense of the Department of Health and Social Security (DHSS) (HC 473 1969) especially as the cost was not insubstantial. Goudie (1972) estimated that the total cost of rent allowances to council tenants in 1968/9 was £105 million, £15 million more than the total for housing subsidies paid out that year. Finally, a choice would have to be made as to who should bear the cost of rebates: local authority tenants, ratepayers or taxpayers, or whether the cost should be shared amongst two or more of these groups.

The amount households had to pay in rent depended on the relationship between the minimum rent set for the dwelling, the household income and a basic expenditure allowance (needs allowance) which was determined so as to maintain comparability with DHSS benefits. Local authorities could improve upon the national scheme by using the '10 per cent tolerance': they could spend up to 10 per cent more than they would have done under the statutory scheme providing they were prepared to meet the costs of this locally. Under the scheme it was possible that some families would not pay any rent although this depended on both the rent level and the limitation on the amount of rebate payable. And to ensure the limit on the amount of rebate payable did not adversely affect tenants in high-rent areas discretion was given to the Secretary of State to grant permission for authorities to have a higher rebate or a lower minimum rent and a number of London authorities subsequently altered their schemes in this manner (Legg and Brion 1976). Lansley (1979) shows that under the scheme low-income households which paid average or above-average rents gained most and that for most other tenants housing costs rose. Those on average earnings only gained if they were paying higher rents and where their rents were below average their housing costs increased considerably.

It was made clear that supplementary benefit claimants would be entitled to rebates on the same basis as other tenants but the administrative process by which this was effected was extremely complex with different arrangements for the first eight weeks of a claim from those operating thereafter (Hill 1984b). Only the minimum rent was taken into account in calculating tenants' entitlement to benefit and the council had to give a rebate to cover the difference between the minimum rent and the full rent. The effect of this decision was to transfer costs that had previously been met by social security payments onto the housing service and because of the new subsidy arrangements effectively onto ratepayers and local authority tenants rather than taxpayers.

The government were quite determined that the total cost should not fall on the taxpayer and stated in the White Paper: 'The Government considers that a 100 per cent Exchequer subsidy for rebates would be wrong in principle, call into question the financial independence of local housing authorities and fail to reflect their responsibilities' (Cmnd 4728 1971, para. 53). But the government had promised not just rebates for public sector tenants but a similar scheme of rent allowances for tenants of private landlords and housing associations. Prior to the 1972 Housing Finance Act allowances had been available to tenants in the private sector only in Birmingham where the Corporation had taken powers under a Private Act in 1969. While the government was not prepared for the taxpayer to meet the full cost of rebates they were prepared to meet the cost of rent allowances — at least initially. The subsidy which would cover 100 per cent of allowances under the model scheme in 1972/3 would, however, be reduced by 1976/7 to 80 per cent, and the remaining 20 per cent could be met by the ratepayers. However, the ratepayers' contributions would only continue for as long as the HRA remained in deficit as any surplus on the account would be used to cover rebates and then allowances. Ultimately it would be possible for local authority tenants to pay for both rebates and allowances out of profits made on the housing account.

Local authorities were to be responsible for the administration of both the rebate and allowance schemes, the former to come into operation in October 1972 and the latter the following January. Despite the staggered start to ease the workload it was a tremendous task, especially given the scope for administrative discretion in determining personal income, taking account of 'exceptional personal circumstances' and for private tenants, considering whether the dwelling was suitable for the needs of the individual. There were also direct cash payments to be made to private tenants of which authorities had little previous experience. As the Act came into force on 27 July 1972 authorities were not surprisingly rather concerned about the tight timetable and over the necessity to reassess rebates every six months (twelve months for pensioners) and although some of the burden was placed on the tenants to claim their rebate and submit the necessary documentation, details of the scheme were to be provided and distributed to all tenants. The administrative load would depend on the numbers applying for rebates and allowances and this in turn was a product not just of the effectiveness of the publicity but of the level of rent. Prior to the Act about 10 per cent of local authority tenants were in receipt of rebate but this was expected to rise to about 40–45 per cent of public tenants and 30 per cent of private tenants by 1975/6 (Goudie 1972).

The division of responsibility which resulted in supplementary benefit claimants receiving help from two different sources added to the workload as papers had to be transferred between agencies and led to a deterioration in the relationship between the local authorities and the DHSS as the almost inevitable disputes arose. Some of the problems were resolved when the system was changed so that from April 1974 the full unrebated rent could be taken into account when assessing supplementary benefit and the tenant made responsible for payment of the rent to the council (DOE Circular 154/73). However, the authority remained liable for the cost of the rebates and a transfer had still to be made to the DHSS to cover the sum of the rebates of tenants in receipt of supplementary benefit. This situation was not redressed until 1978, by which time pressure was mounting for the removal of housing allowances from the supplementary benefit scheme (Donnison 1982; Hill 1984b).

Where private tenants were eligible for rent allowances they were treated differently to their counterparts in the public sector and from home owners. If the local authority responsible for administering the scheme felt that the dwelling occupied was larger than the tenant required or situated in an area of high property values where the tenant was living from choice rather than necessity the allowance could be cut. There was no suggestion that rate rebates or tax allowances should be so reduced, even though occupancy levels were known to be lower in owner-occupied housing.

Although rent allowances were available for the first time to the private sector, the scheme did not cover all tenants. Private furnished tenants were excluded, even though they were acknowledged to include some of the poorest households, because their rents were outside the fair rent system and it was felt that without the same degree of control over rents being charged, any allowance would simply be absorbed in higher rents. In addition, assessing allowances for furnished tenancies would have been more difficult as there would be a need to establish the proportion of rent that was attributable to the provision of furniture and then exclude this.

As a result of pressure from the poverty lobby the Conservatives subsequently conceded the principle that tenants of furnished accommodation should be eligible for rent allowances and the anomaly was rectified by the Furnished Lettings (Rent Allowance) Act 1973. However, the allowances, payable from April 1973, were only available to families with dependent children, pensioners and disabled persons with a residential qualification of three months, single persons over 30 years of age with a residential qualification of six months and to anyone in hardship. These provisions were extended by the Labour government in 1974 so that allowances were available to all furnished tenants. Once this had been done it was difficult to deny that there should be some control over the level of rents towards which allowances were being paid and the Rent Act 1974 accordingly extended protection to tenants of furnished accommodation.

Along with FIS and the new pension scheme implemented by the Social Security Act 1973 the rebate and allowance schemes were all that was achieved by the Conservative government in the social security field. Although preparations for the tax-credit scheme were well advanced they were lost with the election in 1974 (Donnison 1982).

A Universal Housing Allowance?

The legacy of the 1970–74 Conservative government was further dislocation rather than the hoped-for harmonisation cf the income tax and social security system. Their consciously selective policy led to a growth in means-tested benefits and added to the problems of the 'poverty trap' and poor take-up of benefits. The pressure on supplementary benefits was such that Donnison (1982) considered there to be a danger of general breakdown of the whole system. Yet despite this there was neither consistent pressure for change nor a commitment to reform on the part of the new Labour government.

Despite their manifesto promises to achieve greater equality through tax reforms, specifically by the introduction of taxes on wealth and capital transfer (Labour Party 1974a; 1974b), Labour's priorities were the implementation of a new pension scheme and the introduction of child allowances. There was therefore little chance of any major restructuring which might delay this legislation especially as the failure to realise the tax-credit system had highlighted the technical complexity of reforms of such magnitude, the public expenditure implications and the difficulty of completing the task within the lifetime of a government. Failure brought few electoral benefits.

Although Labour had opposed the introduction of rent rebates and allowances as an undesirable extension of means testing they did not repeal this part of the Housing Finance Act 1972 because of its popularity with the electorate. However, their availability created what became known as the 'better off' problem because claimants were uncertain whether to claim rebates or supplementary benefit. David Donnison, appointed Chairman of the Supplementary Benefits Commission in 1975, was convinced this problem could only be resolved and the supplementary benefits scheme simplified if housing assistance were taken outside of the scope of supplementary benefit. It would be possible to institute a much simpler means test if housing costs did not have to be assessed and it would eliminate the obligation to subject about 130,000 people to an elaborate test to receive benefit which only paid for their rent. Nearly a tenth of the staff administering supplementary benefit were required to deal with the housing element alone (Donnison 1982).

There was little logic in retaining two separate schemes to provide assistance with housing costs, with the DHSS paying rent to clients who in turn paid their landlords and the Department of the Environment (DOE) through the local authorities providing rebates of rent. As individuals found it difficult to decide which scheme would be best for them the result was large numbers of people misclaiming benefits and forfeiting their rights. Donnison (1982) maintains that about 300,000 in receipt of supplementary benefit would have been better off receiving rebates while 100,000 had the reverse problem and that the existence of the two systems resulted in people in similar circumstances receiving different amounts of housing aid.

While Labour fulfilled their electoral promises on pensions and child allowances they failed, for the second time in less than a decade, to reform housing assistance. The Social Security Pensions Act 1975 which came into force in 1978 was a revised version of Labour's earlier superannuation scheme which was lost when the government fell in 1970. This was superimposed on the Conservatives' pension plan which had been partially implemented by 1975. The Child Benefit Act 1975 brought in an enlarged tax-free family allowance for all children, including the first. It did not, however, phase out the child tax allowances although the anticipated savings from doing so had been the justification for the measure. In the event resistance to the withdrawal of tax allowances, even though in this instance the redistribution was within the family from fathers to mothers, resulted in concessions. Allowances were retained for a longer period and the scheme was less ambitious than the original proposals.

This approach could have provided a precedent for the reform of housing assistance and was the essence of Donnison's contribution to the review of supplementary benefits begun in 1976 and discussed in the Supplementary Benefits Commission's Annual Reports of 1976 and 1977 (Cmnd 6910 1977; Cmnd 7392 1978). He saw a need both to unify the system of payments to tenants and to bring owner-occupiers within the scope of the scheme. This would have allowed the ending of tax relief on mortgage interest payments and some of the savings could have been used to cover the costs of aligning the DHSS and DOE benefits. Without this there would have been too many losers and not enough gainers to make the idea politically saleable; no government would have welcomed a scheme that suggested taking money away from elderly ratepayers. However, there was a further reason for the integration proposals: more and more owner-occupiers were becoming supplementary benefit clients and any reform which left them out would still leave the DHSS wrestling with some of its most difficult calculations of housing costs (Donnison 1982).

By 1978 it was evident that Labour did not intend to institute either a tax-based universal housing allowance or a unification of the supplementary benefit housing allowance with rent and rate rebates. Before the review team's report 'Social Assistance' was published in 1978, 'Peter Shore agonised for a fortnight before we were allowed to include a chapter, already drastically shortened by his officials, proposing the reform of housing benefits' (Donnison 1982: 114). The government's negative attitude cannot be entirely attributed to the hostility of DOE officials to this kind of reform as surprisingly little on this subject emerged from Labour's review of housing policy. This review began in 1974 when Anthony Crosland, then Secretary of State for the Environment, announced an inquiry into housing finance. It was his belief that the distribution of housing assistance was causing deep and bitter resentment: home owners were seen to be getting a better deal than tenants; not only did they have the benefit of tax concessions but, as a result of inflation, their homes were rising in value (Crosland 1975). The review failed to appear in the anticipated 12 to 15 months as a result of disagreements both among those responsible for producing the report and in Cabinet (Nevitt 1978). While Crosland evidently preferred some redistribution of subsidy others were aware of the political mine-field of tampering with tax reliefs for home owners (Harloe 1977); apprehensions that would have been heightened by Labour's by-election defeat in July 1975 which was attributed to voters' fears for the abolition of mortgage tax relief (Kilroy 1978). After Crosland was replaced by Peter Shore in April 1976 the decision was taken to post-pone publication and widen the scope of the review to include all aspects of housing policy and thereby lessen the prominence to be given to financial issues. Even from the early stages 'there seemed to be scant concern about the poor amongst those working on the housing review and no reforming drive coming from the top' (Donnison 1981: 6).

When the Green Paper (Cmnd 6851 1977) was published in June 1977 its proposals were of a very conservative nature and suggestions for fundamental financial changes were rejected. Four sets of proposals had been considered in the search for more equitable forms of assistance towards housing costs:

(i)   fixing the price of housing according to current value rather than historic costs;
(ii)   replacing general assistance by increased rebates or allowances;
(iii) introducing a universal flat-rate housing allowance; and
(iv)   maintaining existing forms of general assistance but distributing them more fairly.

However, all were rejected in favour of the status quo because 'the decisions and family budgets of millions of households have been shaped by the expectation that existing arrangements will continue in broadly their present form' (Cmnd 6851 1977, para. 2.14). The only viable explanation for Labour's indifference to the claim for greater equality is an 'almost fanatical belief in owner-occupation as a cure for almost all problems' (Nevitt 1978: 333) and the urgency of securing home owners' votes. Advocates of a universally available housing allowance were particularly disappointed that Labour did not take their ideas on board (Hill 1984b).

The government's failure even to secure a partial unification of rent and rate rebates with supplementary benefits was probably due to their desire to retain a specifically identifiable rate rebate which they believed gained them political support: the same grounds which they chose to introduce rate rather than rent rebates in the late sixties. 'It is still difficult to know what might have emerged had Mr Crosland not been succeeded by a man ambitious for the leadership of his party, and apparently more sensitive to the prejudices of party activists than to the public good' (*Financial Times* 18 May 1978) but Shore's political judgement may have been correct. Webster (1980a) on observing that the Housing Policy Review was not even debated at Conference suggests that there would have been very little backing for a Secretary of State interested in financial reform, except from a handful of intellectuals. Any change would offend some entrenched interest and it was to minimise giving such offence that the government chose to conserve the existing system.

Housing Benefit: An Illusion

The 1979 Conservative Party Manifesto had restated the Party's commitment to the tax-credit scheme but it would now only be introduced as and when resources became available. It was soon evident that this time would be a long way off: within a year of taking office earnings related supplement on unemployment benefit was abolished and child benefits, short-term national insurance benefits and pensions were allowed to fall in real terms in an attempt to contain a social security budget which was under severe pressure as a result of rising unemployment. In this context Ministers were prepared to make changes to the social assistance and housing assistance schemes only where they could be achieved at 'nil-cost' (Donnison 1982; Timmins and Walker 1984). The Social Security Act 1980 implemented some of the proposals formulated during the supplementary benefits review, producing a simpler system with less discretionary payments. The requirement of a 'nil-cost' reform ruled out increases in the scale rate and resulted in a redistribution of benefit amongst the poor although the change made in the legal basis for decisions about supplementary benefits was beneficial and increased individuals' rights as discretionary and secret rules were replaced by regulations laid down by Parliament (Donnison 1982).

The Conservatives reviewed the situation with regard to housing benefit in 1979 and the reform of supplementary benefit was followed with a consultation paper 'Assistance with Housing Costs' (DOE 1981b) which proposed a unification of rent and rate rebates with the supplementary benefit housing addition. It was claimed that a unified housing benefit would solve the 'better off' problem, make the scheme easier to understand and be fair for recipients in similar circumstances and for those both in and out of work. However, it soon became evident that a primary consideration was the possibility of shedding about 2900 civil servants by making local authorities responsible for administering the scheme. Local authorities would need much smaller increases in staff because of the savings that would result from easier rent collection and in the longer term removal of the housing element would permit further simplification of the supplementary benefits scheme and reductions in staff.

Because of the different tests of income and means, alignment of the rebate and supplementary benefit schemes could not be achieved without either an increase in expenditure or a large number of 'losers'. As the 'nil-cost' constraint ruled out the former and the latter was politically unacceptable the 'solution' was to drop 'unified' from the housing benefit scheme and effectively leave the two schemes running together (McGurk and Raynesford 1982). Supplementary benefit recipients would have their housing costs met in full by the local authority after they had been 'certificated' by the DHSS while those whose income was above supplementary benefit level but who were entitled to help with housing costs would receive standard housing benefit depending on their household composition, income and housing costs. The 'tapers' used in assessing the benefit were originally to be adjusted so that those who gained from the new scheme would be offset by those who lost — initially estimated at 2,150,000 losers compared with 810,000 who would gain (DOE 1981b). However, those who would incur the most substantial losses were those who had previously had part, but not all, of their rent met by supplementary benefit, a group which included large numbers of occupational pensioners, a natural Tory constituency. As a result of pressure from the poverty lobby the scheme was altered prior to implementation and the tapers adjusted to shield pensioners from the full extent of the loss and a top-up payment 'housing benefit supplement' was introduced for those who would be better off on supplementary benefit. This was to be paid by the local authority but assessed by the DHSS (Hill 1984b) and by 1933 almost half a million claimants were eligible (Parliamentary Debates (Commons) 1984, vol. 67, cols 381–3). Despite such expedients the Social Security and Housing Benefits Act 1982 made a fundamental distinction between the two categories of claimant. Only supplementary benefit claimants had a right to have their rent met in full. Standard housing benefit recipients were entitled to assistance with a proportion of their housing costs but that proportion could be altered and the tapers manipulated to favour one social group at the expense of another (Harvey 1982).

Housing benefit was introduced in two stages: a partial start in November 1982 with the scheme becoming fully operational from April 1983. Because of the decision to introduce an enabling Bill with the detail to be covered later, between August 1982 and April 1983 no fewer than nine separate sets of regulations were published, some amending those issued only a few weeks before. Donnison (1982) had previously pointed out that it took weeks, and sometimes months, to provide rebates so the success of the new scheme would depend upon authorities getting the benefits to claimants quickly enough to prevent people with high rents who suddenly became unemployed from getting into serious difficulties. Nevertheless at no time during this period did the government appear to seriously question the local authorities' ability to administer the scheme, the number of staff and the amount of training they would require or the time it would take to acquire the necessary technology and develop the related software. This contributed to what the Social Security Advisory Committee was later to describe as a 'remarkably troubled birth' (Timmins and Walker 1984).

A number of administrative difficulties arose during the first year of operation. Faced with an increasing number of cases, delays in receipt of DHSS certificates, larger numbers of short-term claimants than had been anticipated, changes in tapers and benefit levels and rent and rate rises, authorities were unable to make payments without unreasonable delays – often weeks or even months (Bradley 1984; Hill 1984b). As a result while their own tenants built up arrears, tenants of private landlords and housing associations were actually left without the money to pay their rent. Private tenants were evicted and housing associations, which claimed their arrears increased by 57 per cent during the six months following the introduction of housing benefit, were left with serious cash flow problems. Some claimants were subsequently over-paid due to DHSS delays in cancelling certificates or because papers were lost in transit between the offices involved. The additional administrative costs of the scheme, estimated at £20.2 million for 1983/4, turned out to be £52.5 million, an increase of 160 per cent, and were likely to be even higher at an estimated £60.7 million in 1984/5 (*Guardian* 3 April 1984).

This was because local authorities, encouraged by the government's pledge to reimburse them for additional administrative costs (DHSS Circular 2/82) and faced with an increased caseload and complex assessments, recruited more staff than had been saved at the DHSS.[1] By 1985 about 3500 additional staff were employed by local authorities to administer the scheme rather than the 1500 predicted when the scheme was launched. And although savings of around 2500 DHSS staff were initially made, about 500 were re-instated once the scheme was underway (Parliamentary Debates (Commons) 1984, vol. 68, col. 472). The result was a scheme more costly to administer than the range of benefits it replaced (HC 638 1984), without any improvement in either delivery or equity.

Furthermore inequalities are likely to increase as a result of planned reductions in housing benefit. In 1983 the government announced proposals to make savings of £230 million on the housing benefit budget. Although the reason they gave was the need to reduce the un-expectedly high administrative costs it soon became clear that reductions of this scale, which if implemented, would have resulted in 2.8 million (including 1.3 million pensioners) being worse off and 600,000 (including 270,000 pensioners) losing benefit altogether, could not be ascribed to such a cause. The problem was that one million more people were claiming housing benefit than the govern-ment expected when the scheme was introduced. Following signs of growing disquiet on the government backbenches some limited con-cessions were made. The reduction in the level of benefits was delayed, the tapers modified to protect pensioners and an independent review of housing benefit was instituted.

The housing benefit review began in April 1984 along with three other reviews of aspects of the social security system: supplementary benefits, provisions for retirement and benefits for children and young people. The limitations of its remit to 'examine the structure and scope of the scheme to ensure that it is as simple as possible, and that help is concentrated on those most in need' excluded the possibility of additional resources or of including home owners and at best promised to achieve some improvement in local authority operations. Despite this the question of whether councils should continue to administer the scheme and the desirability of unification of the tax and social security systems or the payment of a universal housing allowance were raised in the ensuing debate. However, the government was looking to the review to provide an answer to the problem of the enormous growth in social security payments.

Income maintenance, along with housing, came to the forefront in debates about the economy in the late seventies and early eighties when governments were under increasing pressure in their attempts to maintain macroeconomic strategies by restraining public expenditure. Rising unemployment made it difficult to keep within planned expenditure targets but the problem was exacerbated by reductions in unemployment benefit and high rents which forced large numbers of people onto supplementary and housing benefits, a trend which has resulted in increased dependency upon means-tested benefits and more people being caught in the poverty trap. Having failed to include home owners in the housing benefit scheme, except for rebates of rates, there is the unresolved problem the DHSS faces in paying a housing addition covering mortgage interest and an allowance for insurance and repairs to the growing number of home owners in receipt of supplementary benefit; more than twice as many in 1982 as in 1979 (Table 3.1).[2]

Table 3.1   **Payment of supplementary benefit to meet mortgage interest charges (Great Britain)**

Year	Claimants	Amount added in assessment[1] (£ million)
1974	84 000	11
1975	98 000	20
1976	123 000	27
1977	124 000	33
1978	105 000	26
1979	98 000	31
1980	134 000	71
1981	196 000	124
1982	235 000	170

[1] The estimated amount of money added in the assessment includes mortgage interest and ground rent.

Source: Parliamentary Debates (Commons) 1984, vol. 65, cols 510–11.

While the urgency of addressing these issues is greater than in the late sixties or early seventies, paradoxically the chances of finding a solution are much less. The 1983 Conservative government was elected on a manifesto that for the first time in over a decade made no commitment to a tax-credit or similar scheme (Conservative Party 1983) and the decision to hold four independent reviews of social security suggested they would condone little more than piecemeal reform. This approach has a measure of political realism: the time it would take to achieve a major overhaul of the system would extend beyond the lifetime of the government. Furthermore the sheer complexity of the task because of the interactions between different elements in the system is a formidable deterrent. While housing benefit has exposed the delusion of 'nil-cost' reform, there is no indication that the electorate is prepared to pay through higher taxation. Neither is new technology a panacea; the prospect of computerisation of personal taxation may provide an opportunity for restructuring but housing benefit revealed what chaos could ensue when software was inadequate or not available on time.

However, the most fundamental impediment is the absence of agreement on the direction reform should take. There are widely conflicting beliefs about the main purpose of the social security system: whether it is the relief of poverty, the enhancement of efficiency or the reconstruction of a new social order (Atkinson 1983). Such a divergence of views accounts for the failure of the Commons Treasury and Civil Service Committee to agree upon a report on the structure of personal income taxation and income support before Parliament was dissolved in 1983.

During the seventies a pattern of provision emerged in which separate arrangements were made to assist tenants on low incomes with their housing costs. At first this support had to be found from within the housing budget but it was gradually accepted that this was an element of income maintenance to be funded under the social security programme. With the limited prospects for structural reform the distinction between means-tested housing-related benefits for tenants and tax reliefs for home owners is both likely to remain and to continue to be reinforced by the division of supplementary benefit claimants into two groups with different rules and different institutions processing their claims. In the process the freedom local authorities had previously enjoyed over the granting of rent rebates was lost with the introduction of a mandatory scheme in 1972. They were, however, allowed to vary the amount of support provided, within limits, and the DOE adopted a *laissez-faire* approach which allowed them to exercise considerable discretion in the administration of the scheme. The transfer of responsibility from the DOE to the DHSS with the introduction of housing benefit has made significant inroads into this discretion as the 'DHSS seem much more inclined to see rule making for local authorities in much the same way as they see rule making for the centralized supplementary benefits scheme' (Hill 1984b: 306).

The inequities arising from the differences between the rights enjoyed by tenants and home owners and between certificated and standard housing benefit recipients must be partly attributable to Labour's repeated failure to grasp the nettle and reform housing finance. Even if the 1966–70 Labour government cannot be blamed for their failure to recognise the opportunity for radical reform presented by linking housing subsidy to interest rates with the attendant possibility of incorporation into the tax system and of equating assistance for tenants with that provided for home owners, they could have introduced a fair and equitable rent rebate scheme. Despite Labour's professed opposition to any extension of means testing the Conservatives' national rent rebate scheme was left intact and remained unscathed despite the reviews of housing policy and supplementary benefits initiated at the start of their term of office. Labour's rejection of the claim for equity and their uncertainty about the form of residential property for a socialist society accounts for their failure to respond to the case made for a universal housing allowance.

4 Housing Subsidy and Housing Costs

When Anthony Crosland remarked that: 'We have a system of subsidies which distribute aid to housing in a whimsical manner' and noted the need for a system which would 'at least . . . eliminate some of the more unjustifiable inequalities' (Crosland 1975: 128–30), he was reflecting upon all the tenure groups and not tenants in isolation. However, his wider perspective was not shared by either his colleagues in the Labour Party or the Conservatives and government programmes were almost exclusively confined to the public sector where, it was believed, council tenants were over-subsidised and able to pay more for their housing and public landlords were inefficient and in need of financial management. Governments therefore sought to reduce housing subsidies, both Exchequer and rate fund contributions, by raising rents. And as this had to be accomplished without undue hardship to poorer tenants they had to adopt, as Chapters 2 and 3 have shown, not only new approaches to rent determination but a national scheme for rent rebates.

The Housing Finance Act 1972

The 1970 Conservative government realised that a substantial reduction in the subsidy bill would only be achieved if they could curtail existing subsidies and ensure that in future payments were not made whenever new investment took place, regardless of authorities' ability to finance the development. They felt in the long term only those areas with high costs or a continuing programme of building would need Exchequer or rate subsidy and that tenants who could afford to do so should meet all or a higher proportion of their housing costs. 'The Government's central policy of subsidising people, not bricks and mortar' (Cmnd 4728 1971, para. 41) would be carried out through the national rent rebate scheme and a new form of deficit subsidy. Although different levels of subsidy had been paid under the Housing Act 1961 depending upon the state of a notional HRA, the introduction of deficit subsidies marked a radical departure in subsidy design and the HRA, the account on which all transactions arising from the ownership and management of council housing were recorded, assumed a new importance over and above its role in rent fixing and became a focus of debate. The income and expenditure on the HRA, as well as the notional sums involved, was subjected to much closer scrutiny and manipulated by both central and local government in the battle over resources.

The subsidy design had to meet five main objectives:

(i)   to contain the growth of subsidies so that they remained at their current level until 1975/6. Thereafter it was hoped that the amount of subsidy could be reduced.

(ii)   to increase the proportion of direct rent assistance;

(iii) to redistribute subsidies to areas with the greatest housing need;

(iv)   to remove financial disincentives to slum clearance and encourage alternative uses of the land to local authority housing; and

(v)   to facilitate long term planning by making provision for 1981/2 and beyond;

and to achieve these ends eight new subsidies were introduced. As the whole basis of subsidy entitlement was to be changed, provision had to be made for a period of transition as well as a new permanent system of support. Three of the new subsidies — Residual, Transition and Operational Deficit — were to be temporary and would phase out existing subsidies over two to three years. All authorities would be entitled to Residual Subsidy into which all existing subsidies were to be consolidated. This would be withdrawn in a controlled manner as it was replaced by rent income as rents progressed to 'fair rent' levels. However, if rent rises were insufficient to cover the reduction in Residual Subsidy then a proportion of the difference would be met by Transition Subsidy and where, as was likely in authorities which had large deficits under the old system and which were in the habit of making large rate fund contributions, there was a remaining deficit, a third subsidy, Operational Deficit, would meet the contingency.

The major new permanent subsidy, in addition to those to cover rent rebates and allowances, was Rising Costs. This was to be payable when costs on the HRA rose faster than rent income. As it was felt that 'fair rents' would ultimately eliminate any deficit on the HRA and would actually generate surpluses, where there was an entitlement to Rising Costs Subsidy it was only to be paid for a limited period. So that, for example, if an authority was entitled to Rising Costs Subsidy in 1972/3 it would be paid for ten years whereas if a similar entitlement were to arise in 1975/6 or later years it would only be paid for a five-year period.

Nevertheless to prevent subsidy becoming open-ended local

authorities became subject to more detailed control over their general expenditure levels, including spending on management, maintenance and improvement; these controls were in addition to the established capital cost controls, operated through the cost yardstick system, which were retained (Hepworth 1976). This was to be achieved by basing entitlement to Rising Costs Subsidy not upon actual expenditure on, say, loan charges or maintenance, but on the increase in 'reckonable expenditure' over the immediately preceding year. Thus by defining reckonable expenditure the government might not only limit the size of the subsidy bill but influence the pattern of local authority expenditure as councils would be reluctant to spend on unsubsidised items. To avoid the necessity for checking individual authorities' expenditure formulae were devised that allowed figures to be set for each main class of authority. For example, for 1973/4 and subsequent years limits for expenditure on repair and maintenance and supervision and management were derived by averaging expenditure per dwelling for the preceding three years for each class of authority and adding a sum to allow for inflation; this was meant to encourage authorities to bring costs down towards the average costs for their type of authority.

As originally drafted the Bill only provided for the payment of Rising Costs Subsidy during the first two years 'if for the year 1972–73 or the year 1973–74 there is an increase in the local authority's reckonable expenditure which exceeds £6 multiplied by the number of Housing Revenue Account dwellings as at the end of the year' (Clause 4(2)(a), Housing Finance Bill, November 1971). These provisions were felt to be particularly onerous not only because of the sum involved but also because the authorities would not know in advance the basis upon which reckonable expenditure would be determined. Effective lobbying resulted in an amendment being forced upon the government after the Lords stages which provided for the first year's subsidy to be based on the actual increase in expenditure in 1972/3 over 1971/2. As the Exchequer's share of the increase was to be 90 per cent this provided an opportunity for local authorities to increase their expenditure in 1972/3 in the knowledge that most of the increase over 1971/2 would be met by the government. This was one of the reasons why subsidies increased rather than diminished after the Act.

These subsidies were all credited to the HRA (Figure 4.1) but, with the exception of Residual Subsidy, were only payable if there was a deficit on the account. Furthermore the subsidy design was such that they would meet only a proportion of any deficit. One of the government's principal concerns was the control of profligate authorities and so they ensured that any deficit arising as a result of an authority's housing activities should be shared between the Exchequer and the ratepayers, as an incentive to economy. Provision was therefore made for a mandatory rate fund contribution to be linked to each subsidy. In

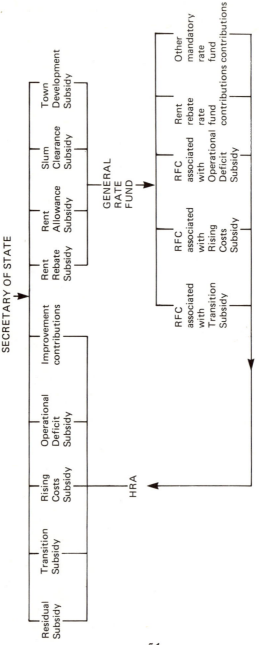

SECRETARY OF STATE

Residual Subsidy · Transition Subsidy · Rising Costs Subsidy · Operational Deficit Subsidy · Improvement contributions · Rent Rebate Subsidy · Rent Allowance Subsidy · Slum Clearance Subsidy · Town Development Subsidy

HRA

GENERAL RATE FUND

RFC associated with Transition Subsidy · RFC associated with Rising Costs Subsidy · RFC associated with Operational Deficit Subsidy · Rent rebate rate fund contributions · Other mandatory rate fund contributions

HRA = Housing Revenue Account; RFC = rate fund contribution.

Source: Department of Environment Circular 76/72.

Figure 4.1 Diagrammatic representation of the relationship between subsidies, the Housing Revenue Account and the General Rate Fund

54

addition, to prevent authorities from deliberately creating or increasing the size of their deficit, limits were placed on the size of the working balance and on the amount of capital expenditure that could be financed from revenue (to 2 per cent of total HRA expenditure). The Act laid down the share of the deficit that would be met by the Exchequer and over time an increasing proportion would have to be found by the ratepayers. Overall these requirements would result in some authorities making a rate fund contribution for the first time in many years since they had ceased to be compulsory in 1956.

Although the Rent Rebate and Rent Allowance Subsidies were paid into the General Rate Fund they were intimately linked to the state of the HRA. Rent Rebate Subsidy would only be paid where the 'surplus' on the HRA was insufficient to cover the costs of rebates and even then, as Figure 4.1 shows, there was provision for a contribution from the rates, set initially at 10 per cent but to increase to 25 per cent by 1975/6. In addition to this linked contribution, ratepayers would have to cover the costs of administering the scheme and extra expenses incurred if the authority chose to make use of the 10 per cent tolerance and go beyond the requirements of the model scheme.

Perhaps the least controversial of the new subsidies was the Slum Clearance Subsidy. This also marked some break with the past, although perhaps not as great as was sometimes suggested (Cullingworth 1979). While previous subsidies had been tied to local authority redevelopment, in future aid was to be available regardless of the future use to which the site was put, to the extent of 75 per cent of the difference between the costs of acquiring and clearing the land and the value of the cleared site. Although the changes could be explained in terms of equity, that an activity that produced benefits for the community should be financed by the community as a whole, it is much more likely that the change was prompted by a desire to see the cleared sites used for housing for owner-occupation rather than developed for public housing.

Some of the most acrimonious exchanges arose over the arrangements made for the expected surpluses. Some Conservatives clearly expected the windfall profits to be so great that they were 'hoping to obtain sufficient revenue to justify a lowering of taxes' (Nevitt 1971: 17). Accordingly the Act provided that once subsidies and rate fund contributions had been eliminated from the HRA any surplus was first to be offset against the authority's entitlement to Rent Allowance Subsidy, although this would result in local authority tenants subsidising tenants in the private sector and meeting what were clearly national responsibilities for income maintenance. Thereafter, any remaining surplus was to be divided: with the Exchequer keeping half and the rest being returned to the authority for the benefit of the ratepayers on the grounds that 'The Exchequer will relieve ratepayers of

Table 4.1   Central government subsidies and rate fund contributions to local authority housing 1970/1 to 1979/80 (England and Wales)

£ million

	Central government subsidies			Rate fund contribution	Total housing subsidy
	Subsidies excl. rebates	Rebates	Total		
1970/1	159	—	159	56	215
1971/2	187	—	187	40	227
1972/3	184	61	245	94	339
1973/4	237	132	369	88	457
1974/5	486	153	639	176	815
1975/6	632	166	798	232	1030
1976/7	835	212	1047	227	1274
1977/8	894	248	1142	242	1384
1978/9	1055	266	1321	305	1626
1979/80	1225	408	1633	444	2077

Source: DOE Housing and Construction Statistics.

most of any deficits in the Housing Revenue Account and initially of the whole cost of rent allowances. The Government therefore considers that the Exchequer should share in any surplus arising in that Account' (Cmnd 4728 1971, para. 64).

In the event these provisions were largely superfluous because, rather than being maintained at their existing level or reduced, subsidies continued to increase steeply, along with rate fund contributions (Table 4.1). The results of this are shown in Table 4.2 in terms of the fall in the proportion of HRA costs met by rents. While there was an initial sharp rise in the proportion of outgoings met by rents in 1972/3, there was a decrease thereafter and this would have occurred even without the intervention of the Labour government and their decision to halt the progression to 'fair rents' by imposing a rent freeze (Cmnd 6851 1977).

Although rents increased as predicted and kept pace with earnings (Table 4.3), the annual increase of £26 per dwelling was insufficient to match accelerating inflation and the rising costs of management, maintenance and loan charges (reflecting land and tender costs and higher interest rates) (Cmnd 6851 1977). The higher level of council house building that followed the 'Barber boom' and the change of direction in economic policy would also have added to these costs but in addition local authorities appear to have taken the opportunity to replace lifts,

Table 4.2 Ratios of rent to Housing Revenue Account outgoings
1970/1 to 1983/4 (England and Wales)

	Gross rents	Rents net of all rebates	Net rents and certificated rebates
(1964/5		73)	
(1969/70		70)	
1970/1		72	
1971/2		72	
1972/3	77	69	
1973/4	73	59	
1974/5	60	47	
1975/6	57	45	
1976/7	53	44	
1977/8	56	46	
1978/9	53	43	
1979/80	50	38	
1980/1	49	38	
1981/2	66		57
1982/3	69		59
1983/4	72	39	60

Notes:
1 It is difficult to obtain figures for gross rents (before deduction of rebates)
prior to 1972/3 but as rebates in 1971/2 were only about £18 million compared
to net rents of £572 million, the lack of gross rent figures prior to 1972/3 should
not affect the comparison too much.
2 Rents are of dwellings only and outgoings are net of transfers to the Grant
Redemption Fund and other income to show the amount to be raised from rents
of dwellings, subsidy, or rate fund contribution.
3 Figures for 1981/2 and subsequent years are not comparable with 1980/1 and
earlier years because net rent income includes payments from tenants in receipt of
supplementary benefit from the DHSS. Previously reimbursements to the DHSS
were required. Separate figures for certificated rebates are only available for
1983/4.

Sources: Table IV.12 Cmnd 6851 1977; DOE Housing and Construction Statistics; CIPFA Housing Revenue Account Statistics.

Table 4.3   Rents, index number of rents, average earnings and general price level 1970 to 1983 (England and Wales)

Indexes 1974 = 100

	Rents[1] (£ a week)	Rents Index	Earnings[2] Index	Index of Retail Prices[3]
1970	2.27	60	61	67
1971	2.48	66	67	73
1972	2.75	73	75	78
1973	3.44	92	87	86
1974	3.75	100	100	100
1975	4.16	111	127	122
1976	4.77	127	151	145
1977	5.52	147	165	170
1978	5.85	156	187	183
1979	6.40	171	213	202
1980	7.71	206	261	246
1981	11.39	304	295	276
1982	13.50	360	324	301
1983	14.05	375	351	313
1984	14.70	392	375	330

[1] Average weekly unrebated rents of local authority dwellings for April of each year, except for 1973 where the figure is for May and 1974 which is for January.

[2] Full-time men 21 years and over (adult rates for 1984), all occupations, April figures; Great Britain.

[3] April figures, United Kingdom.

Sources: Table IV.13 Cmnd 6851 1977; DOE 1982c; 1983; 1984.

install central heating, undertake major capital repairs and improve some of their older estates as well as taking on extra staff, in the knowledge that such expenditure would be underwritten by the government. The increase in expenditure on management and maintenance was most marked in 1972/3 and was over and above what can be accounted for by general inflation (Cooper 1984).

There were several reasons why authorities spent more. The Act not only provided subsidy for the first time for repairs and maintenance and supervision and management but councils were able to take advantage of the decision to pay Rising Costs Subsidy on the actual increase in expenditure between 1971/2 and 1972/3. By increasing their expenditure they would not only have increased their subsidy in 1972/3 but also for subsequent years as the 1972/3 spending level was the base from which reckonable expenditure would be computed for subsequent years. It would have been to a local authority's disadvantage not to have as high a figure as possible. Furthermore in a situation in which rents were being forced up against the will of many councillors it was natural for them to look for ways to mitigate the effects of the rent increases and one way was to compensate the tenants for the higher charges with better services and higher standards of maintenance. This also had the added advantage of delaying the withdrawal of subsidy as higher levels of expenditure kept the HRA in deficit.

Throughout their period of office the Conservatives supported the sale of council houses by removing restrictions and increasing discounts. However, their concern to achieve and maintain high levels of sales was not solely due to a preference for home ownership but because the interest from capital receipts from sales would be likely to reduce any deficit on the HRA (Craven 1975). In the event this strategy was not very successful as they were unable to sustain the peak of over 60,000 sales reached in 1972 but it formed a precedent for the 1980s. The rise in the cost of rebates was also a precedent, if of a rather different sort, and was an important component in the rise in the subsidy bill. The cost of rent rebates increased from £61 million in 1972/3 to £166 million by 1975/6 and would have reached an even higher figure had the Conservatives' policies continued after 1974 (Cmnd 6851 1977), unless the government had pushed up the amount of rent increase. This might have helped reduce the gap between rents and costs but given the economic conditions, even with much greater rent increases it would have taken a long time to bring about an appreciable change in the size of the subsidy bill.

The government were more successful in redistributing subsidies than in controlling the total amount. Before the Act about 10 per cent of Exchequer subsidies were used to provide rebates for poorer tenants and the remainder, together with any rate fund contributions, was used to keep down the rents of all tenants, whereas in 1972/3 rebates comprised 22 per cent and by 1973/4 34 per cent of all subsidies. It was also the case that subsidies went increasingly to high-cost areas, especially inner London. In seeking to make the housing service profitable and to redistribute assistance the government had established the principle that surpluses on housing activities could be used to provide for income maintenance both for council and private tenants within and outside of the local authority area and that any remaining surpluses could be used to finance non-housing activities.

Despite the government's failure to achieve all their objectives, they succeeded in producing a system that was more effective in controlling local housing decisions than the one it superseded. Although Labour was committed to a repeal of the Housing Finance Act 1972 they were reluctant to relinquish the power it afforded central government. Furthermore in some respects the 1972 Act actually represented Labour's position: it had been developed from the finance review undertaken by the previous Labour government and would re-emerge in the subsidy proposals in the Housing Policy Green Paper (Cmnd 6851 1977) of the next Labour government. Its lasting contribution was the curtailment of the subsidy commitments of earlier generations. It was dangerous to maintain that old promises were sacred if current circumstances justified change.

The Labour Government's Interregnum

The lack of an apposite programme forced Labour to return to the pre-1972 situation. The long hard battle, both inside and outside Parliament, over the Housing Finance Act 1972 and the unexpectedly early decision to hold a General Election after the Conservative government had completed only three full years in office only partially explains their disarray. Merrett (1979) attributes Labour's reluctance to offer the electorate a comprehensive plan to their failure to implement their National Housing Programme during their previous term of office and hence to their disillusionment with centralised planning but there is no evidence for this and in any case such 'failure' might have been overcome by adopting different strategies and setting more realistic targets. It seems more likely that it was lack of agreement over the future direction of housing policy that forced them back to the rent and subsidy arrangements in existence in the late sixties. While there were elements within the Labour Party that supported the Conservatives' stance others still felt that the generous subsidies characteristic of the Crossman period and paid under the Housing Act 1967 were the answer to the problem. Certainly many Labour councillors would have been unhappy with anything less than repeal of the 1972 Act.

Pending the outcome of the housing finance review 'temporary' arrangements were made. As part of these the system of rebates and allowances was left unchanged including the subsidy arrangements and the balance of contributions between the Exchequer and the rate fund. Seventy-five per cent of the 'standard amount of rent rebates' (i.e. rebates falling within the model scheme) was met by the Exchequer and all remaining costs (25 per cent of the standard amount of rent rebates, rebates granted in excess of the standard amount and the costs of administration) by the ratepayers. Many local authorities considered it to be unjust that they should have to bear the burden of what was essentially provision for income maintenance but the government was not prepared to shoulder the additional costs, justifying their position with reference to future action: in the longer term 'We shall have to examine our definitions of housing subsidy and housing finance . . . and consider rebates and rent allowances in future as part of the cash social security scheme' (Parliamentary Debates (Commons) 1974 Standing Committee A, col. 206). Other subsidies — Rent Allowance and Slum Clearance — were also left untouched.

The Housing Rents and Subsidies Act 1975 brought in a new subsidy system designed to meet four objectives:

(i)   to restore local authorities' freedom to decide their rent levels and therefore the amount of contribution from the rates;

(ii) to restore the rule that local authorities should not make a profit on the HRA;

(iii) to enable local authorities to maintain the higher levels of investment the government wished to see without imposing an unacceptable burden on tenants or ratepayers; and

(iv) to 'raise the total subsidy for local authority house building to that granted to owner-occupiers on their mortgage payments' (Labour Party 1974a: 8).

Although the government wished to see an adequate level of general support for all authorities they were aware from past experience of the dangers of escalation of the subsidy bill that could result from a universal subsidy. Accordingly they accepted a formula which combined both 'producer' and deficit elements. To this extent the new system was built on the foundations of the 1972 Act but there were important differences:

(i)   some subsidy would be available to all authorities regardless of the state of their HRA;

(ii) local authorities would determine the distribution of costs between tenant and ratepayer. There were no compulsory rate fund contributions apart from the mandatory contributions to cover a deficit on the HRA and in respect of rebates and costs charged to the HRA for amenities which were of benefit to the whole community; and

(iii) the authorities would be allowed to retain existing subsidies.

The three producer elements — Basic, Supplementary Financing and New Capital Costs — were to be available regardless of the state of the HRA. Basic element consisted of the existing subsidy entitlement for 1974/5 and would therefore meet loan charges on existing properties while Supplementary Financing element covered the effects of inflation on these costs and helped those authorities which as a result of refinancing loans had to pay higher rates of interest. The latter element met 33 per cent of the increase in debt charges over those payable in 1974/5, a generous sum in Webster's (1977) opinion as in many authorities rent income would have been sufficient to cover such an increase. However, the decision to meet a third of the increase in costs was explained in other terms: 'This seems to us a fair proportion of the burden to be shared between the tenant, taxpayer and ratepayer, and is not too far from the additional relief given to an owner-occupier when . . . the interest on his mortgage rises' (Parliamentary Debates (Commons) 1974, vol. 881, col. 909).

As deficit subsidies were considered responsible for the lower levels of output under the Housing Finance Act New Capital Costs element was to meet 66 per cent of the 'reckonable expenditure' on land acquisition, construction, improvement and acquisition of dwellings falling on the HRA each year. The choice of 66 per cent was of necessity arbitrary. The subsidy needed to be high initially but could be lower in the long term as rents would meet an increasing proportion of costs.

However, at local level the contribution that could be made from rents towards the cost of new projects would vary and such considerations forced compromises on the subsidy designers (Webster 1977).

Under the Housing Finance Act 1972 authorities, such as Islington and Liverpool, with high costs and large building programmes whose HRAs had remained in deficit had received 75 per cent of their costs under Rising Costs Subsidy. There was therefore pressure in individual cases for the level of contribution to be raised. However, the circumstances of most authorities and the necessity to provide some incentive for economy suggested both keeping the proportion down and defining reckonable expenditure very tightly. To avoid the necessity of unacceptably large rent increases in areas where the subsidy would be inadequate High Costs element was to be payable from 1976/7. There was no detailed discussion of the operation of High Costs element in the debates on the Bill and from the little information available it was almost impossible to determine which authorities would be eligible. As a result concern was expressed by some Members that it would only assist the London Boroughs, and to allay their fears Gerald Kaufman explained: 'We are going to negotiate with the local authorities about the matter. We have a breathing space this coming year during which the high cost subsidy goes into abeyance and is replaced by the special element. We will try to work out something more satisfactory to the local authorities' (Parliamentary Debates (Commons) 1974, Standing Committee A, col. 183). The crucial decisions were yet to be made. As it happened they were remade each year and the result was a different level of subsidy without any explanation being given for the variation.

The control of rents was an important part of the government's counter-inflation strategy and so local authorities had to be helped both over the effects of the rent freeze and subsequently to keep the amount of any rent increases down. Consequently Special element was to be available for 1975/6. It was to be paid for one year only and thereafter consolidated into Basic element. Although no provision had been made in the original legislation a second instalment of Special element was paid in 1976/7 under the Remuneration, Charges and Grants Act 1975 although this time it was not incorporated into Basic element in subsequent years. This concession, which added £68 million to the subsidy bill, was to meet the claim of local authorities that High Costs element was insufficient compensation for complying with the guidelines in the White Paper 'The Attack on Inflation' (Cmnd 6151 1975) and limiting their rent increases to 60 pence per week. An authority's entitlement to Special and High Costs elements was not based on actual costs and revenue but as with the 1972 Act system on what government felt should be taken into account. A notional HRA had to be drawn up with admissible items on the expenditure side and expected income on the other. Expenditure on management and maintenance was based on actual expenditure for 1975/6 updated annually to take account of relevant pay and price increases. It was a device that allowed any increase in real terms over the previous year to be disregarded and became in effect a cost limit which could be used to control local housing expenditure. Income was adjusted by adding a 'local contribution' which varied in amount from year to year: there was an assumed rent increase of £23 per dwelling per annum (45 pence per week) for 1975/6 and £31 (60 pence per week) for 1976/7 and for subsequent years. Special or High Costs elements met a proportion of the deficit on the notional account. Where councils wished to claim High Costs element they were obliged to increase their rents by at least the guideline amount. The system was certainly more generous than the one preceding it but it did not turn out to be simpler and with constant adjustments to Special and High Costs elements it proved almost impossible for local authorities to calculate their subsidy entitlement (Webster 1977).

The government found it increasingly difficult to control the level of subsidies which increased significantly from 1974/5 (Table 4.1). Most of the Exchequer subsidy was paid in Basic and New Capital Costs elements, with the proportion paid as New Capital Costs increasing from 22 per cent in 1975/6 to 43 per cent by 1977/8. Although High Costs element was a less significant component in the subsidy bill a surprising 145 authorities applied for this in 1977/8, showing that it did not turn out to be a subsidy only available to the London Boroughs.

The government's inability to control the subsidy was due to a number of interrelated factors which included both the subsidy design and an incomes policy in which rent increases were kept deliberately low in order to restrain wage demands. As had occurred under the 1972 Act, inflation and rising interest rates added to the costs to be met by the Exchequer both directly and indirectly as general price rises in periods of wage restraint encouraged the take-up of housing-related benefits. This together with the adjustment of the needs allowance which was raised, for example, four times between April 1973 and

December 1975, increased the cost of rebates and allowances. Because the subsidy was designed during a period in which costs and interest rates were rising sharply and the government wished to provide some kind of subsidy floor so that tenants, like home owners, would be guaranteed a measure of assistance regardless of means, no provision was made to claw back Basic element or limit entitlement to New Capital Costs element should either rents increase or costs fall and authorities be able to finance their housing programmes from their own resources. In the absence of such provision the only way the government could have contained New Capital Costs element would have been to reduce the level of new investment. Consequently when the rise in costs began to slow down and interest rates to fall from 1977/8 the government was unable to benefit from this (Smith and Howes 1978).

In terms of their own objectives the government was more successful in holding down rents. This was achieved by a combination of rent freeze and rent guidelines, subsidy payments, the reintroduction of the non-profit rule and the decision that from 1974/5 rate fund contributions to the HRA would be eligible expenditure for Rate Support Grant (RSG) at 66 per cent. Although rents continued to rise they fell in relation to earnings (Table 4.3) and failed to keep pace with rising costs on the HRA, falling from just under 70 per cent in 1972/3 to just over 40 per cent by the end of Labour's term of office (Table 4.2).

Furthermore, apart from the handful of authorities which were dependent upon High Costs element, the size and regularity of rent increases was once more in the hands of local authorities. After 1974/5, the year of the rent freeze, some authorities reverted to a low rents policy with no or minimal adjustments from year to year while others implemented substantial rent rises. The result was great variation in practice, for example, some authorities (including Islington, Lambeth, Tower Hamlets and Manchester) did not raise their rents at all during 1975/6 while others delayed their increase until October 1975 or later (including Camden, Greenwich and Hackney) and then only increased rents by 40 pence or so per week. Elsewhere authorities made two increases (107 out of 344 authorities including Leeds, Newcastle, Liverpool and Coventry) and the amount of the increase was higher overall (exceeding £1.50 per week in Bromley, Kensington and Chelsea and Merton). In 1976/7 increases were more evenly spread and generally there was only one. Few authorities made no increase at all but the amount was inversely related to the level of increase during the previous year (Cmnd 6851 1977; Cooper 1984).

Labour's temporary arrangements lasted much longer than the permanent system they replaced and led to a number of unanticipated longer-term effects: rent differentials increased, the gap between rents and costs widened and the subsidy bill increased alarmingly. Not only did Labour unwittingly overturn the one real achievement of the

Housing Finance Act 1972, the establishment of the principle that past subsidies were not sacred, but also effectively institutionalised continuing political controversy about the State's contribution to individuals' housing costs. Although new proposals were made as a result of the review of housing policy they never reached the statute book.

Their experience in office evidently convinced Labour of the need for a subsidy that would achieve the same objectives as the Conservatives had sought in 1972: that could take account of both local needs and resources; that was flexible enough to adjust to changing interest rates and costs; that would concentrate financial assistance on needy areas and reduce the size of the subsidy bill. Given these objectives it was not surprising that the proposals in the Housing Bill 1979 had much in common with the earlier legislation although they also incorporated features of the Special and High Costs elements paid under the 1975 Act. Entitlement to subsidy would depend on the status of a notional HRA and if this showed a deficit all or part of this would be met by subsidy. Although the setting of a subsidy floor was discussed no firm decision was taken on whether there would be an automatic entitlement to subsidy in order to retain some degree of equity between owner-occupiers and local authority tenants (Cmnd 6851 1977). Neither were any estimates of the effects of the new system published although such forecasts were available (Kilroy 1978), possibly because it was likely that for all types of authority except Inner London Boroughs there would be reductions and savings in the overall total (Howes 1978). There is little doubt that Labour would have used the system to reduce the cost of subsidies but they were prepared to set a limit to the rate of withdrawal to ensure that rents did not rise faster than average earnings, that allowance was made for reasonable building and running costs and that the housing service was not used to generate profits. Greater savings would have been possible had they been prepared to abandon the non-profit rule and adopt national rent pooling. While Labour were prepared to adopt a subsidy design that had much in common with the Conservatives' they drew the line at the unpopular profit-sharing provisions.

Housing Subsidy: The Merry-go-round

The Conservatives inherited a relatively impoverished public sector and a growing subsidy bill. Had the experiences of 1970—74, the failure of 'fair rents' and deficit subsidies to create a profitable public sector, not been enough to convince them that the answers lay in a drastic reduction in the amount of council housing and subsidies and much higher rents Labour's omissions would have led them to the same conclusions. Even had they wished to do so they could not have adopted the same approach as in 1972. There was little to be gained from objective methods of rent fixing and the 1975 Act had shown that there were other tools for achieving the same effect; rent guidelines could be set at any level, high or low. However, by dismantling the 1972 Act system Labour had returned local authorities' freedom to determine rate fund contributions as well as rents and these were underpinned by RSG as a result of the Conservatives' own actions. This would have to be changed if rent increases were not to lead to subsidy by the back door of rate support. At the beginning of the seventies they had thought it possible to divert profits from public housing to finance rent rebates and allowances and other central government services. By the eighties they were much less sure: they could no longer isolate housing support from income maintenance because of decisions taken on the funding of supplementary benefit recipients entitled to rebates of rent and proposals for reform of both supplementary benefit and housing benefit were well advanced. If profits could not be tied to housing assistance, care would have to be taken in the way the 'tax' was levied if confrontation was to be avoided.

In conception the 1980 Housing Act subsidy was very similar to that devised by Labour in 1979, although its implementation would not necessarily have had the same effect as the main parameters in the subsidy equation were amenable to considerable adjustment and the system could be used to generate very different levels of subsidy. The government claimed that it would achieve the objectives that had eluded them in 1970–74, a reduction in the excessive level of housing subsidy and in the inefficiency they believed was rife among local authorities. Therefore the system had been designed to direct subsidy to areas unable to finance their housing costs locally and to increase central government control over the recurrent expenditure of local authorities thereby improving efficiency and restraining 'indiscriminate purchases which can easily result in a waste of public money' and 'unduly extravagant' schemes (Parliamentary Debates (Lords) 1980, vol. 411, col. 646).

The government's first major departure from existing policy was to remove the automatic entitlement to subsidy and make it available only where there was a deficit on the housing account. An authority's entitlement would be calculated:

> by taking the amount of subsidy entitlement for the previous year or nil or the appropriate negative amount if there was no entitlement, called the base amount (BA), and increasing or decreasing it according to whether the change in their reckonable expenditure for the year of account, called the housing cost differential (HCD), is greater or less than the change in their reckonable income, called the local contribution differential (LCD). (DOE 1982a, para. 7)

This can be represented by the formula:

HOUSING SUBSIDY = BA + HCD - LCD

where   BA = base amount
            HCD = housing cost differential
            LCD = local contribution differential

Whether an authority would be eligible for subsidy therefore depended upon an equation in which the government controlled the variables. When the subsidy was first paid in 1981/2 BA was defined as the aggregate of subsidies paid the preceding year under the 1975 Act. As the government had reduced entitlement more drastically in 1980/1 than in previous years by assuming a rent increase of £94 per dwelling per annum in the calculation of High Costs element, these reductions were reflected in BA for 1981/2 (Gibson 1981). For subsequent years BA was the existing subsidy entitlement or nil or a negative amount, depending upon the outcome of the calculation. To BA had to be added HCD which represented the difference in reckonable expenditure on capital programmes, mainly debt charges, and management and maintenance between the year of account and the preceding year. To 'encourage a proper sense of efficiency and economy in the taking of their investment decisions' (DOE 1980c, para. 13) it was decided that for 1981/2 and subsequent years only 75 per cent of loan charges and capital expenditure financed from revenue would be reckonable for subsidy, a decision which had the additional merit of reducing an authority's entitlement or deterring them from incurring such expenditure.

The management and maintenance allowances could be manipulated in the same way. In the early stages of the development of the subsidy system it was proposed that regression analysis be used to determine an appropriate management and maintenance allowance for each authority, but this was subsequently rejected in favour of a simpler method based on actual levels of expenditure. The allowance for 1980/1 was based on the authority's average expenditure over the three years 1978/9 to 1980/1, the figures having been adjusted to allow for inflation. For later years the amount was increased by an annual percentage set by the Secretary of State: 9 per cent for 1981/2, 7 per cent for 1982/3 and 1983/4 and 5 per cent for 1984/5 over the figure for the previous year (DOE 1981c; 1982b; 1983; 1984). Any costs above these amounts were not reckonable for subsidy. By keeping the inflation factors as low as possible additional savings could be made on the subsidy bill and by excluding any increase in expenditure in real terms authorities would be encouraged to keep within the guidelines and to look for economies in the provision of these services. Any costs above the amounts reckonable for subsidy would have to be met from rents or rate fund contributions.

The LCD, the difference between reckonable income in the year of account and the preceding year, was also derived from notional figures. Gross rent income for 1980/1 was defined as the reckonable income for that year and the criteria for determining the notional increase as 'among other things . . . past and expected movements in incomes, costs and prices' (Section 100, Housing Act 1980). The government interpreted 'among other things' as including the need, in their view, to reduce public expenditure, to safeguard capital programmes within a reduced housing budget and 'the incidence of those housing costs which authorities bear from local income unsupported by Exchequer subsidy' (DOE 1980b, para. 9). On this basis decisions were taken about the increase in local contribution for 1981/2 and subsequent years and in all cases it was assumed that the increase would be met entirely from rents (DOE 1982b; 1982c; 1983; 1984). The notional rent increase over the preceding year was £2.95 per dwelling per week for 1981/2, £2.50 for 1982/3, £0.85 for 1983/4 and £0.75 for 1984/5, representing increases of 50, 20, 6 and 5 per cent respectively.

If LCD increased more rapidly than HCD then the amount of subsidy payable would be reduced and the greater the difference between them the more rapid the withdrawal of subsidy. Gibson (1981) has shown how such a reduction was achieved in 1981/2:

> The average national figure for the initial amount for management and maintenance in 1980—81 is estimated at £283 per dwelling. Therefore, on average, there is a (£283 x 9/100) [as each local authority's initial amount is to be uplifted by 9%] £25 increase in reckonable expenditure on management and maintenance. The 'increase in local contribution' for 1981—82 is, however, much larger at £2.95 per dwelling per week or £153 per dwelling per year. Thus for each dwelling in the average HRA in 1981—82 which enters the calculation the increase in the deficit due to the comparison of the notional changes in management and maintenance and rents is

---

Change in management and maintenance component of reckonable expenditure	minus	Change in reckonable income	
£25	minus	£153	= minus £128

> . . . for nearly all housing authorities it is the above difference . . . which will have been the main determinant of the loss in subsidy between 1980—81 and 1981—82. (Gibson 1981: 17—18)

Unlike the situation in 1972 when Residual Subsidy was protected and the other subsidies were only withdrawn when there was a surplus on the HRA and by implication they were no longer needed, the 1980 Act provided for their removal irrespective of local requirements. However, it proved more difficult for the government to recoup the profits that arose as rents were increased than it did to cut the payments made. As a result of lobbying by the Local Authority Associations it was agreed that when the subsidy calculation resulted in a negative entitlement no attempt would be made to reclaim the subsidy in the year of account but the negative figure would be carried forward as BA to be offset against any future entitlement. The clawback arrangement was therefore much less direct than under the Housing Finance Act 1972 when surpluses on the HRA had to be remitted to the Exchequer and the new scheme allowed local ratepayers rather than taxpayers to benefit as profits were transferred to the rate fund. Having made this concession the government attempted a less direct approach to achieve the same end.

Rate support for housing expenditure
The achievement of the government's central objective, the reduction of public spending on housing, was seen to depend on the curtailment of both Exchequer subsidies and rate fund contributions and making good such losses from increased rents. This result was achieved by more subtle means than those tried in 1972, as local authorities were not compelled to make specific rent increases but rather induced to do so. Several mechanisms were employed to achieve this end including the withdrawal of support for rate fund contributions to the HRA. RSG had been made available for this item of expenditure in 1972 when such contributions were made compulsory. However, had it been allowed to continue there would have been less incentive to increase rents rather than rates as the full burden of housing costs would not have fallen on the ratepayers. The 1980 Local Government, Planning and Land Act made alternative provision for such rate support in the new Block Grant which was payable from April 1981 in place of the Needs and Resources elements of the RSG.

An authority's entitlement to Block Grant was based on an assessment of Grant Related Expenditure (GRE). This sum represented the cost of providing a standard mix of services and was calculated from a number of factors, one of which, Indicator E7, covered housing costs falling upon the rate fund. This indicator represented the notional HRA deficit and was arrived at after the government had decided what proportion of its assumed rent increase could be used to reduce the level of rate fund contributions. For example, in 1981/2 the government assumed a rent increase of £3.25 per dwelling per week (£2.95 per dwelling per week was the notional increase for subsidy purposes and a further £0.30 was added to cover increases in non-reckonable expenditure). As much of this increase was needed to offset the reduction in subsidies the government decided only £171 million would be available to reduce the aggregate of rate fund contributions from £408 million to £237 million (at 1980 survey prices) (Gibson 1981). The £237 million was then distributed among authorities on the basis that they were charging an average rent equal to the average rent in their region. Those authorities which had lower-than-average rents were therefore discriminated against in a way that was designed to encourage them to raise them to average levels.

The lower the E7 figure the greater the rate finance required at any given level of expenditure and so although rent policy was left to local authorities' discretion there was considerable pressure upon them to increase rents. This pressure was greatest upon those authorities given a negative E7 figure, implying that a notional profit was available for transfer to the General Rate Fund. As this profit reduced the authority's GRE less grant would be payable and in effect an authority's 'negative subsidy entitlement' would be clawed back. Although it was not as easy as it had been under the 1972 Act to identify the redistribution of profits on the HRA, authorities in this position, mainly small Conservative-controlled District Councils, protested at the 'tax' and as a result it was agreed that no authority would be given a negative E7 figure in 1984/5 (Walsh 1983), thus effectively restoring their right to the profits.

Although authorities were free to spend any surplus on improving the housing service they could also under Section 134 of the Housing Act 1980 transfer such a sum to the General Rate Fund and use it for any purpose proper to that fund including holding down the rates. In 1980/1 18 authorities were making transfers from their HRAs to the rate fund and by 1983/4 the number had increased to 78, with 89 proposing to make such transfers in 1984/5 out of over 300 councils in surplus on their HRAs. The councils making such transfers were predominantly District Councils, for example, Slough, Tonbridge and Malling, South Oxfordshire and Cheltenham, but included the London Boroughs of Bexley, Bromley, Havering, Hillingdon and Kingston; and Dudley, St Helens and Wirral Metropolitan Districts. Neither were the sums involved insubstantial, £17.8 million in 1981/2, £20.8 million in 1982/3 and an estimated £26.2 million in 1983/4. One authority in particular, East Cambridgeshire, gained notoriety by raising more revenue from its stock of 5200 dwellings than it did from the rates and in so doing revealed the extent to which the government had gone beyond the 1972 position with council tenants paying not just their housing costs but even subsidising their better-off neighbours in providing a whole range of local authority services (*Guardian*, 13 October 1982).

As an additional incentive to councils to increase rents rather than rates a taper was built into the Block Grant. The GRE figure for each authority was taken as a threshold and there was a different level of support for each £1 increase in expenditure depending upon whether or not the authority's spending was above this figure. Authorities whose expenditure exceeded GRE – and rate fund contributions to the HRA counted as expenditure – were penalised by a correspondingly greater reduction in grant. However, as some authorities had been spending below their GREs the system proved ineffective in controlling the aggregate of all authorities' expenditure and so an *ad hoc* adjustment was made by introducing additional expenditure targets. From 1981/2 individual authorities were set an expenditure target based on their level of past expenditure and grant penalties were imposed where this was exceeded (Smith 1983). The government decided to exclude HRA transfers to the rate fund when determining whether or not an authority was overspending in relation to its expenditure target. As this artificially reduced the spending target it resulted in a number of largely Conservative-controlled authorities which had rigorously followed government advice on the raising of rents being penalised as overspenders in 1982/3. This embarrassing anomaly was subsequently rectified but is a further reason why a relatively low rent increase was set for 1983/4 and illustrates the way in which the system was becoming increasingly difficult to control.

The government were not as successful in controlling rate fund contributions which increased from £321 million in 1979/80 to £504 million by 1983/4 as they were in scaling down subsidies. However, the new system did enable them to contain this increase; rate fund contributions increased by only 20 per cent between 1981/2 and 1983/4 compared with 31 per cent between 1979/80 and 1981/2 (Table 4.4). One of the reasons they were not as successful as they had hoped to be was that the control systems began to break down when some of the higher-spending inner city authorities like Camden, Southwark and Manchester lost entitlement to RSG and it was no longer possible to penalise them for making contributions from the rates until a mechanism for rate-capping was established by the 1984 Rates Act.

The balance between rent and subsidy
Exchequer subsidies fell from their peak of £1423 million in 1980/1 to £290 million in 1983/4, a reduction of over 80 per cent from the introduction of the new system in 1981/2. By 1983/4 most authorities had lost their entitlement to subsidy, apart from a minority of London Boroughs and Metropolitan Districts, and only 87 councils claimed subsidy in 1984/5 (Parliamentary Debates (Commons) 1984, vol. 69, cols 65–6). The greatest losers were those which had undertaken little or no new building during the preceding decade, along with urban authorities with large holdings of stock in relation to their development programme which were penalised by the inadequate allowances for

Table 4.4   Central government subsidies and rate fund contributions to local authority housing and rent rebates 1979/80 to 1983/4 (England)

	Central government subsidies to local authority housing (£ million)	Rate fund contributions to local authority housing (£ million)	Rent rebates[1] (£ million)
1979/80	1274	321	238
1980/1	1423	430	317
1981/2	906	420	490
1982/3	507	434	944
1983/4	290	504	1968

[1] Figures include the cost of help with rent for tenants in receipt of supplementary benefit, from November 1982 for some and from April 1983 for all cases, Great Britain.

Sources: Table 2.7, Table 2.12, *The Government's Expenditure Plans 1984—85 to 1986—87*, Cmnd 9143 1984.

Table 4.5   Rate of rent increase 1979/80 to 1984/5 (England and Wales)

	1979/80	1980/1	1981/2	1982/3	1983/4	1984/5
	£ per dwelling per week					
Average unrebated rent	6.48	8.18	11.51	13.59	14.04[1]	14.94[1]
Assumed average increase as compared with previous year	0.42	1.80	3.25[2]	2.50	0.85	0.75
Actual average increase as compared with previous year	0.58	1.70	3.33	2.08	0.45	0.90
Percentage increase	10%	26%	41%	18%	3%	6%

[1] Estimated figure.

[2] Composed of £2.95 increase for subsidy purposes and £0.30 to cover non-reckonable expenditure.

Sources: DOE 1983; 1984.

revenue expenditure on management and maintenance. Leicester, for example, received £11.8 million in general subsidy (excluding Rent Rebate Subsidy) in 1980/1 and if the 1975 Act had remained in operation would have received £12.8 million in 1981/2. Instead the council collected £8.2 million, losing £4.6 million in subsidy.

Local authorities generally made good these losses from rents rather than from the rates; and rent increases of over 130 per cent between 1979/80 and 1984/5 took the majority of councils into surplus on their HRA. The pattern of both recommended and actual increases was somewhat erratic: substantial rises of 26, 41 and 18 per cent in 1980/1, 1981/2 and 1982/3 were followed by lower increases of about 3 and 6 per cent respectively in 1983/4 and 1984/5. Nevertheless rents increased much faster than both earnings and retail prices (Table 4.3).

Table 4.5 shows how closely average increases corresponded to government guidelines. There was less pressure to conform after 1981/2 as by this time most authorities had lost their entitlement to subsidy and the RSG controls were weakening. What action an authority took on rents would depend on whether it decided to create a surplus on the HRA or not. While some councils evidently chose to make a profit out of housing others saw no justification for further increases and may have kept rents down by choosing to invest capital receipts from council house sales, rather than spend them on capital programmes, in order to credit the interest to the HRA. Forrest and Murie (1984b) show this was the fastest-growing item of income on the HRA, having increased from £81 million in 1979/80 to £494 million by 1983/4 and suggest it has become as important in relation to rents as rate fund contributions. In these circumstances 152 out of 367 English authorities were able to declare no increase in rents for 1984/5 and a further 14 reported having made reductions (Parliamentary Debates (Commons) 1984, vol. 53, col. 656).

The modest rent increases assumed for 1983/4 and 1984/5 marked a dramatic reversal in rent policy. The government attributed the change to a fall in the level of pay settlements: a weak explanation when there had been no previous attempt to keep increases in line with inflation and where the increase of 6 per cent was below the government's own forecast for the growth in average earnings for 1983/4. Their embarrassment over the block grant penalties and the publicity surrounding councils using housing surpluses to subsidise better-off ratepayers may have caused them to temper the rate of rent increase in the period up to the 1983 General Election. However, this does not explain why the trend continued in 1984/5 and a correspondingly small increase (60 pence per dwelling per week) was recommended for 1985/6.

The real reason for the change was the impact government rent policies were having on the social security budget. As the numbers

Table 4.6   Rent rebates and local authority tenants receiving supplementary benefit 1970 to 1983 (England and Wales)

	Number granted rent rebate (thousands)	Local authority tenants receiving supplementary benefit (thousands)	TOTAL (thousands)
1970	350	1023	1373
1971	350	1120	1470
1972	270	1168	1438
1973	765	1105	1870
1974	840	1134	1974
1975	940	1103	2043
1976	995	1176	2171
1977	1005	1269	2274
1978	985	1302	2287
1979	980	1266	2246
1980	1095	1312	2407
1981	1305	1513	2818
1982	1383	1694	3077
1983	1440	1593	3033

Notes:
1 The figures for rebates are for October except for 1972 (March), 1973 (December), 1974 (April), 1983 (April), whilst those for supplementary benefit are for November 1972–74 and August thereafter.
2 A mandatory rent rebate scheme was introduced in October 1972.
3 The figures for 1983 are for standard and certificated housing benefit.

Sources: DOE Housing and Construction Statistics; CIPFA Rent Rebates and Allowances; Quarterly Statistical Enquiry.

receiving help with their rent through rebates or supplementary benefit increased so did the total cost of such assistance. Table 4.6 shows a 35 per cent increase in the number of tenants in receipt of housing benefit between 1979 and 1983 and although the rise in the number in receipt of supplementary benefit is related to the growth in unemployment there was a similar increase in the number in receipt of rent rebate (standard housing benefit from 1982). By 1983 almost 60 per cent of council tenants were receiving assistance.

The higher rate of take-up and the increase in the average amount of rebate from £3.65 in 1979 to £7.94 in 1983 (an increase of 118 per cent) led to the reintroduction of a large-scale and open-ended subsidy at a time when housing subsidies on revenue deficits were being phased out. While housing subsidy fell to £290 million in 1983/4 £1968 million was being spent on housing benefit (Table 4.4) so that the proportion of housing costs met by net rents was the same in 1983/4 as it had been in 1979/80 (Table 4.2). Table 4.7 shows in some detail how the proportion of rents actually payable by tenants was likely to be less than 50 per cent by 1984/5. To this extent the new subsidy system failed to achieve the government's objectives: to improve efficiency and to eliminate the waste of public money. In their haste to raise rents and reduce public expenditure they failed to appreciate the number of poor people in council housing and the economic justification for maintaining low rents and limiting the number entitled to rebates. With a high proportion of poor tenants direct assistance is more efficient than indirect aid because of the administrative costs of assessing each individual's entitlement. As further savings could only be made by reducing individuals' benefits, a policy known to be unpopular both with the Party and the electorate, there was the supreme irony that the government recreated the very problem the 1980 Housing Act was designed to eradicate: a rising subsidy bill not easily susceptible to government control.

Furthermore as profits on authorities' HRAs were partly generated from housing benefits as more and more councils made transfers to their rate funds so it became increasingly clear that 'the DHSS in the name of welfare ends up subsidising ratepayers who often own their own homes' (*The Times*, 2 February 1983). And with a national subsidy available for the poorest households and no objective system of rent fixing or national ceiling for rents, there was even the possibility that local authorities would make differential rent increases in order to increase the payments for housing benefit and hold down the rents of those not in receipt of assistance towards their housing costs. In 1982 Sheffield City Council planned to raise the rents of its 32,000 tenants in receipt of supplementary benefit and to leave the rents of the remaining 63,000 tenants unchanged (*The Sunday Times*, 20 November 1983). The DHSS refused to pay the extra element which the council explained was the result of a new division of responsibility for repairs so that the rent rise only applied to tenants who did not elect to carry out minor repairs. However, should the DHSS's objections be overcome and the scheme widely adopted the government will not only have failed to control the state's share of housing costs but will have permitted a return to the irrational rent policies characteristic of the sixties.

'Tax Spending' and the Myth of Self-sufficiency
Although there was an increase in the number of council tenants in receipt of housing benefit, many tenants were not eligible and having lost their entitlement to a general subsidy they received no assistance towards their housing costs. Consequently, the only way in which they could obtain state aid was to buy their council house and take advantage of the discount and tax relief on mortgage interest payments.

Table 4.7 Gross rent income local authorities 1981/2 to 1984/5 (England and Wales)

	1981/2		1982/3		1983/4		1984/5	
	£m	%	£m	%	£m	%	£m	%
Net rent income	2678)	86.1	2965)	84.7	1888) 53.5)	83.6	1798) 49.9)	82.2
Certificated rebates[1]	)		)		1065) 30.1)		1161) 32.3)	
Standard rebates[2]								
Subsidy	383	12.3	476	13.6	510	14.5	562	15.6
RFC	43	1.4	53	1.5	57	1.6	62	1.7
Rebates excess (RFC)[3]	7	0.2	8	0.2	12	0.3	18	0.5
Gross rent income	3111	100.0	3502	100.0	3532	100.0	3601	100.0

1 Certificated rebates are those paid to tenants in receipt of supplementary benefit from the DHSS.
2 Statutory rent rebates are financed 90 per cent by government subsidy and 10 per cent by mandatory rate fund contributions.
3 Rebates paid in excess of the statutory scheme must be met by a rate fund contribution.

Source: CIPFA Housing Revenue Account Statistics Estimates.

By 1982, largely as a result of rising rents, average council rents were almost the same as average mortgage payments for tenants who had exercised the right to buy. Being a tenant evidently did not pay in circumstances where their assistance was withdrawn while community support for the house buyer was maintained.

The trend towards relatively more favourable treatment of home owners was a characteristic of the 1970—84 period. Despite persistent fiscal crises, 'tax spending' on home ownership was allowed to grow to unprecedented levels while both its regressive nature and its ineffectiveness in improving access to owner-occupation were disregarded. By permitting house prices to rise higher than they would otherwise have done it inflated the level of total mortgage costs and effectively offset the benefit of the initial tax deduction (Boddy 1980; Ball 1983).

The cost of tax allowances on mortgage interest payments, a relatively minor concern in the 1960s, doubled between 1968/9 and 1972/3 under the impact of rising prices and interest rates (Klein *et al.* 1974). Yet the Heath government made no proposals for reform apart from a change in the system of administering tax relief and option mortgage subsidy which would result in all recipients paying interest net of tax relief (Cmnd 5116 1972), a reform not effected until mortgage interest relief at source (MIRAS) was introduced in April 1983. Subsequently Labour excluded second homes and placed a limit of £25,000 on mortgage advances eligible for tax relief in the March Budget of 1974. Although this had little effect at the time, with continued inflation it did reduce the assistance given to better-off purchasers (Webster 1980b). Those who expected more radical reform to follow the completion of the housing policy review were disappointed: no changes were recommended in the level or form of support for home owners and the prospect of achieving equity in the distribution of housing subsidy was repudiated on the spurious grounds that 'much of the debate on "equity" in housing is sterile: it is an attempt to compare chalk and cheese' (Cmnd 6851 1977, para. 6.41). Any objective comparison, taking into account all payments, costs and benefits for the different tenures, was deemed to be impossible and the limited analysis undertaken to compare home ownership and council housing excluded the more controversial forms of assistance related to the investment aspects of owner-occupation such as exemption from capital gains tax and absence of tax on imputed rental income (Whitehead 1977).

All attempts to reopen this debate by academics such as the Clare group of economists (King and Atkinson 1980) and groups such as Shelter (1982), Catholic Housing Aid Society (Warburton 1983) and the Labour Housing Group (1984) during the late 1970s and early 1980s were unsuccessful. The Conservative governments of 1979 and 1983 refused to consider the issue (Cmnd 8105 1980; Cmnd 8435

1981) although it was raised by the Environment Committee (HC 714 1980) and a proposal was made by the Chancellor of the Exchequer, Sir Geoffrey Howe and the Environment Secretary, Michael Heseltine, for the revival of Schedule A tax (*The Sunday Times*, 24 February 1980). Instead they chose to increase the ceiling on mortgages qualifying for tax relief to £30,000 in 1983.

The cost of tax relief on mortgage interest therefore continued to grow, reaching £2750 million in 1983/4 and an estimated £3500 million by 1984/5 (Table 4.8), without any attempt to redress its regressive impact so that those with the highest incomes and largest mortgages continued to receive the greatest benefits (Table 4.9). If the costs of capital gains tax reliefs were also taken into account the total cost of tax concessions would almost double to £5250 million in 1983/4. Assistance also became increasingly regressive between tenures as the balance shifted progressively in favour of home owners who were generally better off than tenants. While average assistance (Exchequer subsidy plus rate fund contributions) to council tenants fell from £323 per annum in 1979/80 to £188 in 1983/4 and to an estimated £124 by 1984/5, average mortgage tax relief for home owners increased over the same period from £265 per annum to £400 and was likely to reach £500 in 1984/5. The reversal of positions was largely brought about by deliberate acts of policy, withdrawing subsidy and increasing tax relief. However, the level of 'tax spending' is also dependent upon house prices and interest rates. Although rises in interest rates affect costs in both the public and private sectors, local authorities' expenditure does not rise as sharply as home owners' because of their ability to pool the costs of servicing old and new debts.

The reduction of expenditure on public housing has been a common response among Western governments to the world economic recession. Investment in social housing has fallen and general subsidies have been replaced with selective assistance to tenants. Market rents were applied to the public sector, for example, in France, Germany, Australia and New Zealand during the seventies and personalised housing assistance either introduced or extended (Kemeny 1981; Kennedy 1984; Pearsall 1984; Van Weesep 1984; Williams 1984). In Britain apart from the Labour period when subsidies increased because rents were held down and public housebuilding was encouraged as part of the government's counter-inflation policy Conservative governments sought to increase rents in order to bring down the cost of subsidies. Although their first attempt, the Housing Finance Act 1972, was unsuccessful and subsidies increased despite planned rent rises, they subsequently engineered such a substantial growth in rent income that there was little scope for further reductions in direct subsidies to council tenants. Rising costs and inflation, frequently in double figures during the seventies, were among the reasons why it proved so difficult to control current expenditure. The problem was eased during the eighties as inflation was

Table 4.8 Tax relief on mortgage interest and option mortgage subsidy 1969/70 to 1984/5 (United Kingdom)

£ million

	Tax relief on mortgage interest	Option mortgage subsidy
1969/70	235	9
1970/1	285	12
1971/2	310	17
1972/3	365	26
1973/4	507	49
1974/5	687	73
1975/6	856	105
1976/7	1090	140
1977/8	1040	150
1978/9	1110	140
1979/80	1450	190
1980/1	1960	214
1981/2	2050	265
1982/3	2150	300
1983/4	2750[1]	–
1984/5	3500[1]	–

[1] Estimated figure including option mortgage subsidy after MIRAS introduced in April 1983.

Sources: DOE Housing and Construction Statistics; Cmnd 9143 1984; Parliamentary Debates (Commons) 1984, vol. 58, col. 82 and vol. 65, cols 61–2; 1985, vol. 78, col. 63.

Table 4.9 Average costs of mortgage interest tax relief in 1984/5 (United Kingdom)

Marginal tax rate* per cent	Averages in £ mortgage size			
	£15 000	£20 000	£25 000	£30 000
30	525	700	900	1 100
40	700	950	1 200	1 450
45	775	1 050	1 350	1 650
50	900	1 150	1 450	1 800
55	950	1 300	1 600	2 000
60	1 050	1 400	1 750	2 150

*After taking into account mortgage interest relief.

Source: Parliamentary Debates (Commons) 1984, vol. 65, cols 61–2.

brought under control, to below 5 per cent by 1984/5, and rent rises kept above or equivalent to the inflation rate.

One of the marked differences between Labour and Conservative administrations was their approach to rent determination, rent levels and the profitability of public housing. The Conservatives were convinced that the only way to higher rents would be to limit local authorities' discretion, whether this was achieved by 'fair rents' and Rent Scrutiny Boards or complex administrative mechanisms. As their legislation was directed towards those councils which would not adopt their policies voluntarily they devised procedural and financial sanctions and although initially these were used rather reluctantly, after 1979 they were applied some vigour. In 1972 the non-profit rule was abolished to ensure the progression to 'fair rents' and although it was subsequently restored by Labour on both ideological grounds and as part of their bargain with the trades unions this provision was repealed by the 1980 Housing Act. There is little prospect of its restoration. Back in 1972 it was intended that as the HRA moved into surplus, with the income from higher rents and the interest from the proceeds of council house sales, the profit would be used to meet the costs of rebates and allowances for tenants and that the housing service would become self-sufficient as a result. This did not happen: the hoped for profits were not realised and the problems created by making councils responsible for the rents of tenants in receipt of supplementary benefit eventually led to the expenditure being charged to the social security budget. The principle that assistance towards housing costs ought to be considered as part of a programme of income maintenance rather than housing provision was finally accepted with the introduction of housing benefit in 1982. These changes meant that in future HRA profits could not be used directly for such purposes. However, the decision to manipulate authorities through the grant and subsidy systems rather than apply formal legislative controls made it difficult for the government to apply HRA profits to any of their purposes and after several abortive attempts to claw back these sums they appeared to be content to let councils use surpluses as they wished even if the outcome was inequitable.

Although means-tested housing assistance was financed under the social security programme the system was administered by local housing authorities. This administrative arrangement together with insensitive rent policies intensified dependency in the public sector as well as increasing expenditure as subsidy and administrative costs continued to rise. A greater proportion of tenants had to rely on means-tested benefits in order to meet their housing costs and many lost any control over their housing payments. Before the introduction of housing benefits tenants eligible for supplementary benefit received cash payments from the DHSS from which they were able to pay their rents to the local authority. The tenant could therefore decide when and how much rent was paid. Under the new system these tenants simply ceased to pay rent as it was paid direct to the local authority. The increased reliance of council tenants on means-tested benefits brought into sharper focus the contrast between the two main sectors. Support for home owners was provided discretely through the tax system. They were thus protected from any overt means testing and the social stigma associated with this form of provision while tenants appeared to be the more privileged group. And as tax concessions were not challenged when public expenditure was reviewed they had a right to assistance whereas the poorer tenants were denied a guarantee of support as well as equitable treatment when the decision was taken that there would be no subsidy floor. Neither Labour nor the Conservatives found the courage to tackle the growth in 'tax spending' or the political will to integrate housing assistance for tenants and owner-occupiers. Few countries have achieved a totally integrated approach but some, like France and Germany, do have more comprehensive policies and forms of personalised housing assistance for which both tenants and home owners are eligible (Donnison and Ungerson 1982).

The pursuit of profit has not only led to unintended consequences but to more profound contradictions emerging between different elements of Conservative housing policy. While loyal councils dutifully following government guidelines suffered unwelcome penalties as their RSG was reduced, some ratepayers got unexpected bonuses as tax-payers' money voted for welfare benefits was diverted to the rate fund. The Party that had once pledged itself to rationalise rents presided over a period in which variations in rents increased rather than diminished once government financial support was withdrawn and local councils could choose whether to continue to raise rents. Ironically the proceeds from council house sales provided the resources for 'low' rents in the mid-eighties.

Raising rents in the hope that tenants would buy their council houses when the majority were in receipt of housing benefits could not fail to inflate the cost of assistance to the extent that it cancelled out the savings made in housing subsidy. In the face of the evidence it is difficult to argue that selective provision has been more efficient than the more universal forms of assistance it replaced. Not only do the numbers in receipt of housing benefit suggest there must be a limit to the scope for extending the right to buy but there is also a profound contradiction between a form of income maintenance which increases dependency and removes the basic responsibility for rent payment and the tenants' charter which, as Chapter 6 shows, was introduced to provide tenants with greater independence and control. The Conservatives created a dependent rather than a self-sufficient public sector and a regressive financial framework between tenures while at the same time claiming to be granting tenants rights equivalent to home owners. Tax reliefs have become of major political significance, and not just in Britain but in many other countries such as Denmark and the Netherlands, where tax uncollected now exceeds all other forms of housing assistance (Donnison and Ungerson 1982; Haywood 1984; Van Weesep 1984). The trend is not only difficult to reverse as owner-occupation is extended to successively lower income groups but tax concessions become an important electoral issue when, as in Australia in 1980, home owners have difficulty in meeting mortgage repayments at a time of rising house prices and high interest rates (Williams 1984). The Conservatives' decision to increase the ceiling for tax relief on mortgage interest in 1983, an election year, shows the importance they attributed to such concessions in maintaining the owners-occupiers' vote. As this form of income support was essential if lower-income households were to be enabled to buy, the Conservatives' endorsement of universal home ownership helps explain the contradiction between burgeoning 'tax-spending' and an economic strategy which relied on curtailing public expenditure and cutting taxes.

Likewise, the recession which was the justification for pruning public expenditure programmes was the cause of higher expenditure on housing benefit as a result of rising unemployment and falling real incomes. Confronted by such unplanned expenditure governments responded with adjustments to planned programmes necessitating seemingly constant changes in the direction of housing finance and resulting in variations in the level of subsidy, reversals of rent policy and modifications to housing benefits. An environment was thereby created in which it was difficult, if not impossible, for local authorities to operate an efficient housing service.

The arena in which local authorities had to operate was very different from the past: in the course of just a decade they lost their rights to determine the level of rents, rebates and expenditure on management and maintenance. Not only did they lose their entitlement to subsidy but on occasions had profits arising on their housing accounts commandeered for non-housing purposes. Whatever governments stated to the contrary, and in 1979 the Conservatives like Labour before them had promised 'to reduce substantially the number of bureaucratic controls over local government activities' (Cmnd 7634 1979, para. 1), they were interested only in extending their own control rather than in delegating to councils to enhance local choice and flexibility. In the ensuing conflict with central government local councils were undoubtedly the losers, and although some of the troops resisted valiantly if to little effect in 1972, they were battleworn and weary by the 1980s as a result of having to wage war on too many fronts.

5 The Place of Public Property

The new balance which emerged between public and private housing and within the public sector between local authority and other forms of social housing was a product of both public investment and sales policies. Decisions about the relative size of the public sector were justified by the role it was expected to perform and by preferences for individualised private ownership or collective social provision, in turn derived from beliefs about the influence of residential property ownership upon social structure. Although the debates were conducted primarily in terms of the rights of individuals to security, freedom and choice, the shortcomings of local authorities as landlords and the need to curtail public expenditure also vindicated this compulsory sale of council houses.

There were several ways in which the state could have rectified what was perceived to be an inequitable distribution of real estate. In addition to compulsory transfer of land, changes could be made to the administrative or legal frameworks or to the tax system to encourage the redistribution of property. Taxes could be levied at a rate sufficient to induce some landowners to relinquish their holdings, for example, a high rate of taxation on residential properties would act as an incentive to those currently under-occupying to sell and move to a less highly rated dwelling. Although taxation could be used in this way the redistributive process would be prolonged and would depend upon the long-term maintenance of the tax regime. Any tax system is subject to modification with changes of government and there are the additional dangers of evasion and the consequent delays in exposing and closing loopholes in the legislation and procedures. The difficulties of this approach are illustrated by the attempts of the Liberal government to change the distribution of property through the imposition of land taxes in its budgets of 1909 and 1910. These measures yielded very little and were repealed in 1920 (McKay and Cox 1979). On the other hand, a combination of rent controls and taxation of rent revenue forced sales of privately rented property although the measures were not explicitly designed to end private renting (Nevitt 1966). Similarly, the 1925 property legislation removed those restrictions inherited from feudal and pre-feudal times which either prevented the transfer of land or created uncertainties as to legal title which made it unmarketable. Once land transactions were made easier by the removal of anachronisms like copyhold tenure and a reduction in the number of legal interests and estates, the way was open for the break-up of the great estates of the landed aristocracy (Megarry and Wade 1975; Massey and Catalano 1978).

However, compulsory transfer of land had proved to be the most effective mechanism and had been used successfully in the Leasehold Reform Act 1967 to secure for long leaseholders of houses either the freehold or an extension of their term at a reasonable price. A rapid change in tenure could only be accomplished through such a transfer as then new investment was adding only about 2 per cent to the housing stock each year. Furthermore, as there was limited scope for the conveyance of substantial amounts of privately rented property any major change could only be achieved by the redistribution of council housing: whether to individuals or associations of individuals such as companies, condominiums, co-ownership societies, co-operatives and housing associations.

The Labour and Conservative parties were not so divided on the ethics of the transfer as upon the mechanism for achieving it. Both parties accepted the case for council house sales although Labour wished to confine them to situations in which there was no shortage of rented housing and insisted that they should be at the discretion of the local authority. There was also a consistency in their approach to public investment: in the methods adopted to control council house building and the support they gave to housing associations. However, this stemmed more from Labour's confusion over the place of public housing than a genuine consensus on the form of residential property needed for modern urban society.

Public Investment and Controls on Capital Spending

The determination of successive governments to control both housing expenditure and the activities of local authorities prompted their instigation of new administrative systems to control housing investment. The reduction in the output of public sector dwellings between 1972 and 1974 and after 1977 is a barometer of their success (Table 5.1) but they also scaled down local spending on house renovation and mortgage lending. Whereas the Heath government had planned lower levels of council house building on the basis of the progress made towards the relief of housing problems and the prospect of a surplus of dwellings, Labour promised to restore total production to 400,000 units per annum and intended a sizeable contribution to come from the

Table 5.1 Permanent dwellings completed by public authorities 1970 to 1984 (England and Wales)

	Local authorities	% of all	Housing associations	% of all	New towns and government departments	% of all	All public sector
1970	125 456	86.4	8 249	5.7	11 477	7.9	145 182
1971	107 817	83.1	10 335	8.0	11 626	8.9	129 778
1972	86 479	84.2	7 252	7.1	8 941	8.7	102 672
1973	72 388	80.8	8 607	9.6	8 639	9.6	89 634
1974	89 196	80.0	9 440	8.5	12 911	11.5	111 547
1975	110 735	80.1	13 927	10.1	13 651	9.8	138 313
1976	112 028	80.0	14 618	10.4	13 537	9.6	140 183
1977	108 483	73.6	24 581	16.7	14 259	9.7	147 323
1978	87 799	73.5	21 644	18.1	9 980	8.4	119 423
1979	69 732	73.2	17 225	18.1	8 291	8.7	95 248
1980	71 079	72.2	19 863	20.2	7 501	7.6	98 443
1981	49 411	65.4	17 152	22.7	8 988	11.9	75 551
1982	29 859	67.0	11 235	25.2	3 452	7.8	44 546
1983	30 024	66.4	13 703	30.3	1 494	3.3	45 221
1984	28 663	65.1	13 599	30.9	1 772	4.0	44 034

Source: DOE Housing and Construction Statistics.

public sector. However, recurrent economic crises led to a reversal and the programme was cut in 1975 and 1976. Although the marginal surplus at the beginning of the decade had reached half a million dwellings by 1976 Labour considered the existence of local housing shortages to be sufficient justification for further production of state housing. Nevertheless they were prepared to leave the introduction of the Housing (Homeless Persons) Act 1977 which ensured those in greatest need had access to council housing to a Liberal, Stephen Ross, who had won a place in the ballot for Private Members' Bills, as no room could be found for the Bill in the government's programme (Donnison and Ungerson 1982).

Subsequent Conservative administrations planned the reduction in council house building as part of a strategy by which public would be replaced by private activity. However, low levels of completions in the public sector were paralleled by a slump in the private sector in the early 1980s and this gave rise to speculation about an impending housing crisis with the All-Party Environment Committee forecasting a shortfall of half a million dwellings by 1985 (HC 714 1980; Ball 1983; Labour Housing Group 1984).

Tighter controls on housing capital spending began with Labour's need to reduce public expenditure in 1975. In view of their decision to intervene in local housing investment the paternalism of the Labour Chancellor, Denis Healey, was somewhat misplaced: 'A sizeable proportion of these savings will fall on programmes administered by the local authorities . . . I do not think it would be right to leave them to face it without closer guidance and help from Ministers' (DOE Circular 51/75). Initially they made their changes to the Public Expenditure Survey Committee (PESC) planning system in a rather *ad hoc* way by introducing cash limits for spending departments set as a proportion of the previous year's expenditure and in 1975/6 and 1976/7, using powers provided in Section 105 Housing Rents and Subsidies Act 1975, limits were imposed on local authorities' lending for house purchase and on acquisition and improvement of the existing stock. Existing procedures such as the housing cost yardstick (HCY) and controls on borrowing were retained to restrain investment in new housebuilding and were strengthened in 1976 when the general consent for purchase of land was withdrawn and DOE authorisation had to be sought prior to inviting or accepting tenders (DOE Circulars 45/76 and 80/76).

These measures proved inadequate and in 1977 a more comprehensive system of housing investment programmes (HIP) was introduced (DOE Circular 63/77). Each local authority was required to submit its bid for housing investment for the coming year and these were considered in the context of such factors as housing need, assessed according to a general needs index (GNI), and national priorities, such as inner areas policy. Allocations were made out of the sum available nationally for expenditure on housing. The allocation was made to three spending blocks: local authority investment, improvement grants and lending to housing associations, with limited virement between blocks and tolerance over financial years; enabling the government to control the distribution as well as the total sums spent on housing. Labour claimed that the purpose of the system was to ensure that allocation of resources matched the incidence of housing need and to provide authorities with greater freedom over the use of those resources. Nevertheless it was difficult to disguise the extension of central government control into areas that hitherto had been left to local discretion when, for example, in 1978/9 the government accepted 69 per cent of bids and approved only 48 per cent of proposed expenditure on improvement grants and lending for house purchase. The statement by Reg Freeson, Minister for Housing and Construction:

> even when the crisis fully recedes and we have less need for controlling things so tightly as in recent years, I hope and believe that the strategy and investment programme approach will continue and develop. My regret is we did not introduce it at a time when we did not also have to bring in a cash control system. (HC 600 1978: 18)

was unlikely to convince local councils that the government was not seeking unlimited powers when the opportunity to remove redundant controls like the HCY and borrowing approvals was not taken and the new system was simply imposed on the old.

The 1979 Conservative government strengthened the HIP system by replacing the three spending blocks with a single allocation which became the legal limit for housing capital expenditure under the Local Government, Planning and Land Act 1980. From April 1981 spending limits were set for each authority under five headings: housing, education, personal social services, transport and other services, and powers were given to the Secretary of State to monitor expenditure and order any authority that was in danger of exceeding its allocation to stop spending. Although the housing allocation could be increased by diverting resources from other blocks, such expenditure did not attract subsidy. The only alternative for councils who wished to spend over the limit was to supplement their allocation with capital receipts from sales of land or dwellings.

For services other than housing borrowing approval was set at the level of the block allocation, obviating the requirement for individual loan sanctions. However, specific approval was needed for the acquisition of dwellings and housing land and in addition all schemes were subject to a new project control procedure (DOE Circular 7/81). From April 1982 purchases of land and the construction, renovation or acquisition of dwellings had to be justified by value-for-money criteria and borrowing approval would be withdrawn if the cost of the scheme was considered to be so high or so disproportionate to any likely benefit that the use of scarce resources was unjustifiable. Unlike the former system when the HCY was used to control expenditure no details of the criteria used to evaluate projects were published, thereby affording the government greater opportunity to ensure that approved projects accorded with their own housing strategy (Jeffries 1982). The government also wanted local authorities to maximise house sales to influence the rate of reinvestment of the ensuing capital receipts. It was for this reason that, despite all of these additional controls, they allowed local authorities discretion over the timing of this expenditure; this led to years of underspending on national cash limits interspersed between years of overspending.

Although the case for selling council houses was argued on grounds other than finance, the claim that it would result in long-term savings was given prominence in the 1979 Manifesto (Conservative Party 1979) and in election speeches by Party leaders. However, when detailed plans for the legislation began to emerge it was admitted that it was not possible to say whether sales would result in financial gains or losses as it depended upon what assumptions were made. When Members of Parliament pressed for more detailed information they were told that it was not available, although it was subsequently admitted that a study of the effects of council house sales had been completed in July 1978. As losses of the order of £700 to £2700 per dwelling sold were estimated to arise by the end of the century the government's reluctance to publish these findings was understandable. Instead they undertook their own appraisal which enabled them to draw attention to the beneficial results for both local authorities and the Exchequer (DOE 1980a) despite virulent criticism of the assumption that rents would not increase faster than earnings. As there were no difficulties in setting the preconditions — rents could be set any level the government chose, as subsequent events were soon to show — it is unlikely that the financial issues had much impact upon the government's decision to sell. Rather, having decided upon the right to buy, they looked for suitable financial arguments to make their case respectable.

Once the sales policy was established there were compelling financial grounds for its continuation because capital receipts could be used as an alternative to borrowing to finance the housing investment programme and would help reduce the Public Sector Borrowing Requirement. The approach had been tried by the 1970–74 Conservative government but had been unsuccessful at that time because they were unable to sustain a sufficient level of council house sales. Whether local authorities used their capital receipts from sales (and from repayment of loans to housing associations or for house purchase) to finance housing investment or to reduce their borrowing or to lend on to someone else it would reduce the councils' own borrowing and that reduction would reduce the total PSBR for the year in which the receipt was received. Such reductions were taken into account when the government planned public expenditure and so if authorities chose to spend their receipts in later years it could upset their calculations. However, the government were more concerned initially with persuading councils to use the receipts for new investment than they were with the timing of expenditure and so they amended the HIP system in April 1981 to allow authorities to enhance their allocation by a sum related to their capital receipts. They could add a sum equivalent to 100 per cent of the receipts from the sale of land, unimproved dwellings and shared ownership sales and 50 per cent of receipts from house sales. The other 50 per cent was added in to the basic HIP allocation (DOE Circular 9/83). In addition to this right to augment their HIP allocations they were allowed to carry forward unspent receipts to future years. The new provisions therefore placed individual authorities outside the cash limit system they were collectively considered to be within.

Annual cash limits had always made long-term planning problematical and had led to underspending because councils were reluctant to enter into contracts they might be unable to honour and consequently when slippage occurred on their building programmes they had no other projects to which they could divert the resources. However, the complexity of these arrangements was compounded after April 1981 so that underspending in 1981/2 and 1982/3 was followed by overspending in 1983/4 and 1984/5 and the threat of a moratorium on the letting of contracts, along the lines of the one imposed in 1980/1 (DOE Circular 19/80). In the event this was rejected in favour of voluntary restraint – the government in effect was prepared to condone overspending rather than have to deal with further contraction in the already beleaguered construction industry.

Initially councils failed to spend up to the new limits because of the difficulty of accurately forecasting the level of receipts in advance and because receipts accrued in areas with modest investment programmes. The DOE also consistently underestimated the outturn of capital receipts and so a lower figure was added to authorities' basic HIP allocations, which contributed to the underspending. As a result the formula was changed in April 1984 so that a sum equivalent to 60 per cent of receipts from house sales could be redistributed through the basic HIP allocation. Despite this 'supplement' the basic allocation represented a further reduction in real terms and this encouraged authorities to spend their capital receipts including those that had accrued from earlier years. The drawing on these reserves precipitated the overspending in 1983/4 and 1984/5 and the subsequent request to councils to restrain their spending at the same time as they were being encouraged to maximise their receipts from house sales. Accordingly

Table 5.2   Housing expenditure 1970/1 to 1978/9 (Great Britain)

	£ million at 1974 survey prices				£ million at 1979 survey prices				
	1970/1	1971/2	1972/3	1973/4	1974/5	1975/6	1976/7	1977/8	1978/9
CURRENT EXPENDITURE									
Subsidies to local authorities					1152	1210	1379	1279	1384
RFC to local authority housing					350	341	264	244	302
Subsidies to new towns					98	128	143	157	164
Subsidies to housing associations					14	19	21	21	23
TOTAL GENERAL SUBSIDIES	428	403	372	518	1614	1698	1806	1701	1872
INCOME RELATED SUBSIDIES			132	218	492	473	526	565	556
Option mortgage	18	22	33	54	150	175	196	188	170
Administration	15	12	14	18	68	59	80	57	78
TOTAL CURRENT EXPENDITURE	461	437	551	808	2325	2404	2609	2511	2676
CAPITAL EXPENDITURE									
Local authority gross expenditure					4461	3927	3412	2936	2596
Local authority receipts					– 294	– 408	– 410	– 505	– 567
TOTAL LOCAL AUTHORITY					4167	3519	3002	2431	2029
New towns gross expenditure					264	327	318	244	199
New towns receipts					– 17	– 20	– 20	– 19	– 28
TOTAL NEW TOWNS					247	307	298	245	171
Housing Corporation schemes					184	272	357	356	383
Other capital					231	204	– 4	– 5	– 4
TOTAL CAPITAL EXPENDITURE	1836	1556	1496	1932	4829	4302	3653	3027	2579
TOTAL	2297	1993	2047	2740	7154	6706	6262	5538	5255

Note: Detailed analysis not available for earlier years.

90

Table 5.3 Housing expenditure 1978/9 to 1983/4 (England)

£ million at outturn prices

	1978/9	1979/80	1980/1	1981/2	1982/3	1983/4 (estimated)
CURRENT EXPENDITURE						
Subsidies to local authorities	1004	1274	1423	906	507	290
RFC to local authority housing	200	321	430	420	434	504
Subsidies to new towns	87	101	115	117	117	120
Subsidies to housing associations	19	24	28	39	43	31
TOTAL GENERAL SUBSIDIES	1310	1720	1996	1482	1102	945
Administration	85	120	137	132	139	165
TOTAL CURRENT EXPENDITURE	1395	1840	2133	1614	1241	1110
CAPITAL EXPENDITURE						
Local authority gross expenditure	2248	2595	2258	1919	2432	2743
Local authority receipts	- 501	- 448	- 568	- 976	-1725	-1725
TOTAL LOCAL AUTHORITY	1747	2146	1691	943	707	1018
New towns gross expenditure	130	161	165	115	71	78
New towns receipts	- 20	- 20	- 19	- 38	-63	-73
TOTAL NEW TOWNS	110	141	146	77	8	5
Housing Corporation schemes	324	397	495	492	680	624
Other capital	- 4	- 4	- 3	1	4	3
TOTAL CAPITAL EXPENDITURE	2176	2680	2328	1514	1399	1650
TOTAL	3571	4520	4461	3128	2640	2760

Source: Table 2.7 Cmnd 9143 1984.

91

the prescribed proportion of capital receipts was decreased from 40 to 20 per cent for 1985/6 to give central government greater control.[1]

Notwithstanding the government's difficulty in both boosting sales to provide resources for the housing programme and keeping housing expenditure within cash limits, by 1982/3 capital receipts were accounting for over 70 per cent of local authorities' housing investment compared with 17 per cent in 1979/80 and just under 7 per cent in 1974/5 (Tables 5.2 and 5.3). However, it was 70 per cent of a much reduced total which had fallen in real terms by 60 per cent between 1979/80 and 1982/3. After 1982/3 council house sales had passed their peak and the level of housing investment was under threat from diminishing capital receipts (Table 5.3). Hence the provision in the 1984 Housing and Building Control Act to boost individual sales (see Chapter 6) and the encouragement given to local authorities to sell whole council estates to private developers.

Capital investment had also fallen between 1974/5 and 1978/9 when within a limited housing budget resources were diverted from capital programmes to current expenditure as additional subsidy was needed to hold rents down as part of a government policy for controlling inflation (Table 5.2). The total resources available for housing investment fell after 1974/5 but within this declining total additional resources were made available for housing association schemes. Tables 5.2 and 5.3 also show how they received an increasing amount of subsidy and that this was maintained even after 1979/80 because of the decision to avoid radical reform of the system of support established in 1974, even though housing association housing cost far more than council housing because of the limited scope for pooling rents or subsidies.

Housing Associations and the Public Purse

Prior to 1972 associations received subsidy on a basis similar to that for local authorities and in return entered into rent agreements with local councils, which determined their rent levels. In 1972 they were brought within the fair rent system and although there was no obligation to charge the full fair rent, had they failed to do so they would have prejudiced any claims for subsidy. As it was expected that rents would rise to fair rent levels, subsidies paid under the 1967 Housing Subsidies Act and earlier legislation were withdrawn and replaced by a new system of deficit subsidies. While the withdrawal of existing subsidies was tempered, as it was for local authorities, by transitional payments, the new building subsidy was rather less generous as its rate of withdrawal exceeded that to be applied to the council sector. The subsidy which was calculated on a scheme-by-scheme basis was paid for ten years as a decreasing proportion of the initial deficit. This was calculated as the difference between the income from the scheme for the year immediately following its completion and the reckonable expenditure for that year. All of the loss was met for the first year but the proportion of the initial deficit reduced to 10 per cent in the tenth year.

The Conservative government had a rather ambivalent attitude towards the voluntary housing movement. Their rents were to be fixed in exactly the same manner as private landlords but they would be entitled to subsidy albeit at a lower level: 'It is in the movement's best interest that its members should be financially strong and engage on the major enterprise of new building only from a sound financial base secured by charitable money or surpluses from properties already owned' (Cmnd 4728 1971, para. 75). Associations were trying to shake off their charitable image and rely less on gifts and donations (Best 1973) and therefore with rising land and building costs they regarded the measures as posing a considerable threat to their future development. However, this attitude on the part of the government towards the housing association movement was to be short lived.

The Conservatives' intention in 1970, as in 1979, was to replace public with private provision. Yet by 1973 it was evident that the free market approach was not working. There had been marked fluctuations in activity as house prices and interest rates first rose and then slumped and as a feast of building societies advances was followed by a famine (Boddy 1980; Boleat 1982; Merrett 1982). A White Paper in 1973 acknowledged the need for additional house building but had reservations about relying upon local authorities: 'the trend towards a municipal monopoly of rented housing is unhealthy in itself' (Cmnd 5280 1973, para. 37). Accordingly the government, having committed themselves to galvanising the housing association movement, published a Housing and Planning Bill with proposals for a new grant which when subsequently enacted by Labour was to prove to be so generous 'as to be beyond the wildest dreams of the most ardent supporters of voluntary housing' (Cullingworth 1979: 122).

Labour took immediate action to help associations over the rent freeze by slowing down the withdrawal of subsidies under the Housing Finance Act 1972 and by introducing housing association grant (HAG). This new form of assistance was paid as a capital sum on the completion of a scheme, whether new building, acquisition, improvement or repair, to meet that proportion of the 'qualifying capital costs' which could not be met from a loan serviced by the expected surplus of income (from fair rents) over running costs. Revenue deficit grant (RDG) was available for those associations which had deficits on their annual revenue account from earlier schemes. This grant alone cost £51 million over the first five years for which the scheme was in operation as it was claimed by over 500 associations per annum. The grants were balanced by new systems of supervision involving registration with the

Housing Corporation and for allocating grants and loans from the Corporation to accord with government priorities (DOE Circular 70/74).

The justification for the incorporation of what had been the Conservatives' proposals was that associations would provide a useful additional resource adding variety and flexibility to the private rented sector. They would complement council housing: 'Housing associations can and will have a growing role in supporting local authorities, particularly in meeting special needs and in the worst areas of housing stress' (Parliamentary Debates (Commons) 1974, vol. 873, col. 48). The generosity of the subsidy was successful in stimulating housing association activity and output increased markedly after 1974 to reach in excess of 40,000 units per annum in 1977; a level very much higher than was ever achieved before and which would have been exceeded had not restrictions imposed on public expenditure inhibited expansion after 1976. Yet even during the period of retrenchment associations increased their share of total public sector housing activity, in the case of new building from 10 per cent in 1974 to 24 per cent in 1977 and for rehabilitation from providing 7 per cent of improved dwellings in 1974 to 35 per cent by 1977 (Arden 1983). The notion of complementary agencies was a weak one and did little to explain associations' preferential treatment in the allocation of resources especially as this represented a significant break with tradition. However, it does indicate that Labour failed to establish any clear policy position on the public sector and that they had growing doubts about the future of local authority housing.

After a relatively short period of time it was evident that the HAG system had serious defects. High interest rates and inflation had made it difficult to forecast accurately trends in rents and in management and maintenance costs and as a result associations reaped uncovenanted financial benefits through overpayments of grants (HC 622 1978). In 1977 proposals were made to remedy this situation: there was to be a new form of deficit subsidy and a new basis for rent fixing, with associations free to determine their rents subject to government advice. However, by the time a Bill was drafted in 1979 the government had a change of mind and decided to keep the existing grant with a provision for the recovery of surpluses through a requirement to establish a grant redemption fund (GRF). While this change might be partly attributed to successful lobbying by the housing association movement, it was undoubtedly due to a growing realisation that a deficit system would be difficult and costly to administer to a large number of associations many of which had only modest development programmes. These provisions were adopted by the Conservatives and formed the basis of the Housing Act 1980 although the 'fair rent' system was retained in preference to a new method for rent fixing.

The bipartisan support for housing associations was maintained by successive Conservative administrations which guaranteed the continuation of a generous subsidy even though it might be clawed back at some time in the future through the GRF and allowed associations' share of capital expenditure to increase relative to local authorities'.

Although associations' programmes were initially curtailed by cuts in public expenditure they were subsequently fully restored to pre-1979 levels as a result of their successful lobby of Members of the House of Lords and in 1982/3 they benefited from local authority underspending when additional resources were allocated to them to avoid a shortfall on the national cash limit. Where sums accrued in GRFs they were used initially to offset revenue deficits and reduce payments of RDG and thereafter sums were paid (with interest) to the Secretary of State who added an equivalent amount to the Housing Corporation's gross programme to enable further investment to take place (Parliamentary Debates (Commons) 1984, vol. 54, cols 671–2).

As a result of these measures and the complementary cuts in local authority programmes 25 per cent of the 44,546 public sector completions in 1982 were by housing associations, whereas they had contributed only 6 per cent of the output in 1970 (Table 5.1). The position was similar in respect of renovations (Arden 1983). Because of the increasing importance of the housing association programme within a declining housing capital budget, in April 1982 a new system for an approved development programme (ADP) for housing associations, similar to the HIP system, was introduced. Prior to this Housing Corporation allocations had been made on a unit total basis but this made it difficult to control the level of expenditure in any one year. The new system, based on a cash allocation, was designed to improve on this but it proved ineffective without the moratoriums imposed in 1982/3 (before the decision was taken to reassign resources allocated to councils) and 1983/4. However, it was effective in allocating resources according to national priorities.

The Corporation's programme was related to a number of expenditure blocks for different categories of rented housing and the home ownership initiatives. These, along with the GNI, were the basis of allocations made to individual associations which showed a change in emphasis between 1982/3 and 1983/4 away from rented housing to improvement for sale and shared ownership and within the rented provision from general to special needs. Such a move was not universally welcomed within the housing association movement which began a search for private funds to supplement the public support for 'fair-rented' housing.

The Conservative governments' programmes represented their view that public rented housing was needed only for the small minority of people who were unable to compete in the market and when faced with a choice of agency to provide such accommodation they preferred housing associations even though they were more costly. Associations were easier to manipulate: they had no local mandate or rate fund to fall back on and there was little doubt about their willingness to co-operate: 'In recent years Governments have led many horses to water, only to discover they will not drink. Not so the voluntary housing movement' (Geoffrey Finsberg quoted in National Federation of Housing Associations 1979). Labour's intention may have been different but the effect of their policies was surprisingly similar; the role they saw for the council sector was not at all clear.

The Right to Sell and the Right to Buy
The 1980s witnessed 'the sale of the century' but the policy of selling council houses had been gaining prominence since 1967 (Forrest and Murie 1984a). Committed to giving every encouragement to home ownership as 'the most rewarding form of house tenure' (Cmnd 4728 1971, para. 14) and convinced by the successful campaigns in Birmingham of both the feasibility of council house sales on a large scale and of its political expedience (Griffin 1971), immediately upon assuming office the Heath administration began to dismantle the restrictions Labour had imposed. A new general consent was issued but the level of sales was disappointing (DOE Circular 54/70). This was attributed to unwillingness on the part of Labour-controlled councils to sell, regardless of what demand to buy might exist among their tenants; although it was evident that the rate of take-up was as dependent upon costs as the aspirations of tenants to become home owners (Murie 1975). Nevertheless the situation prompted a Conservative Member to introduce a Private Member's Bill during 1973/4 session to give tenants a statutory right to buy and this approach was adopted by the Party and a promise made in the 1974 election manifestos (Conservative Party 1974a; 1974b) that tenants with three or more years' residence would have a right to buy at a price a third below market value (with a five-year pre-emption clause).

In the event a Labour government was returned to office to provide every family with 'a decent home'. Although this was a very vague commitment it was implied that it went beyond standards of occupancy and repair. Security of tenure would be extended to furnished tenants and agricultural tied cottages abolished (Labour Party 1974a) and there would be similar protection for council tenants (Labour Party 1974b). Furnished tenants were brought within the scope of the Rent Acts in 1974 and because it was felt that this would hasten the decline of the private rented sector plans were made to compensate for a reduction of 100,000 units per annum with additional council housing. At this time it was the government's view that 'housing is essentially a social service and that apart from the owner occupier who lets off part of his home – the future lies with the social landlords, that is local authorities and housing associations. Since coming into office the Government have therefore gone all out to step up the activities of both' (Reg Freeson quoted in Cutting 1977).

The Minister for Housing and Construction, Reg Freeson, had a long-standing interest in the co-operative movement and had been personally involved in sponsoring one of the few existing housing co-operatives and had been impressed by tenant management in public housing in the USA (Harloe and Martens 1984). It was on his initiative that a working party had been set up under Harold Campbell to explore the prospects for co-operative housing and although its report was not produced until late in 1975 (DOE 1975) an interim report was available and would have formed the basis for these provisions. The Minister was keen to promote co-operative housing in a variety of contexts 'as an essential part of a Socialist housing policy for the future' (Parliamentary Debates (Commons) 1975, vol. 884, col. 380) but was so committed to the concept of public ownership that although he made it possible for local authorities to set up housing co-ops on their estates without loss of subsidy under the Housing Rents and Subsidies Act 1975 he would not be party to their establishment with full freehold of the land (Parliamentary Debates (Commons) 1975, vol. 884, col. 388). However, funds were not made available for such schemes to be developed on any scale and local authorities and housing associations were subsequently advised to develop co-ops on an experimental basis only (DOE Circular 8/76). Even without the 1976 financial crisis it is hard to envisage co-operative housing as the solution to the problem of providing a 'decent home' for the vast majority of council tenants. It was a diversion from the real issues of tenants' rights and the problems of financing housing.

On their return to office in 1974 Labour changed the advice on sales (DOE Circular 70/74) but not the regulations. Sales policy had not been highlighted in either of the election manifestos produced that year and only a general promise had been made to the effect that the government would place more emphasis on housing and move away from 'a free for all market' (Labour Party 1974a; 1974b). DOE Circular 70/74 set out more clearly the government's position, emphasising the role of council housing to rent in meeting needs. There was to be no alteration in the terms of the nature of the general consent but an attempt was made to persuade authorities to consider local conditions before deciding to sell. The expansion of owner-occupation was not to be at the expense of the public sector and local authorities were urged to refrain from selling housing:

> In areas where there are substantial needs to be met for rented dwellings, as in the large cities, the Secretaries of State consider that it is generally wrong for

local authorities to sell council houses. There may be areas where the sale of council houses into owner-occupation is appropriate, in order to provide a better housing balance, but this should not be done so as to reduce the provision of rented accommodation where there is an unmet demand. (DOE Circular 70/74, para. 35)

Murie (1975) considers that no more was necessary to limit sales in the major urban authorities under Labour control. However, with the general consent unchanged the opportunity was there for Conservative-controlled authorities which wished to sell. In London the GLC and the 18 London Boroughs in Conservative control, by selling to sitting tenants and newly completed dwellings and relets, provoked protests within the Parliamentary Labour Party and the NEC. However, policy remained unchanged, despite rising sales figures, until 1979 when Peter Shore, Secretary of State for the Environment, reluctantly announced new restrictions to prevent 'indiscriminate and irresponsible' sales of stock at very high discounts by some Conservative-controlled authorities. Shore had a strong preference for home ownership; speaking in Newcastle in 1976 he had stated that owner-occupation: 'not only makes economic sense for the individual and the community, it also satisfies deep seated aspirations in our people' (quoted in Harloe 1977: 147). The policy on sales reflected the underlying tensions in the Party between those with a traditional allegiance to council housing who held the view that sales would reduce the stock necessary for letting and the apostles of owner-occupation. In 1975 Peter Walker had advocated free transfer of ownership for council tenants of more than 20 years' standing and the 1976 Conservative Party Conference pledged the implementation of the right to buy as one of the first acts of a Conservative government. These were warning signs for Labour that a radical new policy had to be adopted if they were not to be outflanked by the Conservatives in marginal constituencies.

In an influential pamphlet Frank Field reasoned that 'for those concerned with the twin principles of extending human freedom and creating a more equal society there may be some very considerable advantages to be gained from the wholesale transfer of council houses to their tenants' (Field 1975: 3). However, such an approach would have divided the Party and antagonised local councils. Haines (1977) describes a compromise plan put to the Prime Minister in 1976 for 'life enfranchisement'. Tenants would be enabled to purchase a life lease at a discount on historic cost while the local authority would retain the reversion. Crosland declined to react to the scheme on the grounds that his Department was carrying out a major review of housing finance and he did not want to commit himself to a view in advance of that and other Ministers were hostile, fearing both the opposition of Labour councillors and the NEC. The political advice from advisors at the DOE was for caution, it was felt there were few votes to be won and that it would be at the cost of 'the most appalling demoralisation' among Labour Party activists (Haines 1977: 107). Haines suggests that the scheme was finally killed off by civil servants who changed its form so that the cost of purchase would be higher and because it was known by March 1976 that Harold Wilson intended to resign and little thought was being given to anything other than choosing his successor. In a bitter postscript Haines says: 'If Labour loses council housing votes in future, they will know whom to blame' (Haines 1977: 111).

In this context Labour's support for the 'half and half' scheme pioneered by Birmingham Corporation Labour councillors was surprising as it involved selling the freehold. The Housing Rent and Subsidies Act 1975 authorised such shared ownership schemes whereby tenants acquired a long lease based on a premium which represented part of the freehold value of the dwelling and paid a rent on the remainder with the option to buy the full share of the equity. Initial outgoings would be higher than renting and tenants would have the added responsibility of undertaking the repair and maintenance of the dwelling but in recognition of this they could benefit from the capital appreciation of the dwelling. Even without a full share in the equity tenants could sell their part-share and with the rewards buy their way into home ownership elsewhere. Although it was claimed that shared ownership introduced 'a new and variable form of tenure' (Parliamentary Debates (Commons) 1975, vol. 887, col. 200) suggesting it was an end in itself and a possible alternative to more traditional forms of housing it was a further component in the inexorable expansion of owner-occupation.

While little was being done for tenants councils were encouraged to build for sale, especially 'starter homes' designed for first-time buyers (DOE 1977a) and a new savings bonus and loans scheme was introduced. Both France and West Germany had subsidised savings schemes for potential home owners which influenced Labour Party thinking (Harloe and Martens 1984). Within a year of the proposal in the Green Paper (Cmnd 6851 1977) the House Purchase Assistance and Housing Corporation Guarantee Act 1978 introduced a scheme for first-time buyers of dwellings within prescribed price limits. After saving for two years they would be eligible for a cash bonus, of between £40 and £100 depending on the amount of their savings, and an additional loan of £600, providing they had saved an equivalent amount. The loan was to be free of interest and repayable after five years.

The government's optimism over these proposals was out of all proportion to the impact which they could reasonably be anticipated to make and by the end of 1984 only about 18,000 people had received benefits under the scheme (Parliamentary Debates (Commons) 1984, vol. 68, col. 31). It would have been surprising if this assistance had enabled prospective purchasers to keep pace with rising house prices

over their savings period and there was little evidence to suggest it
would allow 'the market to adjust to increased demand for lower priced
houses' (Cmnd 6851 1977, para. 7.40). Despite pressure from the building societies the government would not allow the scheme to operate
retrospectively thereby ensuring that no costs would be incurred until
1980. In the meantime they had the advantage of having what they
considered to be a vote winner, even if it had been dismissed by the
Opposition as a 'derisory and cynical piece of window dressing'
(*Financial Times*, 3 December 1977). However, the homeloan scheme
paled into insignificance as a vote catcher beside the right to buy. The
Conservatives had learned from their experiences between 1970 and
1974 that the creation of a society of home owners would depend not
only on the aspirations of tenants but on measures which would bring
owner-occupation within the means of those on marginal incomes.
Accordingly they planned a number of low-cost home ownership
initiatives which along with the right to buy they thought would bring
about the 'biggest single extension of home ownership the country
has ever seen' (Parliamentary Debates (Commons) 1980, vol. 985,
col. 790).

Labour's measures were extended and new forms of low-cost home
ownership, including homesteading and improving for sale, developed
(DOE 1980d; Cmnd 8435 1981). By 1979 a small number of local
authorities and housing associations, notably Birmingham Corporation,
the GLC and Notting Hill Housing Trust, had experimented with a
range of shared ownership initiatives: half and half schemes, community leasehold, leasehold schemes for the elderly and co-ownership
(equity sharing), but their wider implementation had been inhibited by
both legal impediments and apprehension on the part of developers and
financiers over possible losses. The 1980 Housing Act rectified the
deficiencies in the law and created a framework within which councils
and housing associations could offer shared ownership in any of the
circumstances in which they might be selling outright and to encourage
them to do so the DOE and the Housing Corporation produced model
schemes (DOE 1980e; Housing Corporation Circular 14/80 1981;
Cooper 1984).

The 1980 Housing Act also made provision for capital grants to be
paid to local authorities and housing associations towards losses arising
from the improvement and sale of either existing stock or acquired
properties. As the scheme was also seen as a means of securing a reduction in the amount of substandard property this assistance was only
available where the dwellings were in need of substantial repair and
improvement. Although they were free to decide on the extent of the
work to be carried out these restrictions and the prospect of losses,
especially in high-cost areas, deterred both councils and housing associations and the scheme started slowly despite the government's

increasing the maximum contribution payable after only nine months (DOE Circular 20/80; Housing Corporation Circular 18/80 1982). Similar dual objectives underlay the homesteading scheme pioneered by the Conservative-controlled GLC. The provisions in the 1980 Act which allowed authorities to assist purchasers of substandard properties by waiving repayment of interest and deferring repayments of principle on mortgage advances for up to five years were modelled on this scheme. Unlike the right to buy these low-cost home ownership initiatives failed to achieve even modest success (Forrest, Lansley and Murie 1984).

The sale of council houses was the centrepiece of the government's plans for involving public agencies in the advancement of home ownership. For the right to buy was destined to set the framework for housing policy for the next decade, laying the basis 'for perhaps as profound a social revolution as any in our history' (Parliamentary Debates (Commons) 1980, vol. 976, col. 1443). However, their first step, in advance of the legislation, was to amend the general consent to increase the discounts payable to sitting tenants and on voluntary sales to first-time buyers, people moving to take up employment and in other circumstances where there was a 'housing need'. This allowed willing local authorities to develop their sales policies in advance of the proposed legislation and thereby help raise the total level of sales. Otherwise, even if the right to buy reached the statute book by the end of the 1979/80 session, it would have been well into their term of office before sales began to reach anything like the desired level.

The 1980 Housing Act granted to the majority of public sector tenants a personal right to purchase the freehold of a house or a 125-year lease of a flat. The right was linked to the new secure tenancy and was given to secure tenants of at least three years' standing. Although the price had to prove attractive to the tenant, the government also had to recognise that existing owners were under an obligation to sell and that the resulting compromise was unlikely to satisfy both parties. The price was fixed at open market value (with vacant possession) less any discount to which the tenant was entitled. However, to get the scheme off to a flying start an exception was made for purchases during the first six months the Act was in force for which prices were frozen at the valuation on 8 August 1980. The amount of discount tenants were entitled to depended upon the length of their tenancy. If this was less than four years the discount was 33 per cent of the value of the dwelling, increasing by 1 per cent for each additional year to a maximum of 50 per cent, subject to a prescribed maximum of £25,000. This approach was justified on two counts: it was held to be a common practice in the private sector to give discounts to sitting tenant purchasers and it was claimed that tenants were entitled to compensation for past rent payments (DOE 1979a; Parliamentary Debates (Commons)

1980, Standing Committee F, col. 7). While it was generally accepted that statutory security of tenure gave tenants a stake in the ownership of the property it was a novel idea to compensate a tenant for what amounted to being unable to accumulate wealth as a home owner. There was no basis in property law for assuming that the payment of rent led to the acquisition of extra property rights; rent payment was a reflection of the tenant's interest, it could not transform that interest.

This lends credence to an observation by Murie (1975) that by allowing a once-and-for-all sale the Conservatives were subscribing to a view that there is a natural right to the ownership of residential property. The right to buy is a right that can only be granted once: once the existing stock of dwellings has been sold the properties will be removed from the rented sector and will not be accessible to future generations of tenants. The granting of such a right, which appears to derive from the mere act of occupation, could be derived from natural rights theories. Natural rights are rights that can be shown to exist in a state of nature, antecedent to the development of societies and positive law (Ginsberg 1965; Macpherson 1978; Phillips 1979).

Philosophers such as Locke postulated a right to property by virtue of the law of nature through which it was argued a man had the right of property in his own person and in that in which he 'mixed his labour', including the portion of soil which he reclaimed by occupation and tillage (Hobhouse 1966). It is difficult to apply theories based on the form of original acquisition or the mixing of labour with materials to the question of the redistribution of property that is already in somebody's possession or to a society in which goods are rarely produced by individuals for their own consumption but collectively through a process in which many contribute a share of their labour. Existing public sector tenants could not be seen as the original occupants of the land or as the builders of the dwellings. Yet the discounts were related to occupation and to the number of years they had held a tenancy. As the time spent as a tenant did not have to be continuous nor in the same dwelling nor with the same landlord it was clearly implied that property rights were acquired through the act of rent payment and occupation. Such a right, not acquired by process of law, but apparently by custom, possibly reflects a new justification for residential property but a justification that has marked similarities to natural rights theories. Furthermore by suggesting that the new law is simply regularising a state that already exists, that the tenants already possess such rights by virtue of rent payment, the role of the state as redistributive agent is apparently minimised, as is the extent of the losses of the existing proprietors.

The sales policy was also radical in the extent to which it departed from previous limitations on discounts and restrictions on resale. Despite a long-established principle that discounts should not reduce the price below historic cost, the rule was relaxed except for dwellings built or improved after 31 March 1974. The date chosen was not exactly arbitrary as it was thought to be difficult, if not impossible, to ascertain all costs incurred prior to this date because of local government reorganisation. However, newly built or improved dwellings could be sold below this cost floor if market value was below cost and, if this did not reduce the price to a level which tenants in high-cost areas could afford, the Secretary of State had discretion to waive the cost floor provisions. In addition pre-emption clauses which gave authorities the option to buy back former council houses when they were put on the market were dropped in favour of provisions for repayment of all or some of the discount where the property was resold within five years. These provisions were applied without any test of means.

Although discounts appeared over-generous to the Opposition, the government considered them justified by the responsibilities for repair and maintenance the purchaser was taking on and the amount of subsidy paid to public tenants. As council housing was seen as 'one of the least efficient ways' of providing homes for people it was worthwhile to provide 'an expensive incentive at the beginning in order to enable people to jump from a rented situation to the owning situation' (HC 383 1981, para. 180). This jump also required a right to a mortgage and an option to buy. Without the right to a mortgage there would be no guarantee that tenants of Labour-controlled authorities would be able to borrow the money to buy, especially as the building societies had made it clear that they would only be able to provide a relatively small proportion of the advances required. Even with this provision and the arrangement whereby tenants could buy with up to three members of their family they might be unable to complete the purchase because they had insufficient income to secure the mortgage. For such a case the Act provided an option to purchase. On payment of a £100 returnable deposit tenants could buy at any time within a two-year period from the date of the initial application to buy at the valuation determined at that date. Schemes of this kind had been used by a number of Conservative councils in the late 1970s to enable tenants to save towards a known purchase price.

These provisions were extended in the 1984 Housing and Building Control Act to try to maintain a high level of applications to buy because by 1982 there were signs that the sale of the century had passed its peak. Accordingly discounts were extended from 32 per cent for those who had been tenants for a minimum of two years to 60 per cent for tenants of 30 years' standing. Those unable to afford outright purchase were given a right to buy on shared ownership. The ultimate step would be to make a free gift of the properties and this might be the only way in which many tenants will become owners.

Property and Power: A Duty to Sell

In granting tenants a right to buy a reciprocal duty was placed on public landlords to sell, because all property rights in conferring a power on their possessors to have or do something place a corresponding duty on others to let them do or have that thing.

> Rights and obligations, though distinct and opposite in their nature, are simultaneous in their origin, and inseparable in their existence. According to the nature of things, the law cannot grant a benefit to any, without, at the same time, imposing a burden on some one else. (Jeremy Bentham, quoted in Offer 1981: 2)

Prior to the 1980 Housing Act public landlords decided whether or not to sell council houses and on what terms. Even councils which decided to sell on a voluntary basis excluded certain dwellings because of conveyancing difficulties, potential management problems, shortages of dwellings in rural villages or their suitability for use by the elderly and disabled (HC 366 1981). Not only did they lose this property right but the Act laid down a strict timetable and procedures to be followed for sales and provided the Secretary of State with powers to act in default which were 'Draconian' and 'little short of dictatorial' (Parliamentary Debates (Commons) 1980, Standing Committee F, cols 489 and 472).

The Conservatives had been smarting from the legacy of the Clay Cross affair since 1974 and Labour had declared during the 1979 election campaign and at the Party Conference held later in the year that they would oppose sales in whatever lawful ways they could. The Act therefore specified that following the tenant's notice claiming to exercise his right to buy, the landlord had to serve a counter-notice within four weeks either admitting or denying the right to buy. If the right was admitted, under Section 10 a notice stating the price at which the tenant was entitled to buy had to be served 'as soon as practicable'. The landlord was responsible for the valuation but this could be challenged by the tenant and redetermined by the District Valuer. However, the District Valuer's decision would be final; there was no further right for either party to argue their case before an independent arbitrator or a court. If the tenant decided to proceed, once a mortgage had been arranged the dwelling was to be conveyed to the tenant.

Although a dissatisfied tenant could take proceedings against the landlord in the County Court, if the Secretary of State felt tenants were or might have difficulty in exercising the right to buy 'effectively and expeditiously' he could take the whole process out of the local authority's hands and step in to conduct all sales himself. In the process he would not necessarily have had to follow the procedures laid down for the landlord, could demand officers produce documents or information required without having received instructions from their employer and retain any proceeds from sales without the liability to pay to the local authority the interest received from their investment. Any costs incurred would be the liability of the local authority and could be recovered by withholding payments such as housing subsidies due. Landlords were only entitled to 72 hours' notice in writing of the Secretary of State's intention to intervene. However, the Minister, John Stanley, gave an undertaking in Standing Committee that administrative steps would be taken beforehand to indicate to an authority that a notice was being contemplated (Parliamentary Debates (Commons) 1980, Standing Committee F, col. 567).

While it is unexceptional that Ministers should be given a power to act in default of a local authority's failing to perform its duties, the kind of intervention provided for by Section 23, Housing Act 1980, is unusual in allowing the Secretary of State to administer the service directly. The Housing Finance Act 1972 entrusted this function to a Housing Commissioner and the 1976 Education Act provided for the Secretary of State to give directions which could be enforced by mandamus but with the 1980 Act, the Secretary of State became 'the ultimate ground landlord' (Parliamentary Debates (Commons) 1980, Standing Committee F, col. 526) and able to 'actually transfer the ownership of property, built and paid for in the main by local councils, to the tenant' (Parliamentary Debates (Lords) 1980, vol. 412, cols 90–1).

The Labour Party carefully considered how it might best oppose the right to buy but the Act was very tightly drafted and there was little prospect of avoiding its provisions. Even delaying tactics might result in council members being surcharged if it could be established that their actions had resulted in a loss of income. Thinking no doubt of the Clay Cross Eleven Shadow Environment Secretary, Roy Hattersley, advised Labour authorities to 'work to rule' over sales, while complying with the provisions of the law (*Local Government Chronicle*, 5 September 1980). His advice was unnecessary. Opposition to the right to buy was both scant and short lived. While the public had been willing to demonstrate in 1972, by 1980 even local councillors displayed only token resistance: 21 councils had refused to implement the Housing Finance Act yet, despite resolutions to the contrary, no local authority broke the law in 1980 although about 50 councils offered some limited opposition.

Their decision to stay within the law was partly the result of the lesson learnt at Clay Cross, that direct confrontation opened the way for direct control of local administration, and partly because in 1980 there were none of the signs of public outrage characteristic of 1972. Then local councillors who broke the law were actively supported by their tenants whereas in 1980 council tenants sought the government's help to resolve their personal disputes with the council. The lack of solidarity was a product of the division wrought by the right to buy between both council and tenants and prospective purchasers and those unable to buy. There were no grounds for joint action: councils which had spent years building up their housing stock were unsympathetic towards those tenants who wished to buy and thereby reduce the council's holding. Neither could tenants see any justification for councils withholding what were now their statutory rights. And while self-interest prevented anyone able to buy from aligning themselves with the local authority the remaining tenants appeared to be indifferent to whether their better-off neighbours should exercise the right to buy. Labour councils did little to promote solidarity. They failed to mount campaigns to demonstrate the likely impact of sales on tenants' prospects of a transfer and on the availability of accommodation for their sons or daughters or to show how sales could lead to higher rents as management and maintenance costs increased as a result of councils being left with a higher proportion of flatted dwellings and of estates in mixed ownership. Instead they sought to dissuade individual tenants from buying through counselling or distributing literature on the costs and responsibilities of home ownership. The lack of more general public concern over privatising of public housing was a product of the low esteem in which council housing was held and the general support for the Conservatives' view that local authorities were grossly inefficient as both builders and managers.

The additional workload imposed by the right to buy provided councils with ample justification for the delay in processing sales. To cope with the first flush of applications to buy and comply with the strict timetable laid down in the statute they would have had to direct resources from other services as they were already under pressure to reduce spending to avoid being penalised in the rate support settlement. Unlike the situation in 1972 when the government introduced 'fair rents' the administrative problems could not be solved by determining a price for a representative dwelling. Each application to buy had to be individually checked and each dwelling inspected and valued. Discount and service charges could only be calculated after the tenant's housing history had been verified and changes made in accounting procedures to allow costs to be related to individual properties. In cases where the dwelling was built or improved after 1 April 1974 research had to be undertaken to ascertain the cost of building or other works and the sale negotiations, mortgage arrangements, and conveyancing also dealt with on an individual basis.

In opposing the right to buy Labour councils sought both to delay sales and to deter prospective purchasers. Application forms were not made available by Rochdale, Sheffield, North East Derbyshire, Leeds and Thamesdown and as a result tenants had to approach their respective DOE regional offices. In Leeds, for example, the office had visits from 3472 Leeds council tenants up to March 1982, issued 6664 right to buy forms and dealt with 11,500 telephone enquiries (Parliamentary Debates (Commons) 1983, Standing Committee F, col. 810). Insufficient staff were made available for processing applications or valuing the property and where offers were made the Minister was aware of 'a handful of authorities whose tenants have written to Ministers or contacted the Department about the valuations of their local authorities and where, on subsequent investigation, there has appeared a persistent pattern of over-valuation' (Parliamentary Debates (Commons) 1983, Standing Committee F, col. 479). Greenwich sought to deter some prospective purchasers by refusing to sell garages along with the dwelling even where they were within the curtilage of the property and, along with Barking and Dagenham and a number of other authorities, by imposing onerous or restrictive covenants. These included restricting the use of the dwelling to the purchaser and his family, forbidding the keeping of pets and requiring the purchaser to obtain the council's written consent before undertaking any alterations or improvements.

Purchase was also made more difficult where councils issued details of service charges or of structural defects after the Section 10 notice giving the offer price had been sent to the tenant. Although both service charges or structural defects could have affected the capital value of the dwelling the late notification made it impossible for the purchaser to appeal over the valuation. Some councils, such as Lambeth, failed to provide details of service charges, giving prospective purchasers an estimate instead. Uncertainty as well as the level of service charges would be sufficient to deter prospective purchasers particularly if the level of charge was due to the cost of unpopular forms of heating or the provision of facilities such as launderettes, open spaces and tenants' meeting rooms which were considered by purchasers to be of little use and not reserved exclusively for the occupants of particular estates. In addition, completion notices which required a response within 28 days were served on tenants still in dispute with the council over service charges in the knowledge that in the event of the tenant deciding not to proceed with the purchase they would be unable to reapply to buy for 12 months (Parliamentary Debates (Commons) 1983, vol. 39, col. 880 *et seq.*). Norwich City Council went further and tried to exploit a loophole in the Act by only allowing exchanges if the tenant assigned, thereby forfeiting the right to buy.

In cases where the Secretary of State received complaints from tenants the authority received an initial warning before being threatened with Section 23 intervention. Their sales progress was monitored and if they produced satisfactory timetables for processing applications the threat of intervention was removed. By May 1981 39 authorities including Birmingham, Bristol, Camden, Doncaster, Gateshead, Greenwich, Hackney, Hounslow, Leeds, Leicester,

Middlesborough, Newham, Norwich, Wakefield, Walsall and Waltham Forest were all under surveillance but a Section 23 notice was only served upon Norwich City Council, despite the volume of complaints from Greenwich tenants (Cooper 1984). The numbers gradually increased so that by the end of May 1983 over 200 authorities were submitting special progress reports including many Conservative-controlled councils (Parliamentary Debates (Commons) 1984, vol. 60, cols 383–4).

The government's reluctance to intervene in Greenwich suggests a desire to avoid direct confrontation with one of the more powerful and resourceful local authorities, especially as it might have led to joint action by a group of London Boroughs at a time when the Secretary of State for the Environment was already in dispute with eight Labour-controlled councils over the compulsory transfer of GLC housing. Brent, Camden, Lambeth, Lewisham, Hackney, Haringey, Hounslow and Waltham Forest had together taken proceedings in the High Court first to challenge the Secretary of State's right to make an order and later to challenge the manner in which the decision to make such an order was made. Although they lost on both occasions the court actions led to a series of negotiations in February and March 1981 during which concessions were made over the terms of the transfer. The government evidently chose to take action against Norwich because the chances of success were greater and to avoid a further legal battle with London councils. With deteriorating relations between central and local government over the control of local government finance the government wished to contain the conflict to a limited number of fronts. When the Secretary of State intervened in Norwich in December 1981 the council decided on legal action but lost both the initial action in the High Court and the subsequent appeal. They therefore decided not to pursue the case to the House of Lords although given leave to do so.[2]

The strength of the government's position was confirmed when the Secretary of State's right to intervene was established in the course of this litigation yet the government decided to legislate: 'to remove points of obstruction and difficulty placed in the way of tenants exercising their legal rights by certain Labour councils' (Parliamentary Debates (Commons) 1983, vol. 39, col. 985). These measures, originally to be included in a housing bill promised for the 1981/2 session, were dropped in favour of a Bill devoted wholly to housing benefits but were subsequently included in the Housing and Building Control Bill 1982. Although this was lost with the dissolution of Parliament in May 1983, a further Bill was presented in June 1983 after the General Election and reached the statute book in July 1984.

Although the government failed to bring forward evidence on the number of councils which had acted 'improperly' they were nevertheless prepared to legislate to strengthen tenants' rights on the basis of complaints from tenants of a few authorities. The 1984 Housing and Building Control Act therefore contained several measures to limit the discretion of local authorities. Councils were required to make application forms available within seven days of a request to do so, serve offer notices within eight weeks of admission of a right to buy and to comply with additional rules on the terms of sales. Covenants which allowed a landlord to charge for giving of any consent or approval were rendered void and those considered not to conform with Schedule 2 Housing Act 1980 could be excluded from both completed and prospective sales on the direction of the Secretary of State. Furthermore, service charges were limited to an amount that was 'reasonable' and if charged in advance adjustments could be made once the actual costs were known. In addition landlords were only able to charge if the works carried out or services provided were of a 'reasonable standard' and owners were entitled to a certified statement of costs actually incurred and access to records and accounts if they wanted further verification. Further protection was also given to tenants by extending the time allowed for completion. The minimum period before which a landlord could serve a notice was extended from three to nine months and the minimum period in which completion could be required from 28 to 56 days. In addition the bar on reapplication within 12 months where a tenant failed to comply with a completion notice was removed resulting in time limits so extraordinarily long as to defeat the purpose for which they were originally introduced: to keep within reasonable limits the number of active applications to buy.

Although tenants who were dissatisfied with a landlord's decision concerning their right to buy, the time taken to process their application or the covenants proposed for the conveyance or lease were entitled to take their landlord to court, most preferred to appeal to the Secretary of State. It was such approaches that provided the justification for Section 23 intervention; although in the case of St Helens Metropolitan Borough Council the government was prepared to act on behalf of a single tenant. The 1984 Act provided the Secretary of State with additional powers to enable him to offer legal assistance and other help to tenants. Such assistance could be available not only in the limited circumstances where the case raised a question of principle or there was an unusually complex lease or conveyance but whenever there were 'other special considerations'. The Secretary of State would be able to try to resolve the dispute by any means at his disposal, including arranging for the tenant to have the benefit of advice and assistance from a solicitor or counsel (including the Treasury Solicitor). This unprecedented step of taking the tenant's side in a dispute with the landlord (to which the Secretary of State would be privy to confidential details about the case by virtue of his right to information under an amended Section 23 Housing Act 1980) is not only a breach of natural justice but an example of the way in which the government sought to establish direct relations with individuals in areas that would have traditionally fallen within the remit of local authorities or the courts.

Having given tenants rights in law by Parliament it was felt tenants should be placed in a position to exercise them without the necessity to go to court: 'It cannot be right that tenants should have to embark on complex and expensive legal proceedings simply to exercise their statutory rights' (Parliamentary Debates (Commons) 1983, Standing Committee B, col. 338). However, these extraordinary remedies were applied in a partisan way. They did not apply to tenants in dispute over the tenants' charter nor to claimants having difficulties with housing benefits. Problems over the introduction of housing benefits resulted in many local authorities failing to make payments or paying the wrong amount and in some cases acting illegally, such as Lincoln City Council which refused to pay full housing benefit to supplementary benefit claimants living in privately rented accommodation (*New Society*, 25 August 1983). Although the claimant's right to benefit was as much a property right as the tenant's right to buy no special provision was made in the Social Security and Housing Benefits Act 1982 for the Secretary of State to step in and assist those in dispute with the local authority. One possible explanation for this is that the Conservatives were only prepared to enforce property rights without the necessity for tenants to have recourse to the legal system where there was an opportunity to out-manoeuvre Labour and win over potential supporters as was the case with the right to buy.

If direct appeal to the individual was a way to increase support the annihilation of local government was considered a small price to pay for becoming the natural party of government. And this contention was borne out by events as the new alliance between government and individuals contributed to the Conservatives' success in the 1983 election and justified further incursions into the powers of the local state. There is, of course, virtually no limit to the power that central government can exert over local authorities through legislation but there has traditionally always been scope for local autonomy. However, this opportunity to exercise discretion has been limited by the erosion of public landlords' property rights. With the loss of the power they give to 'the owner of the unit to use the land and its fixtures in whatever way he will' (Denman 1978: 67), local authorities' capacity to determine their housing policies and management practices has been curtailed. The Norwich case established that the Secretary of State could dictate the rate at which council houses were sold regardless of local decisions and the adequacy of the council's resources to meet existing or new commitments. It was no defence to argue that the council was giving priority to other statutory housing requirements and to policies designed to create employment. There were limits to the Secretary of State's power, he could not determine the manner in which an authority administered sales and in this particular instance direct that the council make use of the services of the District Valuer in arriving at an initial valuation of a dwelling (Court of Appeal 1982: 36—7). However, in practice this was forced upon the council by the deadline set for completion of sales (Cooper 1984).

Throughout the seventies and eighties government's influence upon local housing policies both directly by legislation and indirectly through fiscal controls reduced the scope of local authorities' discretion. However, the 1979 and 1983 Conservative administrations effected a more fundamental change when on points of principle such as choice of tenure or school attended (under the Education Act 1980 parents could express a preference as to choice of school and local education authorities were required to meet parents' wishes as far as they could) they ignored the legitimate claims of democratically elected local councils and granted legal rights to citizens. This stratagem of appealing to the individual over the heads of the local authorities was carried to its logical conclusion in the Rates Act 1984 which allowed councils which exceeded government expenditure targets to be rate-capped and the Local Government Bill 1984 for the abolition of the GLC and the metropolitan counties, both justified on grounds of protecting domestic ratepayers and small businesses from the excesses of profligate councils (Cmnd 9008 1983; Cmnd 9063 1983).

The administrative and legislative powers taken to control the two interrelated processes of housing investment and council house sales provided the mechanism for a reduction in the amount of state housing. Its application, however, has altered the balance of power between public landlord and tenant and between central government and local authority in such a way as to reveal the lack of coherence in the Conservatives' philosophy. While individuals' property rights have been enlarged by the right to buy, the political independence of elected councils has been curtailed and housing associations substituted as providers of social housing despite the likelihood of higher unit costs. Policies justified by individual freedom and choice appear paradoxical in an increasingly centralist state where decisions can only be taken when government approves.

6 Public Property and Private Rights

Although the Conservatives believed home ownership to be the natural form of tenure, their choice was also made on utilitarian grounds because individual ownership was deemed to be the most efficient way to allocate and manage the housing stock and for idealistic reasons as it was felt to foster the social values necessary for a market society to function effectively. That individuals were ready and capable of taking on such responsibilities was never questioned, nor was the universal application of the tenure for it was assumed that the vast majority of people — old and young, rich and poor — could be adequately catered for in the private market:

> There is in this country a deeply ingrained desire for home ownership. The Government believes that this spirit should be fostered. It reflects the wishes of the people, ensures the spread of wealth through society, encourages a personal desire to improve and modernize one's home, enables parents to accrue wealth for their children and stimulates the attitudes of independence and self-reliance that are the bedrock of a free society. (Parliamentary Debates (Commons) 1980, vol. 976, cols 1444–5)

The ultimate justification for property, and for residential property, has always been the individual right to life and not merely to continued existence once born but to a fully human life (Macpherson 1978). It is on this basis that philosophers have justified ownership of things that provide for basic physiological needs and foster the full flowering of human personality. As well as providing shelter residential property performs important psychological functions for the individual. It compensates for the erosion of ontological security (Saunders 1984) and provides a space for exerting power, making decisions, putting plans into action: it is a medium for learning to control the environment and the purpose and direction of life. Home ownership alone among the tenures offers the maximum rights compatible with the same rights for others and the minimum of outside interference. 'A home of one's own' above all else is a 'location in the world where the individual can feel, literally and metaphorically, "at home"' (Saunders 1984: 223) and this accounts for a desire for home ownership which is unrelated to economic factors. Nevertheless it is difficult to prove that outright ownership of the freehold is necessary for the exercise of control within the home or to establish whether rights of disposal, sale, exchange and bequest are needed in addition to those of use and enjoyment for security, personal development or self-fulfilment. It is improbable that men would be robbed of their initiative because the state or the landlord undertook some service on their behalf (Cohen 1978). Furthermore a belief that home ownership was essential for a fully human life would produce a more radical policy than the right to buy. Home ownership could not be restricted to a number of public sector tenants and the opportunity would have to be created for all tenants to purchase.

The Conservatives appeared to be less interested in these aspects of owner-occupation than in the belief that home ownership could influence patterns of human behaviour and in doing so redress the balance of power between individuals and the state. The government's wish to establish the rights of individuals above the bureaucracies of the state (Parliamentary Debates (Commons) 1980, vol. 976, col. 1460) could be interpreted as a desire to relieve tenants from the oppression of public sector landlords whose management style could be considered excessively bureaucratic, insensitive, discriminatory and paternalistic. The inefficiency displayed by public authorities in the management of their housing stock certainly provided grounds for revision. For example, tenants had to wait for long periods for essential repairs and there were even delays in obtaining consent when they wished to undertake the work themselves. They could therefore be no worse off if, as home owners, they had full responsibility for repairs. The belief that home ownership would improve standards of maintenance, geographical mobility and dwelling choice provided sufficient justification for a change in tenure. In view of the Conservatives' desire to reverse the process whereby the balance of society had been tilted in favour of the state at the expense of the individual (Conservative Party 1979) and their belief that: 'In those societies where property is widely owned freedom flourishes. But where the ownership of property is concentrated in the hands of the state freedom is in peril' (Ian Gow, quoted in *Guardian*, 12 October 1984), it is more likely that they regarded an increase in private property as 'an equipoise to political power' (Ian MacLeod and Angus Maude quoted in Murie 1975: 14). Dismantling the public rented sector was seen as one way of undermining socialism.

The redistribution of property would bring about a change in the attitude and behaviour of individuals: 'I can think of no act of social policy more likely to change the attitude of countless thousands of our people than the enfranchisement of council tenants' (Michael Heseltine at the Conservative Party Conference 1979, quoted in Parliamentary

Debates (Commons) 1980, vol. 976, col. 1552). What was expected was independence of character, acceptance of responsibility and self-reliance, qualities necessary both before men were fit to be admitted into society (by implication from the use of the term 'enfranchise-ment') and if the power of the state was to be resisted. The Conservatives believed that by selling council houses they were giving people a real stake in the system: the social stability that would result from their conservatism would be a 'bulwark against Bolshevism'.

It is questionable whether home ownership can change consciousness (Forrest and Murie 1984a) or whether owners are inevitably more conservative (Williams 1984). Nor might a redistribution of residential property be an effective bulwark to state power. Political power is no longer very closely associated with the ownership of land, for the strong links which existed under the feudal system were effectively broken by the 1925 property legislation which allowed the vast landed estates to pass out of the hands of the aristocracy. A government concerned with keeping the power of the state in check could find more effective measures, for instance, the promotion of independent associations like trades unions (Ginsberg 1965). If, as the proponents of incorporalist theory suggest, home ownership fosters political docility by tying workers to mortgage repayments rather than independence of spirit they may have little facility to resist the incursions of the state.

The system of property has to be seen as an integral part of the kind of society the government was seeking to create. Their aim was to roll back the frontiers of the welfare state and the sale of council houses would help achieve this end. Public property would be replaced by private ownership and as this fostered independence so there would be less need for collective social care. People would take increased respon-sibility both for their housing and for the provision of other welfare services currently provided by the state, such as education, health care and social security payments. Sir Frank Griffin, author of Birmingham Corporation's sales policy, had advocated selling more council houses on just such grounds: 'A man who buys a house in the locality, really belongs to the district. He has a vested interest in the secure job, main-taining reasonable standards, in looking after his house and home, in seeing to it that the street is maintained to a good standard' (Griffin 1971: 8). The government saw the right to buy in this broader context: 'The central theme is encouraging the widest response from the largest number of people to help solve their own problems, thus enabling the concentration of public sector resources on those with the most pressing problems' (Parliamentary Debates (Commons) 1980, vol. 976, col. 1444).

This independence was not unrelated to the financial security associated with home ownership: property represented wealth and it was 'because home ownership spreads wealth amongst the people that

Conservatives would like to see more and more families owning their homes' (Bellairs 1976: 190). Dwellings were known to have increased in value and as a source of capital accumulation had provided a return superior to other investments (Pawley 1978). In theory the dwelling could be exchanged to provide an income in old age or on the occasion of any misfortune such as ill health or unemployment or to finance, for example, private education or health care. If home ownership made it possible for individuals to provide for themselves and the experience of ownership made it more likely that they would choose to do so then the way was open for a reduction in public provision.

Private Property and Occupiers' Property Rights
It was on such grounds that the government claimed to be 'reluctant to deprive any class or category of tenant from the right to buy' (Parliamentary Debates (Commons) 1980, Standing Committee F, col. 2357) and were unconvinced of a 'broader overriding community interest' even though a case was put for excluding dwellings in rural areas or designed or adapted for the elderly and disabled. Because of the shortage of council houses and the demand for rented accommodation from low-income households in rural areas the Conservatives had been prepared from the outset to make concessions and had made provision for restrictive covenants which would limit resale of former council dwellings in National Parks and Areas of Outstanding Natural Beauty to persons who had lived or worked in the 'locality' for three years. In response to pressure from an unlikely alliance of Shelter, the National Farmers' Union, Rural Community Councils and Plaid Cymru, a pre-emption clause requiring the owners to offer the property back to the local authority at market value before selling on the open market was added and the areas covered extended to 'designated rural areas'.

Authorities wishing to acquire the status of designated rural area had to make a case to the Secretary of State and the decision was at his discretion. No formal criteria were laid down but it was admitted that the incidence of second homes was taken into account and

> the extent to which a given area could be regarded as a rural area, the need to achieve consistency in making designations as far as practicable and having regard to local circumstances, and the implications for tenants of having the right to buy encumbered by one or other of the covenants set out in Section 19 of the Housing Act 1980. (Parliamentary Debates (Commons) 1981, vol. 998, col. 424)

In the event the boundaries were tightly drawn so that by 1982 parts of only 21 Districts in England had been designated, which included about 30,000 out of over five and a half million dwellings. Examination of the submissions made by authorities designated as rural areas revealed characteristics similar to those of National Parks or Areas of Outstanding Natural Beauty and that in a number of cases, for example, Eden, Kerrier, Purbeck and West Dorset District Councils, they were contiguous with such areas (Cooper 1984).

As it was not the government's intention 'to allow pre-emption as a means of keeping up the stock of council housing simply for its own sake' (Parliamentary Debates (Commons) 1980, Standing Committee F, cols 401–2) nor to unduly curtail the rights of ownership by determining to whom the property was sold or its sale price the two covenants could not be run together, the pre-emption period was limited to ten years and the definition of locality widely drawn to 'ensure that somebody who buys a council house in one of those areas has sufficient people in the locality to which he can reasonably be expected to sell his dwelling. Otherwise there would be a serious effect on the value of the property' (Parliamentary Debates (Commons) 1980, Standing Committee F, col. 449). Such restrictions were unlikely to lead to any reduction in the volume of sales, especially as the imposition of restrictive covenants would reduce the purchase price.

The government were less successful in their attempt to resolve the dilemma of how to preserve specialised housing for letting to elderly and disabled persons while at the same time giving them an opportunity to buy their homes. The 1980 Housing Bill only exempted sheltered housing with special design features, facilities or warden support from the right to buy and although several attempts were made to amend these provisions the government only gave way during the final session in the Commons when it became evident that to do otherwise would delay the passage of the legislation (Parliamentary Debates (Commons) 1980, vol. 990, col. 657 *et seq.*). The result was that in addition to the 300,000 dwellings which were automatically excluded a further 200,000 non-sheltered units could be exempted at the Secretary of State's discretion, provided the dwelling had been designed or specially adapted for occupation by persons of pensionable age and it had been the landlord's practice to let it only to such persons. A rather cumbersome procedure required the landlord to apply to the Environment Secretary for a determination when a tenant applied to buy and to submit the necessary documentation giving details of the authority's intentions when the dwelling was built and a history of previous lettings. Not surprisingly, given the reluctance with which the concession was granted, out of 2047 applications made between October 1980 and February 1983 only 104 dwellings were excluded from the right to buy (Parliamentary Debates (Commons) 1983, vol. 40, cols 74–5).

At the first opportunity the government sought to close what they regarded as a loophole in the 1980 Act and to restore the right to buy to tenants living in non-sheltered housing for the elderly and dwellings adapted for the disabled. However, their 1982 Housing and Building

Control Bill was lost when Parliament was dissolved for the 1983 General Election and they failed to get the provisions in the 1983 Bill through the House of Lords on two occasions. When it looked as if the second Bill might be delayed for a further year they gave way and even agreed to provisions that went beyond the 1980 Act position. The 1984 Act made it mandatory for the Secretary of State to exclude dwellings particularly suitable for occupation by persons of pensionable age where they were let to such a tenant or to a physically disabled person so that, although it had not been the government's original intention, they created new rules which were easier to operate and which might result in a greater number of dwellings being excluded. The government evidently believed that no limitation should be placed on the type of council houses to be sold but their policies were restrained because there were those among their own supporters who felt their passion to be misplaced and that it was against all experience and good sense to try to carry the principle of private property into every corner of social and legal life.

Despite a professed 'deep concern' and 'care about the rights of individuals' (Parliamentary Debates (Lords) 1983, vol. 441, col. 849), the government paid scant regard to the aspirations of tenants when their desire to buy public property clashed with what the government perceived to be private interests. The Conservatives were only enthusiastic about council house sales. Therefore Crown Estate tenants, most housing association tenants and public tenants of properties held on leasehold were all denied a right to buy.

Limiting the right to buy to dwellings on which the landlord held a freehold interest excluded about 50,000 tenants in England and Wales, mainly in South Wales, the North West, London and Birmingham (Parliamentary Debates (Commons) 1983, Standing Committee B, col. 43). The owners of the freeholds ranged from private institutions and individuals to public companies and statutory undertakers yet no attempt was made to limit the exclusion to those instances in which the community's interests were being served nor to allow tenants to acquire a leasehold interest. There was a strong feeling that this stance was inequitable and backbench pressure for a change in the law began to grow after a Lewisham tenant was prevented from buying the leasehold of her council house after she had acquired the freehold in a separate transaction (*Guardian*, 6 October 1982). A promise was elicited from the Prime Minister, Margaret Thatcher, that the right to buy would be extended and the anomaly was rectified by the 1984 Act. A tenant could buy where the landlord had an unexpired term of at least 22 years on a house and 50 years on a flat. The distinction was made between houses and flats because although a tenant of a house could acquire the freehold or an extended lease under the Leasehold Reform Act 1967, these rights were not available to flat dwellers and it was felt necessary to ensure purchasers would acquire a marketable and mortgageable lease.

About 3200 tenants of the Crown Estate were denied the right to buy through the expedient of placing them under the protection of the Rent Acts and hence firmly within the private sector. The Crown Estate was 'part of the hereditary possessions of the Sovereign in right of the Crown. It is not government property, as is that managed by the Property Services Agency for the Ministry of Defence and other public departments; but neither is it part of the private estate of the reigning monarch' (Crown Estate Commissioners 1981). Nevertheless despite such disclaimers it was the opinion of recognised authorities such as Sir William Wood and Sir Frank Layfield that the Crown Estate should be treated as coming within the public sector rather than as a private landlord (Parliamentary Debates (Commons) 1980, vol. 985, col. 106).

The government's position was that even if Crown Estate tenants had been given Housing Act 1980 protection there would be no right to buy as the Crown Estate would be excluded along with other non-housing bodies such as government departments and County Councils, on the grounds that they did not provide housing as their main purpose, were not 'statutorily charged with providing housing out of public funds to meet need' (Parliamentary Debates (Lords) 1980, vol. 411, col. 572) and their assets had not been provided with the help of the taxpayer. Having to their satisfaction established that the Crown Estate was in private ownership the government took the view that they had 'no locus to make decisions about their disposal' (Parliamentary Debates (Commons) 1980, vol. 985, col. 120).

The government's claim that the Crown Estate was not a housing body nor in receipt of public funds can be disputed. Although the Crown Estate Commissioners had a variety of interests, including industrial and commercial enterprises, they managed their residential properties as a separate concern in a manner characteristic of the public sector but possibly with less efficiency as their management practices had not been revised for many years and were still based on methods advocated by Octavia Hill during the last century. Furthermore, since 1760 when King George IV exchanged his private properties for the Civil List the net income from the estate has been paid into the Exchequer and made part of the consolidated fund. It was legitimate to regard the Crown Estate 'as much a part of the public purse as . . . local authority housing or housing association property' (Parliamentary Debates (Commons) 1980, vol. 985, col. 116).

Not only was the government's case for excluding Crown Estate tenants from the right to buy a weak one but there was no logic in their proposition that they only had the right to dispose of assets which had been financed through the public sector when by placing tenants under the Rent Acts they were granting them additional rights at their landlord's expense. The state has the right to redistribute all property but clearly this government had no intention radically to reshape the property system. Had their only concern been the difference in the source of finance for public and private housing they could have overcome the disadvantageous position in which the private owner would have been placed through the provision of adequate compensation. A formula could have been devised to cover the losses resulting from disposal at less than market value and the transaction costs, as it had been in 1967 under the Leasehold Reform Act when owners were required to sell their freehold or grant a 50-year extension to the lease against their will.

The alterations made by the Housing Act 1980 to the law of property were not any less significant because they only related to 'public' property. In fact, the redistribution of property as a result of the right to buy was so substantial that it is difficult to see how it could have been brought about without the precedent of the Leasehold Reform Act 1967 and the years of rent control which enured owners to the transfer of property without compensation. Council housing was not a special case simply because it was provided under a statutory obligation to meet housing needs and financed from public funds; although the disposal of local authorities' properties without compensation for losses suggests a total contempt for their rights as proprietors.

By singling out local authorities and depriving them of their property rights it was implied that their rights differed in some way from those of private individuals or corporations and that they were agents of central government and not independent bodies. However, local authorities are legally independent bodies, popularly elected and with their own powers of taxation. There are limits to their autonomy as they are only able to do those things for which they have been given specific authority by Parliament and are subject to a growing degree of control but this does not undermine their rights as landlords (Cullingworth 1966; Robson 1966; Burgess and Travers 1980). As providers and managers of dwellings local authorities had been given the same kind of powers as were available to private landlords, so that they were able to build and acquire properties and let or dispose of them at will. Although at times they had been subject to administrative controls which determined the price or conditions of disposal, the authorities' legal rights to control their dwellings had never been disputed. The government neither believed their own arguments that the state's right to redistribute property was limited nor held that authorities' property rights differed from those of other proprietors but adopted this posture to subsume their intent to sell council houses as a profession of interest in individuals' property rights.

In justifying the exclusion of Crown Estate tenants from the right to buy the government made it explicit that the right should be available to tenants of bodies whose main role was to provide housing and which had the benefit of Exchequer support. From this it would be logical to assume that the right would have been granted to housing association tenants especially when the Minister for Housing and Construction, John Stanley, had stated: 'In view of the fact that most . . . housing association schemes . . . have been financed from public funds, we think it would be inequitable if the opportunity of home ownership was not also extended to housing association tenants' (*Local Government Chronicle*, 21 September 1979).

However, such an opportunity was provided for only 10,000 tenants, although associations were empowered to sell should they choose to do so. About 300,000 tenants were excluded because certain associations were exempt from the right to buy:

(i)   associations which had not received any grants from public funds for their activities;
(ii)   charitable associations registered with the Charity Commissioners under the Charities Act 1960 or with the Registrar of Friendly Societies under the Industrial and Provident Societies Act 1965;
(iii) fully mutual co-operative and co-ownership housing societies;
(iv)   associations not registered with the Housing Corporation; and
(v)   almshouses.

Of these co-operative, co-ownership and charitable associations were intrinsically public bodies, benefiting from HAG and loans from the Housing Corporation and local authorities.

The only co-operatives exempt from the right to buy were fully mutual par-value societies whose rules restricted membership to tenants or prospective tenants and precluded the granting or assignment of tenancies to persons other than members and which held a leasehold interest in the land. This was to ensure that councils opposed to sales did not evade the Act by setting up management co-ops. With a management co-operative the dwellings remained in local authority ownership while the tenants undertook certain responsibilities, such as rent collection, caretaking, repairs and maintenance, on the landlord's behalf. Mutual co-ownership societies were also excluded by virtue of being self-determining autonomous bodies, in spite of the fact that because their members had a stake in the equity and benefited from any increase in the value of the property they were regarded as a 'stepping-stone' to home ownership. Having taken the decision to allow voluntary sales the government may have felt compulsion to be unnecessary in a situation in which most individual occupiers would vote to become home owners. If this was the case their optimism was borne out by subsequent events. By the end of 1983/4 26,717 co-ownership dwellings had been sold so that only some 9,000 remained in schemes that had been funded by the Housing Corporation (Housing Corporation 1984).

Of greater signficance, in terms of the number of tenants affected, was the exemption granted to charitable associations. To be considered a charity an organisation must benefit the public or an appreciable section of the public and not merely private individuals and these benefits ought to relieve distress or deprivation or improve the quality of life (Goodman Committee 1976). As the provision of housing in this context is considered to be a means of relieving poverty (Longley *et al.* 1979) charitable associations ought to be providing for those on low incomes or in necessitous circumstances, such as the elderly, disabled or those suffering from chronic ill-health (Baker 1976). Because of their contribution to the public good and their dependence upon voluntary contributions, gifts and legacies for funding their activities, charities receive a number of privileges including tax repayments through deeds of covenant, exemption from income and corporation tax, rate reduction on their buildings and exemption from capital gains tax and estate duty. These concessions were extended to housing associations although, as Chapter 5 has shown, they were financed from public funds. Despite opportunities for private giving, charity funds did little more than supplement public monies so that, with the exception of the large Victorian housing trusts, 'for the majority of the movement there are no resources except . . . rents which are limited and Government subsidies' (HC 327 1979, para. 179). It must have been perfectly clear to both sides that associations could not be excluded on the same grounds as the Crown Estate and that, despite denials, they were public bodies:

> Our view is that we are not a nationalised industry or a public authority . . . As independent bodies, we received these Housing Association Grants; but before accepting them we had to comply with a great deal of bureaucracy and a long list of terms . . . . When we took that money, we never for a moment suspected that by receiving it we had changed our status from being an independent body to being a public authority. (Richard Best, quoted in *Guardian*, 6 November 1982)

Consequently the government attributed their decision to the conflict with charitable law (Parliamentary Debates (Commons) 1980, Standing Committee F, col. 15).

The voluntary housing movement exploited these difficulties in the representations they made over the proposed legislation. If their tenants were granted the right to buy, charitable associations would be forced to amend their constitutions or trust deeds because 'it must be extremely doubtful whether the provision of housing for private gain could be considered a legitimate charitable objective' (Page 1979: 6) while charity law only permitted the sale of any asset at the best price that could be obtained. It is unlikely that the government acceded to a view of the unviolability of charitable law. Such attitudes certainly persisted during the nineteenth century when there was a marked reluctance to tamper with existing charities because of a belief that the wishes of the benefactors should be treated as sacrosanct and that if people's wishes were seen to be flouted the supply of donations would dry up. However, since then the law has been amended to allow the revision of charitable objects or the application of funds to other purposes (Nightingale 1973). It would have been perfectly possible for the government to have contemplated some alteration to charity law without cause to be concerned about alienating the supporters of the charities as most of the funds for housing association activities were obtained from the public purse. In view of the extensive changes being made to the law of property, to argue that the old law on charities should be kept because it was difficult to change was particularly weak; especially as granting housing association tenants a right to buy would have provided an opportunity to remove an anachronistic form of housing where personal freedoms and self-determination were limited.

The retention of housing association housing has to be seen as part of a plan to cater for the needs of the minority who would require public rented housing but from agencies other than local authorities. Associations were not only well established as providers of rented housing but were providing similar accommodation to cater for similar households as local authorities (Bird and Palmer 1979). They also had the merit of appearing to be voluntary bodies and therefore compatible with a philosophy of rolling back the frontiers of the state.

The sense of injustice felt by those discriminated against was expressed in the volume of correspondence addressed to Ministers and Members of Parliament. Conservative members had been 'positively inundated' with letters from housing association tenants, one Member alone receiving 166 letters from his constituents and Ian Gow, Minister for Housing and Construction, accepting 53 letters from Members on their behalf (Cooper 1984). Unable to explain why association tenants had been denied the right to buy the government apparently had a change of heart and decided 'that it is unfair to deny the opportunity — perhaps the only chance that they will have to buy a home — to tenants of dwellings that have been provided out of public money and that are directly compatible with the housing stock of other housing authorities and non-charitable housing associations' (Parliamentary Debates (Commons) 1982, vol. 34, col. 62). The legal difficulties had also apparently been resolved to their satisfaction as the Minister admitted what should have been acknowledged throughout that 'the statutory rights . . . take precedence as necessary over the objects of charitable housing associations' (Parliamentary Debates (Commons) 1983, Standing Committee F, col. 303). Nonetheless the 1982 Housing and Building Control Bill provided a right to buy but in a form which would enfranchise only about 80,000 or a quarter of the tenants of charitable associations.

There was already a strong measure of support for housing associations within the Conservative Party and the movement exploited this to the full as they stridently lobbied against the Bill. At the same time a major private landowner, the Second Duke of Westminster, was challenging the government through the European Convention on Human Rights over the forced disposal of freeholds at reduced prices under the Leasehold Reform Act 1967 and the associations therefore also claimed that the Bill breached the Convention in order to draw more public attention to their case. When the relevant clause came up for consideration in the House of Lords the government sustained an overwhelming defeat and decided against reinstating the clause on the Bill's return to the Commons (Parliamentary Debates (Lords) 1983, vol. 441, col. 853). With a General Election in the offing alternative means had to be found to placate association tenants.

The compromise solution, rather than reconciling the parties, was divisive and was greeted with disapprobation. Details of the scheme were not published until late 1983 when the government's second Housing and Building Control Bill was reaching the end of the Committee stage. It provided tenants of charitable associations who had lived in a dwelling financed from HAG for at least two years with a cash grant towards the purchase of an alternative dwelling equivalent to the discount they would have received had they the right to purchase their own home. To forestall any possibility of the grant being sufficient to purchase a dwelling outright it was to be limited to 60 per cent of the valuation subject to a maximum of £25,000.[1] An allocation of £10 million was included in the Housing Corporation's ADP for 1984/5. However, this could only cover a maximum of 25 per cent of eligible applicants and early indications were that within just two months of the scheme coming into operation in August 1984 it was oversubscribed in London.

The arrangements were inspired by Do It Yourself Shared Ownership introduced in January 1983 to enable first-time buyers and others to acquire a part-share in a dwelling being sold on the open market with a nominated housing association buying the other part. The scheme, however, had a relatively short life; the allocation for 1983/4 was quickly spent and the government was unwilling to fund it in 1984/5. Apart from this precedent the transferable discount scheme for tenants of charitable housing associations marks a departure from previous practice. Unlike the sale of council houses, additional public expenditure is incurred and the same dwelling could be the subject of a grant on more than one occasion over a period of years. Consequently, apart from the arbitrary limits set for public expenditure, there is no limit to the potential cost and no compensatory benefit from the generation of capital receipts.

While the scheme might be regarded as fair by tenants who felt their exclusion from the right to buy to be unjustified it will not satisfy those who want to purchase their existing home and will almost certainly be perceived as inequitable by private sector tenants denied any form of assistance and council tenants who were only entitled to discount on the property they were currently occupying. Furthermore, housing association tenants who failed to register an application before the funds ran out or who lived in properties built or acquired without HAG would be disaffected. Disappointed tenants living in similar dwellings funded under different arrangements would fail to see the logic of the government's contention that although associations had received subsidies since 1919 generally on the same basis as local authorities this earlier legislation was different from the Housing Act 1974 (Parliamentary Debates (Commons) 1983, vol. 39, col. 932).

Unless under pressure to do otherwise the Thatcher governments were only willing to sell council dwellings. In all other cases they were sensitive to the fact that: 'These things are not just there to be distributed; they are already attached to people' (Phillips 1979: 75). The property already belonged to someone and it was their wish to protect the interests of 'private' owners. The state as arbiter of the property system was of course free to make any changes provided these could be justified by some basic human or social purpose. The reason for this is that although property is a legal right and the law is made by the state its enforceability depends upon society's belief that it is morally right:

> The legal right must be grounded in a public belief that it is morally right. Property has always to be justified by something more basic; if it is not so justified, it does not for long remain an enforceable claim. If it is not justified, it does not remain property. (Macpherson 1978: 11–12)

However, the relationship between the law and morality is a reciprocal one; law both reflects and influences morality (Phillips 1979). Having promised public tenants a right to buy the government should not have been surprised when housing association tenants claimed the right they had been told was their birthright.

The tension between the principles advanced by the government to justify the right to buy became conflict in practice because of their selective application. The natural right to home ownership was there by implication and an idealistic case made from the link between property and personality and the moral worth of the 'free society'. Such an individualistic perspective could of itself generate the demand for home ownership that government policies were claimed to meet and the

demands for rectification of injustices when the promises were un-
fulfilled. The right to buy was not made more widely available because
of adherence to utilitarian arguments that it was imperative to replace
inefficient public landlords with a more efficacious system for allocation, the market, and a more effective mechanism for management
and maintenance, the home owner. The exclusion of other parts of the
public sector inevitably led to claims that the government found
difficulty in denying because of the more general principles upon which
they pretended the right to buy was based. However, in the political
arena they were defeated by the force of their own false reasoning.
Although it was misleading to claim that the government had no 'locus'
to redistribute private property and the argument that housing
associations were not public bodies was difficult to sustain, the independence and voluntariness of the movement was used by the Lords
as the rationale to justify their flouting the government's first attempts
to rectify these injustices.

The Tenants' Charter

The Heath government had few plans for the public sector apart from
rationalising its finance and despite pressure from the tenants' lobby
little consideration was given to the rights of public sector tenants until
Labour was returned to office in 1974. Unlike some private tenants
council tenants had no legal rights to security of tenure or succession
and only the limited protection of administrative law. Here the burden
was firmly on the tenants to show some administrative law defect in
the public landlord's actions and in practice challenging such actions
in court proved to be virtually insuperable. Their only other recourse
was to the local government ombudsmen, Local Commissioners, introduced in 1974 (Hoath and Brown 1981).

Although Labour made an election promise that council tenants
would be given statutory security of tenure, this programme was not
afforded any priority as the Minister of Housing and Construction,
Reg Freeson, explained several months later: 'Although there is no
immediate plan to introduce such legislation, in due course we shall
look at the question of security of tenure and of tenants' rights in many
respects in the local authority and housing association field' (Parliamentary Debates (Commons) 1975, vol. 884, col. 386). Once more
they appeared to be pinning their hopes on the outcome of the policy
review.

However, the publication of the Green Paper (Cmnd 6851 1977)
only made the government's apparent confusion over the role of public
housing more evident. In the document two conflicting views were
advanced so that it was unclear whether councils were to cater for a
wide cross-section of the population or only for those facing special
difficulties. The first objective was to be achieved by liberalising allo-

cation policies to cater for single people, childless couples, students and other mobile households who were previously housed in private rented accommodation and key workers, young economically active people who could 'make a contribution to the well-being of the community' and doctors, teachers, nurses and other service workers who would widen the social mix of the sector (DOE 1977c; 1978a). The Green Paper also listed those having a special need as including lower-income households, homeless people, one-parent families, battered women, the physically disabled, the mentally ill and mentally handicapped, old people, single people, mobile workers and ethnic minorities, whose problems could only be solved in the public sector and who were to be given priority. Yet 'no data are given in the report that would allow the reader to judge whether or not after the sick, old and socially "deprived" have been housed there will be any council dwellings left for ordinary "able-bodied" workers' (Nevitt 1978: 330).

Even though Labour failed to establish a definitive role for the public sector or endorse the principles underlying public provision because of their acceptance that 'For most people owning one's own home is a basic and natural desire' (Cmnd 6851 1977, para. 7.03), they nevertheless proffered a tenants' charter of five basic rights on the basis that while tenants could not expect the same degree of freedom as owners their rights should not be unreasonably circumscribed. Tenants would be entitled to security of tenure and a right of succession; a written agreement and consultation over the terms of the tenancy; a right to undertake improvements and to reimbursement if the tenancy was surrendered; a right to take in lodgers or sub-let; and a right to 'better management'. Better management was to be achieved through the establishment of a tenants' committee with other unspecified forms of consultation at local level (DOE 1978b), although such arrangements had been amongst the least successful of existing schemes for tenant participation in management (Craddock 1975; Richardson 1977).

Labour's lack of commitment to the future of the public housing and their partiality for council landlords led them to make concessions over, for example, the right to reimbursement for improvements and to two statutory successions and the exclusion from the security provisions of hostel residents, students and other users of 'temporary' accommodation, during the consultation process over the Green Paper and proposed legislation that substantially weakened the charter. Yet in the wake of the growing criticism over the tenor of the Green Paper and content of the Housing Bill 1979 they finally realised the importance of the charter provisions when it was too late and there was no likelihood of legislation reaching the statute book. Security of tenure for council tenants therefore became one of only two manifesto promises that were not honoured in the life of the Parliament (Webster 1980a).

Consequently it was left to the Conservatives to enact the tenants' charter and they made much of the opportunities they were creating for tenants 'to exercise their own personal preferences as never before — by making their own, improvements, by . . . choosing the colour of their own front door, by taking in lodgers, or by subletting part of the dwelling' (Parliamentary Debates (Lords) 1980, vol. 410, col. 20). It was assumed that tenants with greater security would choose to take more responsibility for their own housing and so security was the peg upon which the other charter rights — which were similar to if not the same as those in Labour's 1979 Housing Bill — were hung.

No secure tenancy could be terminated without an order of the court and only then if certain conditions were met. While the grounds on which possession could, or had to, be granted were wide ranging to cover both circumstances in which the tenant was in breach of conditions of tenancy and to give cognisance of public landlords' housing responsibilities, the discretion given to the courts to adjourn, postpone or suspend possession orders subject to conditions, such as the continued payment of rent, was not inconsiderable and further diminished landlords' rights. The charter also provided a right of succession to the tenant's spouse and other members of the family. Although 'family' was broadly defined and included in-laws there would be only one statutory succession and a residential qualification for 'family members' of at least 12 months. This departure from Rent Act principles, where two successions were allowed and the residence required was six months, was explained by the need to enable authorities to manage their housing stock in the interest of those in greatest need.

The right to take in lodgers or to sub-let was closely related to the right of succession as it provided the opportunity for family members to move in with the tenant. Tenants were granted an unrestricted right to have lodgers but had to seek consent before sub-letting, although the consent could not be unreasonably withheld. Authorities would have preferred to exercise discretion over lodgers as well as sub-tenants and argued that this was necessary both for effective management and to protect the interests of other tenants. They based their case on the problems that could arise on high-density estates and in schemes designed for the elderly and disabled where the landlord had adopted a selective allocation policy, possibly aimed at excluding or reducing the number of children. The policy could be circumvented by tenants' use of the right to take in lodgers and as a result life could be made more difficult for the other residents and the development more difficult to manage (Parliamentary Debates (Commons) 1980, Standing Committee F, col. 717 *et seq.*). In practice such problems would rarely arise as the opportunities to exercise these rights would be constrained by the space available. Most public landlords matched household with dwelling size when allocating accommodation so that the situation would only arise in elderly households where children had grown up and moved away leaving their parents underoccupying. Tenants' rights to dispose of the premises in this way were therefore rather limited; neither could they assign because if they did so it would automatically cease to be a secure tenancy and the landlord would be able to recover possession with little difficulty.

The government was more accommodating to public landlords over the arrangements for tenant consultation, the provision of information and the right to improve. The right to improve − which covered alterations and additions to the dwelling, erection of wireless and television aerials and external decorations − was limited by the proviso that the tenant should not make any improvement without the written consent of the landlord and while the landlord could not unreasonably withhold his consent it could be given subject to reasonable conditions. It was made quite clear in the legislation that it would be reasonable to refuse consent both on safety grounds, for example, where the tenant's proposals would interfere with fire precautions or a load-bearing wall, and where there were financial considerations, such as the costs of maintaining a central heating installation or reduction in the value of a dwelling.

To encourage tenants to improve their dwellings they were made eligible for renovation grants and also protected from any increase in rent on account of the improvements. However, the grant would only meet a proportion of the costs and, although there was the additional benefit of tax relief on any loan undertaken for the purpose and the work was at that time zero rated for value added tax, the tenant's contribution might be considerable. No consideration was given to how this work might be financed: the tenant, unlike the home owner would not be able to extend his mortgage and would have to apply for a bank loan or an advance from a local authority or else rely on more expensive non-institutional sources. On the assumption that tenants would be able to afford to undertake such work the government provided an incentive for them to do so by authorising landlords to reimburse at the end of the tenancy for work undertaken after the commencement of the 1980 Housing Act with their written consent providing it had added materially to the value of the dwelling. However, the decision as well as the amount of compensation was left to authorities' discretion and most decided against incurring such additional expenditure.

The charter also gave tenants new rights to be consulted: as individuals on proposals to vary the terms of the tenancy and as members of a group on 'housing management matters'. However, in both instances the scope of the consultation was restricted to matters other than rents, rates and service charges, the issues most likely to unite tenants. In this respect the government departed from Labour's charter and the proposals in their own consultation paper (DOE 1979b).

Local authorities were certainly opposed to the idea, they maintained that tenants would be bound to object to any rent increase and this would result in delays in implementation and higher administrative costs. However, in addition the government expressed some concern over the possibility of creating a precedent which would lead to demands for statutory consultation on all charges levied by local authorities. Although the mechanism for altering the tenancy conditions was set out in the legislation it did not stipulate that collective consultation should take any particular form. It was left to landlords to ensure that those likely to be affected knew of the proposals, had the opportunity to put their views and were informed of the outcome. There was no requirement that landlords should act upon the representations made.

Without guidance on the form the scheme should take or the level of involvement to be achieved the provisions in the Act were so vague that they could be interpreted as requiring anything from full participation with tenants involved in decision-making to simply canvassing individual tenants. Although the government evidently believed some form of consultation would benefit management as well as tenants; having explained that: 'Such consultation has a considerable part to play in reducing vandalism and in preventing the emergence of "difficult-to-let estates"' (DOE 1979b, para. 31), they had not been sufficiently committed to the idea to lay down a statutory scheme for consultation. Only about two-fifths of authorities had a formal participation scheme prior to the Act but the form of the provisions and the lack of any enforcement procedures made extensive change unlikely. Existing variation in the level of participation provided for public sector tenants was therefore likely to persist.

The charter's finishing touch was the right to information: information about the tenancy, the consultation scheme and the landlord's policy on allocation, transfers and exchanges. Unlike the Labour government's proposals there was no requirement to produce a written tenancy agreement but tenants were to receive written details, expressed in simple terms, of the charter rights, the express terms of the tenancy and the landlord's repairing obligations under Sections 32 and 33 Housing Act 1961 within two years. In stark contrast to the right to buy there was no attempt to monitor authorities' response and despite the Minister's assertion that most authorities had fulfilled their obligations under this part of the Act (Parliamentary Debates (Commons) 1983, Standing Committee F, col. 810) research by Cooper (1983), Shotton (1983) and Shelter revealed that some authorities missed the deadline or failed to meet the requirement that the information should be in simple terms and others made serious errors and omissions (Parliamentary Debates (Commons) 1983, Standing Committee B, col. 572). As the form in which the information was provided and the content of tenancy agreements was again left to authorities' discretion, wide variations in the terms of tenancy remained.

While accepting there was a case for increasing tenants' mobility on both social and economic grounds the government rejected the Opposition's case for a statutory scheme similar to the one in their Housing Bill based on 3 per cent of relets. Instead they provided financial backing for a voluntary arrangement developed by the local authority associations at their behest, despite the likelihood that a number of authorities would refuse to participate and tenants' demands to move were unlikely to be met because of the limitation to 1 per cent of relets. Both of these problems had arisen with the Inter Boroughs Nomination Scheme, the voluntary scheme for the Greater London area, and had not been resolved in over two years of operation.

The national mobility scheme was launched in April 1981 and the tenants' exchange scheme the following year. Contrary to predictions, 97 per cent of local authorities had joined the scheme by 1982 along with a number of the larger housing associations. Even so, opportunities for movement were limited to a very small minority, with about 7500 transfers and 8400 exchanges taking place during the first two years of each scheme's operation. The schemes were unable to cater for those wishing to move to a better environment or to improve the quality of their dwelling rather than to take up an offer of employment, not only because of the inadequacy of a 1 per cent quota of a shrinking housing stock but also because of the vulnerability of a voluntary scheme to local authorities' sensitivity to granting tenancies to persons from outside their area when local housing needs remained to be met. The right to exchange provided by the 1984 Housing and Building Control Act in an attempt to remedy some of the deficiencies highlighted by an administrative review of the tenants' exchange scheme may help to overcome this problem. Yet like other charter rights it was subject to the landlord's consent and, although the grounds for refusal were stipulated in the Act, dissatisfied tenants would only have recourse to the courts were consent withheld.

The 1980 charter did not represent a consensus on the rights public tenants should enjoy and in particular it disregarded the widespread concern over the extent of disrepair and the cost of services. Despite substantial increases in rents, tenants had not benefited from corresponding improvements in the quality of maintenance because profits had been diverted away from the housing service (Cooper 1984). However, rather than granting all tenants a right to an effective and efficient repairs service as the Opposition suggested, the government chose an alternative course with a self-help arrangement for those with the resources to exercise such a choice. Under provisions in the Housing and Building Control Act 1984 tenants were given a right to repair which entitled them to undertake repairs which were the landlord's responsibility with a guarantee that they would be reimbursed with a sum not exceeding the landlord's costs. The operational details of the scheme were, however, extremely difficult to design and local authorities' concern that the government guidelines were inoperable led to deferment of the scheme until July 1985. The more fundamental deficiencies would not be overcome even with revised procedures; with over 60 per cent of tenants on housing benefit and no guarantee that tenants' costs would be fully met the majority of tenants would be unable to participate.

To the government the charter was both 'among the most important social advances that have been made this century' (Parliamentary Debates (Commons) 1980, vol. 985, cols 791–2) and 'a vital complement to the right to buy' (Parliamentary Debates (Lords) 1980, vol. 410, col. 20). Yet such reasoning is profoundly contradictory for the creation of a tenancy with most of the attributes of ownership does not so much complement the right to buy as render the latter superfluous. As a social advance the charter did force public landlords to go further than they had done voluntarily in granting tenants certain freedoms but even so it fell far short of what tenants' organisations felt to be existing good practice and of the provisions in Labour's 1979 Bill. And the government diluted even their own proposals between the publication of the consultation paper (DOE 1979b) and their Bill as tenants' freedoms were 'balanced against management considerations' (Parliamentary Debates (Commons) 1980, vol. 985, col. 323), making more concessions over rights to be exercised collectively than over those exerted individually within the confines of the home. Furthermore its impact was limited not only because relatively few tenants had the space to take in lodgers or sub-let or could afford to undertake improvements or repairs but also because, if the landlord refused to give consent or imposed onerous conditions it was incumbent on the tenant to challenge the decision in the courts. Although legal aid was available, unfamiliar and arcane procedures would deter tenants from litigation and if, as the government had argued, it was right that tenants who wished to buy should not have to embark on complex and expensive legal proceedings simply to exercise their statutory rights an equally strong case could have been advanced for the charter.

The charter rights were modelled on the experience of home ownership. The right to security of tenure therefore parallels the owner's entitlement to occupy for as long as he chooses within the limits of the law; for the owner might have to surrender possession, for example, for planning purposes or because the dwelling was unfit and the 1980 Housing Act provides grounds for recovery if, for example, the dwelling was overcrowded or required for someone with special needs. Both forms of residential property entail the right to use and to alter or improve the dwelling to meet the occupier's needs. In some respects, particularly the taking of lodgers, sub-letting and undertaking improvements secure tenants have more freedom than owners buying with a mortgage because of restrictions imposed to protect the mortgagees' interests.

The degree of control home owners can exercise also depends on whether they are freeholders or leaseholders and house owners or flat dwellers. Ground landlords can interfere in, for example, repair and maintenance, particularly but not exclusively if the building is in the form of flats. Flat dwellers will therefore always be subject to more restrictions than house owners because of the arrangements made for the management and maintenance of common areas and services. Despite their status owners may have little choice over the delivery of such services although the Housing Act 1980 gave them the right to verify the expenditure service charges were claimed to represent. Apart from a limited right to have reasonable charges for district heating provided in the Housing and Building Control Act 1984 the secure tenant is in a less fortunate position. There is no facility to question the level of service charges and although the provision for consultation on matters of housing management includes delivery of services it is left to the landlord whether or not to act on the tenants' representations.

Owners have rights of alienation that are denied to tenants which allow them to dispose of their property in what manner, when and to whom they choose. They are free to sell, assign, give away or leave the dwelling to their heirs whereas tenants can only transfer the dwelling when exercising the right to exchange or bequeath it according to the law on succession. Although the charter does not provide the full rights of ownership it offers a measure of freedom and choice and at a lower cost. Rents are generally less than mortgage repayments on an equivalent dwelling and when household incomes are low can be further reduced by housing benefits. A challenge to the Conservatives' belief that home ownership is necessary if people are to enjoy essential rights in residential property is therefore inherent in the concept of the secure tenancy and the tenants' charter.

One of the reasons why the 1980 Act established two systems of residential property offering similar benefits lies in the origins of the tenants' charter. Although the Conservatives claimed the charter as a longstanding element in party policy: 'the adoption of a tenants' charter policy was made by . . . the member for Chelsea (Mr Scott) in 1975 . . . It was then embodied in a Private Member's Bill which was introduced by . . . the member for Birmingham, Hall Green (Mr Eyre) and was introduced in successive sessions' (Parliamentary Debates (Commons) 1980, Standing Committee F, col. 653), the provisions in the Act followed very closely those in the 1979 Labour Housing Bill. While there were differences in the content and scope of some items, for instance, the arrangements for consultation and for mobility, the charter survived with remarkably few major alterations.

Labour had included the introduction of a tenants' charter in their Manifestos for the 1974 elections and its content had been evaluated in consultations on the Green Paper and the proposals for legislation. However, their charter had even deeper roots, in demands made by the tenants' movement in the late sixties and early seventies for a charter of rights that would redress the discrimination in legal and financial status that divided tenants from home owners; demands which could not be ignored by a Party which depended upon the tenant vote. The charter therefore became part of the solution to the problem of how to achieve equity between tenures.

The Party's longstanding position had been to maintain that the public sector was the best solution to meeting the housing needs of a wide variety of people. However, this proposition became difficult to sustain once they had accepted home ownership as the natural form of tenure without measures to promote equality of experience and esteem between tenures. The tenants' charter was therefore modelled on the rights, benefits and freedoms traditionally tied to ownership.

While the Conservatives had no need to reconcile the tenures to achieve their goal of universal home ownership, it cost them little to adopt the tenants' charter. The charter had been the one element of Labour's Green Paper on Housing Policy that had been welcomed almost universally and the Conservative Party in opposition had itself supported the proposals. While this might have induced them to accept the tenants' charter there were also risks in failing to include it in their election manifesto. By not providing benefits for those unable to exercise the right to buy they would have provided ample grounds for Labour to label their policies as unjust. Whereas adopting this strategy would deny Labour an exclusive claim to the charter and hence remove one of the main planks of their housing policy from under them. While correctly sensing that the charter offered an opportunity to win over tenants and to 'dish' Labour the Conservatives also appeared convinced by the argument that by enhancing tenants' status the deficiencies attributed to public landlords would be overcome as tenants took more responsibility for their housing, a perspective that could not be reconciled with the claim that freedom and choice were the prerogative of the home owner and efficient management and maintenance sufficient justification for the right to buy.

The Push to Private Housing
The outcomes of the investment and sales policies pursued between 1970 and 1984 are shown in Tables 6.1 to 6.3. It was a period in which council house sales played a decisive role in both the decline of the public sector and the changing balance between the public and private

Table 6.1   Stock of dwellings by tenure 1970 to 1983 (England and Wales)

	Rented from local authorities or new town corporations		Owner-occupied		Rented from private owners and other tenures		All dwellings
	Thousands	% of all	Thousands	% of all	Thousands	% of all	Thousands
1970	4777	28.2	8 800	52.0	3358	19.8	16 935
1971	4869	28.3	9 029	52.6	3279	19.1	17 177
1972	4895	28.2	9 307	53.5	3174	18.3	17 376
1973	4933	28.1	9 556	54.4	3075	17.5	17 564
1974	5052	28.4	9 727	54.8	2980	16.8	17 759
1975	5198	28.9	9 902	55.1	2878	16.0	17 978
1976	5331	29.3	10 079	55.4	2793	15.3	18 203
1977	5452	29.6	10 257	55.6	2723	1-.8	18 432
1978	5525	29.6	10 469	56.1	2657	14.3	18 651
1979	5565	29.5	10 681	56.7	2593	13.8	18 839
1980	5559	29.2	10 932	57.5	2537	13.3	19 028
1981	5342	27.8	11 449	59.6	2401	12.6	19 192
1982	5159	26.7	11 821	61.2	2339	12.1	19 319
1983	5036	25.9	12 165	62.4	2280	11.7	19 481

Source: DOE Housing and Construction Statistics.

sectors. While sales were high by post-war standards in the period 1971–73 they increased considerably after 1977 to reach record figures in 1982 following the implementation of the right to buy. Very few of these sales have been on shared ownership which like the other low-cost home ownership initiatives proved unattractive (Table 6.3). Table 6.4 reveals both the prominence of compulsory sales which accounted for over 70 per cent of all sales between 1980 and 1983 and the spatial differences in the pattern of sales. Those regions with the lowest proportion of council houses – East Anglia, East Midlands, South East and South West – had the highest rate of sales. These regional variations reflect dwelling type (a higher proportion of flats in the North and Greater London and a nationally lower rate of sales of flats compared with houses), the uneven impact of the economic recession and differences in local political control (Hamnett 1983; Massey 1983; Forrest and Murie 1984a; 1984b).

While housing association holdings continued to grow to about half a million dwellings (about 2.5 per cent of the stock) council housing fell from just over 28 per cent to under 26 per cent of the dwelling stock between 1970 and 1983, having been in absolute decline since 1980 (Table 6.1). This was the result of a high volume of sales exceed-

Table 6.2   Sale of local authority dwellings 1960 to 1984 (England and Wales)

	Local authorities	New towns	Total[1]
1960	1 687	74	1 761
1961	2 349	106	2 455
1962	2 828	100	2 928
1963	2 524	329	2 853
1964	2 564	223	2 787
1965	2 216	273	2 489
1966	3 798	483	4 281
1967	3 200	82	3 282
1968	8 571	155	8 726
1969	7 530	260	7 790
1970	6 231	223	6 454
1971	16 851	2 755	19 606
1972	45 058	15 603	60 661
1973	33 720	7 511	41 231
1974	4 153	737	4 890
1975	2 089	227	2 316
1976	4 879	102	4 981
1977[2]	12 495	365	12 860
1978	29 535	575	30 110
1979	41 095	795	41 890
1980	80 300	4 215	84 515
1981	102 190	3 660	105 850
1982	201 395	5 170	206 565
1983	143 130	4 835	148 145
1984	103 535	4 290	107 825

[1] In general dwellings built for sale are excluded.

[2] Local authority figures to the first quarter of 1977 are reported disposals. Thereafter the figures are estimates including an adjustment for non-reporting authorities.

Source: DOE Housing and Construction Statistics.

ing the amount of new investment which, as Chapter 5 has shown, was much reduced after 1979. In 1980, for example, 80,300 dwellings were sold by local authorities compared to 71,079 completed; the gap widened in 1981 and further in 1982 when 201,395 were sold and only 29,859 added to the stock. The peak year for sales was 1982 and as investment increased marginally in 1983 the gap narrowed slightly with 143,310 dwellings sold compared to 30,024 completed. On other occasions, such as in 1972 and 1973, high levels of council house sales were more than matched by new building (Tables 5.1 and 6.2).

Table 6.3 Sale of local authority dwellings by form of ownership 1979 to 1984 (England and Wales)

	FULL OWNERSHIP SALES				SHARED OWNERSHIP SALES				ALL SALES
	Right to buy and other sales to sitting tenants	Other sales of existing dwellings[1]	Built for sale	All	Sales to sitting tenants	Other sales of existing dwellings[1]	Built for sale	All	
1979			570	41 115			235	550	41 665
1980			1 185	80 575			635	910	81 485
1981	97 055	4220	635	101 910	85	495	335	915	102 825
1982	196 680	3825	485	200 990	60	635	195	890	201 880
1983	135 895	6735	575	143 205	25	285	370	680	143 885
1984	100 020	3140	620	103 780	25	350	705	1080	104 860

[1] Including homesteading and improvement for sale.

Source: DOE Housing and Construction Statistics.

Table 6.4   Council house sales by region 1979 to 1983 (England)

	Right to buy sales October 1980 to December 1983		All sales (right to buy and voluntary) April 1979 to December 1983		Number of council dwellings at 1 April 1982
	Number	As % of stock at 1 April 1982	Number[1]	As % of stock at 1 April 1982	
North	40 544	9.0	43 973	9.7	451 600
Yorkshire and Humberside	37 990	6.4	48 939	8.3	588 849
East Midlands	40 199	10.4	51 316	13.3	386 232
East Anglia	31 008	6.4	58 632	12.1	485 796
Greater London	33 087	3.9	67 269	7.8	856 964
South East (excl. Greater London)	45 671	9.3	76 403	15.6	490 317
South West	32 549	9.5	42 277	12.3	343 399
West Midlands	43 018	7.3	62 832	10.7	585 787
North West	43 752	6.5	63 493	9.4	675 790
England	347 828	7.1	515 164	10.6	4 864 734

[1] Incomplete figures.

Sources: Unpublished data supplied by DOE; DOE Local Housing Statistics.

While the pace of change appears to be slowing down there is no evidence to suggest that these trends will be reversed. No detailed plans for future levels of housing investment have been produced by the 1983 Conservative government but from what has been stated in Chapter 5 it is evident that housing expenditure is especially vulnerable to further cuts, not least because of its dependency upon capital receipts. It is difficult to agree with Clapham and Maclennan (1983) that council house building will be forced upon governments in the 1980s as it was in the 1960s as a result of the reduction in private provision and a growing housing crisis even though private investment did not replace public building as the Conservatives had predicted. The level of sales is equally unpredictable. Total sales exceeded 200,000 in 1982 but this level will be difficult to sustain, even with the 1984 measures, as the figure was inflated by applications made on the introduction of the 1980 Act. Initial applications were very high partly as a result of pent-up demand from tenants previously denied the opportunity to buy and partly because of the government's decision to freeze the purchase price for the first six months of the Act's operation. The level of sales was also a product of the relative costs of renting and buying: applications to buy showed a tendency to increase in the early months of the year when councils announced their rent increases. While further marked increases in rents might help ensure a continuing demand to buy, as explained in Chapter 4 the government have been reluctant to force substantial rent increases upon local authorities since 1983/4, not least because of the increasing number of tenants whose rent is met by housing benefit.

Whether tenants exercise their right to buy will depend on both their household income and the differential between the costs of renting and buying. The latter has already narrowed (Forrest and Murie 1984a) and may continue to do so because the discount scale has been extended by the 1984 Housing and Building Control Act to include for the first time 250,000 tenants of two years' standing and to increase the maximum discount payable to 60 per cent of market value for the 1,400,000 who had held a tenancy for over 20 years (Parliamentary Debates (Commons) 1983, Standing Committee B, cols 144—71). In addition the statute allows the Secretary of State to vary the cost floor date and this power could be used to increase the discount payable on recently completed dwellings. Even with higher discounts it will be difficult to sustain the level of sales because of the extent of poverty in the council house sector. Forrest and Murie (1984b) have argued against those who take this position on the grounds that as most purchasers are in their mid-to-late forties with grown-up families there will be a continuing demand as households reach the stage at which they can afford to buy. Nevertheless the fall in sales after 1982 suggests that those able to have already bought their homes and that even with the 1984 Act provisions it will be difficult to maintain such a high level of sales.

Future patterns of investment and sales may be indeterminate but the framework within which they will be worked out is certain; as with the alterations to the housing subsidy system which effected such a radical transformation in the position of public housing there can be no going back. These changes were not made suddenly, public housing policy had been moving inexorably in this direction since Labour turned away from the claims of social justice and equated owner-occupancy with the natural form of tenure. However, the Conservative governments of 1979 and 1983 developed these strategies with an almost revolutionary fervour. The new legal rights for tenants will be impossible to retract and so the break with the past is complete. Neither is there the political will to restore council landlords' property rights as both parties have sought to increase their hold over local authorities. Indeed Harloe and Martens (1984) have suggested that it is this link between central and local government politics that accounts for the political weakness of council housing and may explain the good fortune of housing associations.

It is difficult to avoid the conclusion, despite frequent statements to the contrary, that the Conservatives were less interested in individual rights than in winding up the council sector and this is borne out by their unsympathetic treatment of tenants of leasehold properties, the Crown Estate and housing associations. Even while enacting the tenants' charter they were hoping that the population of council tenants would decline with more sales. These conflicts cannot be explained: only council housing was to be redistributed and yet the concept of 'enfranchisement' emphasised the importance of home ownership for personal freedom and implied that only owners were fit to be full members of society.

If the politics of property have focused on council housing because of the singular size of the sector — no other market economy has as much local authority housing as Britain (Donnison and Ungerson 1982) — housing associations have been disregarded because of their relative insignificance and their public status overlooked when convenient to treat them as voluntary bodies. Elsewhere in Europe social housing is provided by a wider range of institutions including co-operatives, tenant associations, trade unions and housing associations. In Norway, Denmark, Sweden and Germany, for example, these have been adopted by governments as the principal instruments for the provision of 'public' housing and so the size of the local authority sector is often negligible, as in Denmark where it is about 4 per cent of the housing stock. Where controls are necessary these can be exerted indirectly through building quotas or subsidy, as in Denmark and the Netherlands, or more directly through regulations governing the allocation of housing (Haywood 1984; Van Weesep 1984).

Both Labour and Conservative administrations have promoted housing associations. They have received what have come to be regarded as 'over-generous' subsidies and by various devices have been protected from the right to buy. Even so the movement is small by European standards. Other attempts to provide 'alternative' or 'intermediate' tenures have been surprisingly unsuccessful in contrast to the successes of governments in many parts of Europe in encouraging new forms of tenure, such as co-ownership or shared ownership, to cope with the demand for home ownership among lower-income groups (Donnison and Ungerson 1982). British governments have selected more traditional solutions and, building on the precedents of the Rent and Leasehold Reform Acts and their beliefs in the power of property to vitalise social change, have endowed individuals with new legal rights rather than create new building or managing agencies. The basis for their actions and the resulting restructuring of public housing has been inextricably linked to their vision of the ideal society and their idea of welfare.

7 Parties, Politics and Property

While Labour's dilemma of how to reconcile their collectivist principles with the aspirations of their more affluent supporters for home ownership remained unresolved there was a period of quiescence during which their housing policies drifted towards market provision. Ironically it was the Conservatives' impatient radicalism and conscious pursuit of the free society that increased state intervention as they adopted elaborate devices to manipulate housing investment and subsidies and as spending increased under the pressures of demand for tax reliefs and housing benefits. Rather than the sale of council houses reducing the state's involvement, controls over local authorities multiplied as central government dictated not only the principles by which sales were to be conducted but also the fine detail, down to the covenants to be included in the conveyance. Whereas the state might opt out of direct provision of housing, as was attempted in pre-Mitterand France (Pearsall 1984), even with a system of 'private' property there is no way government can extricate themselves from its finance. Therefore any attempt to do as the Minister for Housing and Construction, Ian Gow, suggested at the 1984 Party Conference to 'set no limit to the opportunities for home ownership in Britain' (*Guardian*, 12 October 1984) will necessitate a more radical redistribution of income and wealth than any government has contemplated hitherto and a complete restructuring of the systems of taxation, income maintenance and housing finance.

In pursuit of universal home ownership governments have paid scant regard to both the unequal distribution of income and wealth and demographic trends. As a result of the growth of pensioner, single-parent and single-person households and of rising levels of unemployment there are increasing numbers of low-income households which will not be able to afford to buy or secure the credit for house purchase. Even with discounts of up to 60 per cent on sales of council houses tenants dependent upon housing benefit were unable to purchase. The enfranchisement of these tenants is therefore contingent upon government guarantees for mortgage advances and DHSS payment of mortgage interest. Alternatively the dwellings could be given away, as Peter Walker suggested during his term as Environment Secretary in 1972, providing further provision was made for assistance towards the costs of repair if the dwellings are not to deteriorate through lack of maintenance. The rejection of an updated version of the Walker plan in 1982 indicates an awareness of this problem: tenants would be unlikely to welcome, even as a gift, dwellings with design faults or other structural defects, as evidenced by the pressure from former council tenants for repair grants or a right to sell back their defective houses. In meeting these claims under the Housing Defects Act 1984, regardless of the implications for public expenditure, the Conservative government revealed just how far they were prepared to go to prevent the image of home ownership becoming tarnished and to keep up the momentum of sales. In a free market the housing opportunities of low-income households would be limited by what they were able to afford as dwellings would always be sold to the highest bidder. Likewise the scope for mobility would be constrained by their ability to buy a suitable dwelling elsewhere from the proceeds realised from the sale of their existing home.

Neither did the extension of home ownership provide the increase in freedom that is the promise of the property-owning democracy. The redistribution of residential property has not built a bulwark against the intrusion of state power. Although it is undeniable that ownership of dwellings has allowed individuals to accumulate wealth, it has been questionable whether such wealth constitutes a source of social and economic power unless it is realised through sales or the use of second mortgages. While claiming to redress the balance of power in favour of individuals, at the same time their influence has been reduced as governments have progressively stripped local authorities of their powers.

This tendency towards centralisation, begun in the late 1960s, has led to a massive erosion of local autonomy and even during the period after 1974 when Labour was supposedly restoring local authority discretion they were in fact gathering and exercising more power for themselves. Councils lost their freedom to determine rents in 1972 and although this power was subsequently restored in 1975 it has since been undermined by the 1980 Act subsidy system. Rent rebates were made mandatory in 1972 and house sales removed from local discretion in 1980. In combination with tighter controls over both current and capital expenditure the loss of local authorities' property rights has allowed central government to exercise an unwarranted influence over local housing policies. The bipartisan support for housing associations as providers for the few whose needs are unlikely to be met in the market place shows a preference for agencies that are less accountable to the public and more susceptible to government manipulation.

Although associations successfully campaigned against the right to buy their building programmes are in the gift of the Housing Corporation. It is to be hoped that Donnison and Ungerson (1982: 67) are correct in suggesting that it is conflicts and contradictions 'which allow the more effective policy-makers, be they politicians or administrators, to seize opportunities for pursuing new objectives and modifying administrative structure and tradition'. If so there is ample scope for reform: a centralist state is irreconcilable with the Conservatives' commitment to a pluralist democracy and the pre-eminence of home ownership is inconsistent with the limitation of the right to buy to the public sector and enactment of the tenants' charter. The reduction in housing subsidy has been negated by rises in housing benefit and the cuts in expenditure on public housing overwhelmed by accelerating tax 'spending' on private owners. The intricate tangle of transfers between subsidy and Block Grant, tenants and ratepayers, central social security budgets and local rate funds, is the antithesis of effective financial management and the system for controlling housing capital finance was in such disarray that the government found it necessary to announce a further review of local government finance in 1984 in the hope of finding an acceptable solution.[1]

The New Welfare State
Although Conservative policies have not restored a free market, nor indeed could they because in modern society 'the market operates in a context which is not given by the nature of things but by political action' (Gellner 1979: 302), they have restructured the welfare state. In its fullest sense the welfare state has ceased to exist as governments have adopted social policies with a greater affinity with capitalism than with socialism and a 'new' idea of welfare more in tune with economic criteria has emerged.

Whereas equity was claimed to be the guiding principle behind the housing legislation of the early seventies, the Labour government subsequently declared this goal to be unattainable and the debate 'sterile'. Consequently privileges have been protected as the values of freedom and choice have gained prominence and as independence and self-help have become more highly prized than co-operation and mutual aid. While inequalities were once questioned they are now acknowledged to be a necessary corollary of the market society and as rewards are given for effort and achievement so the needs of minorities are held in less esteem. It is upon these social values that the new system of property is grounded. The redistribution of state property has resulted in the replacement of a form of residential property where the individual's rights of disposal were limited by one based on individuals holding full ownership rights. This kind of private property provides maximum freedom and choice, and the potential for accumulating wealth, but inevitably at the cost of perpetuating or increasing inequalities. Only home owners have the potential for accumulating wealth and from benefiting from house price inflation (house prices have tended to move upwards relative to both the general index of retail prices and the value of other assets), favourable rates of interest on housing loans, the capitalised value of tax concessions on mortgage interest payments and capital gains, the homeloan scheme and discounts on the purchase of public housing.

And although such gains cannot be guaranteed, and there are areas such as Consett or Corby where there have been large scale industrial closures and redundancies or where dwellings are run down and are a liability and not an asset, generally few households which do not own a dwelling can accumulate wealth on a scale comparable with home owners.

The 1979 Conservative government argued on such grounds that the sale of state housing was therefore an egalitarian measure even though the right to buy at discounted prices was granted almost universally to public tenants without any test of income or capacity to buy in the open market. Hence the better-off tenants acquired an appreciating asset which could be transferred from one generation to the next. The financial effects of sales are difficult to unravel but as Webster (HC 366 1981) has shown, although selling council houses will help achieve a more equal distribution of wealth in respect of a decrease in the share of privately owned wealth held by, say, the most wealthy 5 or 10 per cent, if the extent to which the distribution of personal wealth deviates from perfect equality across the whole distribution is considered there is not necessarily any improvement because, although the position of purchasers is improved in relation to the wealthy, the position of non-purchasers is worsened in relation to tenant purchasers. Furthermore, because of inheritance these differences in wealth will become more significant over time and beneficiaries will be in a better position than non-beneficiaries to compete in the housing market should they choose to do so. Forrest and Murie (1984a) argue that differences in access to wealth will, because of the disadvantageous position of the tenant, lead to social division in society.

Property has the power to shape the lives of both present and succeeding generations. And the greater the individual's share of the rights of ownership the greater the propensity for property to be unequally distributed and for inequalities to be maintained:

> As long as people have the right to trade, exchange or give away their re-
> sources and holdings, and as long as the nuclear family continues to be a
> justifiable social institution, then it is inevitable that the parents' property or
> resources (e.g. the scope of their knowledge) will confer certain advantages
> and disadvantages on their children. These advantages and disadvantages, in
> turn, promote and perpetuate socio-economic inequality. Such inequalities are
> an inevitable result of any moral (or social) system that allows people to exer-
> cise choice as to how and to whom they will dispose of their holdings and
> resources. (Phillips 1979: 251−2)

The effect of inequality in residential property is considerable; it is not simply another element of economic inequality because it helps to determine an individual's life chances. Whereas political power may not be derived from residential property personal power is and provides the medium to exercise those skills which foster self-development. Personality, self-fulfilment and self-respect are equally dependent upon the distribution of the 'new property' rights which provide the guarantees a society is prepared to give to maintain income.

The system of housing support is equally divisive, not only because it is a major redistributive mechanism in relation to income and wealth but also because the home owner is guaranteed tax relief regardless of income while the poorer tenant is subjected to a means test. Tenants have therefore become the recipients of a highly visible form of public assistance as governments have haggled over the amount of resources they were prepared to divert to social security programmes while owners-occupiers' income transfers were made much more discreetly. This may explain why council tenants are still thought to be a privileged group although they have no automatic reduction of their tax liability. It is the association of housing benefit with what appears to be discretionary aid that stigmatises tenants and reduces their status as citizens. Reich (1978: 196) has argued that because 'status is so closely linked to personality [the] destruction of one may well destroy the other. Status must therefore be surrounded with the kind of safe-guards once reserved for personality' and therefore benefits closely linked to status must be held as a right if their purpose is to preserve the self-sufficiency of individuals and to allow them to be valuable members of their families and the community. Although home owner-ship was justified by theories linking property and personality the theory was not applied to housing assistance. Tenants were thus doubly disadvantaged, they were denied the full rights of ownership deemed to be necessary for the full flowering of human personality and without any certainty that their benefits would be maintained they lacked 'a secure minimum basis for individual well-being and dignity' (Reich 1978: 197).

The increasing proportion of tenants that have had to claim benefit has been one of several changes in the system of property which have contributed to the residualisation of the public sector. This process, well documented by Murie (1983), Forrest and Murie (1984a) and Robinson and O'Sullivan (1983), has resulted in:

> a movement from a position where owner occupation was a predominantly middle-class tenure, high quality council housing was used by the affluent working class and private landlordism catered for the poorest sections of the population towards one where council housing serves the vulnerable, low paid and marginalised population with a highly differentiated and stratified home ownership as the mass tenure. (Forrest and Murie 1984a: 65)

These authors point to a strengthening of the relationship between unemployment, low wages, welfare payments, unskilled and semi-skilled work and groups housed in the public sector which has been growing progressively throughout the seventies. The causes are both complex and interrelated: the continuing contraction of the private rented sector, rising levels of welfare dependency as a result of unemployment as well as rising rents, obligations to house the homeless under the Housing (Homeless Persons) Act 1977 as well as the availability of rent rebates which made council housing more accessible to the poor, lower levels of investment in public housing and the sale of council houses. The more affluent tenants with higher incomes, particularly those in skilled manual or white-collar occupations, and those in households with two or more wage earners, have moved out of the sector, either to take advantage of the right to buy or to avoid rises in rent. Becoming home owners was the only way in which they were able to secure some help towards their housing costs.

Residualisation therefore cannot be attributed entirely to Conservative policies. Although it was the Conservatives who broke with the past when attempting to raise rents to market levels and withdraw subsidies in 1972, but for prevarication Labour would have introduced a similar system after 1977. By ducking the issue of financial equity between the tenures Labour opened the way for the right to buy for 'once it was clear that public support for house buyers was not to be put on an equal footing with the support given to tenants, the more affluent tenants were bound to want to join the more privileged of these two clubs' (Donnison and Ungerson 1982: 288). This together with their failure to protect the vision of council housing for all by developing an appropriate legal framework for council housing and a statutory tenancy agreement, allowed the spectre of public housing as welfare housing to arise in default.

While the tenures have become more socially distinct because of differences in residential property rights and the terms and amount of assistance towards housing costs, the physical differences in the standard of accommodation have also become more marked as a result of differential sales of council housing. The more desirable dwellings — houses and bungalows — in the more desirable locations, in rural villages, on small or low-density estates and in close proximity to private estates, are being sold and this could restrict public tenants to less attractive houses or flats in inner city or urban areas (HC 366 1981; Forrest and Murie 1984b). The quality of dwellings will inevitably vary between local authorities as it varies in the owner-occupied sector. However, the contraction of the council sector has increased the probability of the poorest households having to accept the worst accommodation.

Donnison and Ungerson's (1982: 287) more general point that 'It is no longer the mass of working people who suffer the worst hardships; it is a wide variety of unorganized and less popular minorities' has particular relevance for the public sector as the disadvantaged and less able are unlikely to be sufficiently co-ordinated to press for additional resources or improved management and maintenance nor able to achieve similar ends through self-help. While it is debatable whether council housing can produce the solidarity that is claimed for collective provision there have been times of corporate action, such as in 1972. However, such action is less likely in the future because rent rises have little impact on the majority of tenants who are dependent on welfare benefits and because the emphasis on individualism in the tenants' charter is divisive. The right to repair, for example, will allow tenants able to do work for themselves to do so while the remainder will be forced to accept a declining standard of service. With tenants able to opt at any time to undertake repairs the landlord will be left without a fixed level of work to justify the retention of a comprehensive direct labour organisation and would therefore have less control over the timing and execution of repairs. With tenants divided into those who can and cannot undertake the work themselves there will be less likelihood of collective action to press for higher standards. Furthermore there is no right to be consulted over matters of general concern such as rents and service charges but only on specific housing management matters that are likely to be pertinent to a group of tenants and whose interests may well be in conflict with those of other groups. Tenant representatives will find themselves pursuing claims for their estate which may well result in the relocation of resources from other areas. In such situations there is the potential for social unrest and even civil disturbance (Saunders 1984).

This is because Saunders (1984) maintains that tenure is a source of ideological as well as social division. His belief that ownership of housing is significant in shaping people's political values and structuring political alignments is derived from a sociology of consumption which is separate from, if related to, more traditional concerns with class. Distinct political interests are claimed to arise from both the experience of living in the tenure (and here there is a close link with the exponents of property and personality theories) and because housing is a material resource giving access to wealth accumulation. These arguments have been rejected by Ball (1983) and Williams (1984) on both theoretical and empirical grounds, attributing class differences to the means of production and presenting evidence which purports to show that home owners are not a homogeneous group with a common interest. They assert there is no universal experience of owner-occupation nor any certainty of capital accumulation. While this may be true there is little evidence of united action by owners and tenants to press governments for housing reform but rather of more partisan activities such as the rent strikes of 1972. The confused political opposition to massive cuts in housing expenditure since 1979 suggests a society more deeply divided on this issue than on attacks on health, education and social security spending which have been fought by a stronger and more united opposition and not necessarily just by those who would immediately suffer a loss of service (Forrest and Murie 1984a).

Although the evidence is not decisive, voting patterns provide some support for the contention that society is deeply divided on tenure lines and for the notion that home owners are an independent political force (Ball 1983; Saunders 1984) and that political parties perceive a distinct owner-occupier interest that they cannot afford to ignore. It is on the basis of such an interest that the Conservatives conceived of the right to buy as a means of 'dishing' Labour and creating a permanent power base from which to retain office.

For Labour, adjustments to economic recession have been a painful and debilitating process. They failed to preserve the ideals of equity and equality of opportunity that were the foundations upon which the post-war welfare state had been built or even to maintain the status quo. As these traditional values were challenged so a new idea of welfare emerged to inspire the legislative reforms that imposed a system of residential property based on individual rather than state ownership and offering maximum opportunities for the exercise of individual freedom and choice, a system that would facilitate the full and free exchange necessary for a market society to function. Even so the Conservatives did not ensure that everyone was guaranteed a right to buy or an income sufficient to meet the costs of home ownership although social justice demanded the universal enjoyment of these rights. Instead an unequal distribution of residential property was reinforced by a system of housing assistance which perpetuated inequalities in wealth and the opportunities for individual human fulfilment. The restructuring of residential property and redistribution of financial assistance and the concomitant increase in inequality and discrimination has resulted in a more divided society, whether those divisions are perceived as social divisions or immanent ideological cleavages. What is undeniable is that the new system is state directed and not inherently a free market in any sense, in the 'new' welfare state government is more powerful and political freedom has diminished.

Labour's Contracting Constituency

Among the notable consequences of the politics of property has been the electoral decline of the British Labour Party between the General Elections of 1970 and 1983. Over this period Labour's share of the vote fell from 43 to 29 per cent primarily because they lost the allegiance of the skilled working class, those in a position to buy their council houses. Whether or not elections can be won or lost on housing policy alone, it became evident during the seventies that the Party which won the support of this group would be rewarded with electoral success and that housing could play an important part in such a strategy.

Labour had won the 1974 elections on a radical platform but by 1979 voters' attitudes had changed. There are numerous explanations of why Labour did so badly in 1979 and 1983. The electorate were persuaded by Conservatives' promises to reduce taxes, prices and unemployment. During the 1970s the burden of taxation had shifted to income tax and so, faced with a choice between rises in take-home pay and the additional taxation that would have resulted from further government intervention in the economy, they turned away from Labour's proposals (Hood and Wright 1981; Walker 1982). Furthermore the Labour government had failed to deliver the 'social wage' and had cut planned social expenditure while unemployment continued to rise. Coates (1980) feels they expected too much of their supporters who had endured four years of incomes policies and consequent reductions in their standard of living, therefore they underestimated the 'real and understandable resistance on the part of rate- and tax-payers and trade union members to the continuous extension of collective as opposed to individual spending' (Glennerster 1983: 9). Labour failed to hold the support of the unions and with a pay revolt of even greater magnitude than the miners' stand against the Heath government's incomes policy five years earlier there was a degree of public backlash, prompted by irresponsible pickets and scenes on the picket lines which helped to elect the Conservative government on a law and order ticket and on their promise to curb trades unions' power. Labour's failure to deliver on housing, unemployment, inflation and industrial conflict led to a widespread loss of confidence in the capacity of the state to achieve welfare goals and to growing support for more individualist solutions which promised to protect existing privileges (Halsey 1981).

Labour in government 1974–79
Labour's years in office provided neither a solid record of achievement nor an apposite and consistent housing policy on which to fight the election. The government was deeply divided on housing issues, down to the smallest detail. As the radical programme of their Manifestos (Labour Party 1974a; 1974b) had little appeal to those in the government who held almost a free market position the first years of the Labour administration were spent without any clear policy on such fundamental issues as rents, subsidies, the respective roles of local authorities and housing associations, tenants' rights and the place of home ownership in a socialist society.

While waiting in vain for the Housing Policy Review to resolve these dilemmas they embraced the voluntary housing movement and reinstated many of the pre-1972 rules on rents and subsidies in legislation which appeared both inappropriate and backward-looking to many of Labour's traditional supporters. The uncertainty as to how to respond to the growing demand for home ownership was only superseded by unswerving endorsement when it seemed as if to do otherwise would be courting electoral disaster. In the event Labour might have been more effective at the ballot box had they had the political courage to tackle what Crosland had described as 'the dogs' breakfast of housing subsidies'.

While they might have justified reductions in the public sector building programme or the plans for investment in run-down estates and the proposals for curtailing subsidies in the 1979 Housing Bill by recurrent economic crises they were unable to explain their reluctance to increase tenants' rights, having promised statutory security of tenure as early as 1974. By siding with municipal landlords and jealously opposing any independent movement of tenants which threatened their political guardianship of the working class, Labour forfeited their constituency.

Apart from the homeloan scheme Labour only enacted interim measures and their permanent proposals never reached the statute book. The final years, from 1977 to 1979, were characterised by delays and inertia which were evident not only in housing but in all aspects of policy. Potentially embarrassing issues, such as policies for the elderly, the review of supplementary benefits and doctors' pay, the results of the 'Great Debate' on education, were all ignored (Donnison 1982) and no decision was reached on energy policy or environmental protection. Labour were certainly hampered by the political weakness of their governments. In contrast to the Conservatives who had majorities of 31 under Heath, 44 under Thatcher in 1979 and 140 in 1983, Labour was in a minority in February 1974 and their slender overall majority of 4 in October 1974 did not last long and forced the development of the Lib—Lab pact. However, their relationship with the Liberals cannot explain their poor performance as it was just one of a number of constraints upon government policy. Even with signs of a significant revival in the economy by 1977/8, Labour failed to take what with hindsight appears to have been the last chance to improve equity.

Labour's lost elections
In 1979 the Labour Party had little to offer electors as an alternative to the right to buy. Their subsequent opposition to compulsory sales proved to be an electoral liability because of the impression created that Labour's housing policy was nothing more than opposition to home ownership in general and council house ownership in particular. The leadership endeavoured to extricate themselves from this situation by reaffirming Labour's longstanding commitment to home ownership but at the 1980 Party Conference it was resolved that a future Labour

government would repeal the right to buy and give local authorities an option to buy back former council houses when they were first offered for resale, at a price which was to involve no financial loss to the authority in real terms (Labour Party 1980). However, by February 1981 the NEC and the Shadow Cabinet adopted a different attitude towards future policy on the grounds that working out the repurchase price on the proposed terms 'would be very burdensome for the local authority, if not impossible in principle, and would be incomprehensible and seemingly capricious to the former tenant' (Labour Party 1981a, para. 4). Accordingly they suggested authorities should be given a power to acquire properties when they came onto the market and that this should be provided by the retrospective insertion of a perpetual pre-emption clause in the authority's favour. They would then be able to buy the dwelling on first resale at market value (subject to the discount-sharing formula of the 1980 Act during the first five years). There were risks even with this formulation, such a power would be unlikely to be used by Conservative-controlled councils so that 'tenants who had bought would have a significant financial incentive to vote Tory in future elections' (Labour Party 1981a, para. 9). As sales policy was so contentious all that appeared in the 1983 Election Manifesto was a statement that a future Labour government would: 'end enforced council house sales, empower public landlords to repurchase houses sold under the Tories on first resale and provide that future voluntary agreed sales will be at market value' (Labour Party 1983), a policy that appeared at best ambiguous and at worst confused.

Although the Party professed to 'believe that it is as legitimate to rent as to buy, and that public rented and owner occupied sectors should co-exist on a basis of equal social esteem' (Labour Party 1982: 137), their proposals for achieving this end, a rent freeze and the provision of 'so far as is possible, the same legal rights and freedoms as private owners' (Labour Party 1982: 143), fell uneasily from the lips of those who had previously failed to honour such pledges. A rent freeze was small inducement to those dependent upon housing benefit to pay the rent and the Conservatives, who had already delivered on the charter, were also promising to extend it with a right to repair.

Labour were mistaken in assuming that prospective buyers would be prepared to sacrifice what might be their best chance of freedom and independence because others would be denied similar opportunities and for the dubious benefit of greater local democracy. Sales might restrict access to public housing or the possibilities of a transfer and lead to higher rents as management and maintenance costs would increase if councils were left with a higher proportion of flatted dwellings and estates in mixed ownership but the idea that council housing offered the best prospects for equalising opportunities did not equate with tenants' experience of wasteful, inefficient, unresponsive and overly bureaucratic housing authorities. In the circumstances, having failed to introduce a measure of fairness into housing finance, they should not have been surprised that tenants voted to join the more privileged sector.

The Conservatives' belief that home owners and prospective purchasers would transfer their political allegiance was confirmed by events. Crewe's (1983) analysis of voting patterns in the 1983 Election confirms that the majority of those who had bought their council house voted Conservative – 56 per cent voted Conservative, 25 per cent SDP/ Liberal Alliance and 18 per cent Labour. Of those who had voted Labour in 1979, 59 per cent switched to Conservative or the Alliance. Although Labour's vote held up better among council tenants, as sales progressed they would form a diminishing group. Labour had been completely out-manoeuvred by the Conservatives.

Within days of the election, defeated candidates were attributing Labour's rout to their sales policy and Roy Hattersley, the Shadow Home Secretary, and other prominent members of the Party publicly announced that they considered the policy to have been wrong: 'We cannot continue to deny council tenants the right to buy their own house when the sale would do no harm to the community as a whole. We must be careful to respond to the people's needs – not the council's prejudices' (Roy Hattersley, quoted in *Guardian*, 12 July 1983). What Hattersley slightingly referred to as the 'council's prejudices' were what members on the left of the Party regarded as basic socialist principles. Although the Labour Party was not opposed to home ownership as such but to compulsory sales of council houses it was implied that dwellings like other forms of capital needed to be in corporate owner- ship. However, Saunders (1984) suggests that such opposition to sales also derives from a more general fear of individualism and all forms of 'petty property' which produce a bourgeois mentality and is also related to a longstanding mistrust of the private landlord.

Those adopting a more pragmatic perspective were prepared to over- look the conflict between the socialist principles of equality and collectivism and a system of property relations based on private owner- ship. They accepted that opposition to the right to buy was politically untenable, that the world had changed and that the 'old Labourism will not do' (Griffith 1983: 5).

The way was cleared for the Party to revise its sales policies at the 1983 Conference when a motion calling for an end to all council house sales was rejected and by the 1984 Conference Labour was prepared to endorse the right to buy. Even so the decision is unlikely to produce political returns because to retain some credibility with those unable to buy they were unable to condone the payment of discounts on the Conservatives' generous terms. The Party's reconciliation to the right to buy was linked to a new 'right' to choose between renting and buying, prerequisites for which were financial equity and a right to rent which would ensure 'alternative tenures of equal status and esteem' (Labour Party Conference 1984, Composite Resolution 26). Even if rented accommodation were available on demand and there was as was suggested a duty upon an authority to acquire a suitable home to rent when it cannot offer a satisfactory dwelling from its existing stock, it is doubtful whether there would be widespread public support for their plans for large-scale building and municipalisation programmes when public intervention was not endorsed in 1979 or 1983. Neither does their commitment to a progressive distribution of assistance with housing costs as part of a wider reform of income maintenance and taxation appear realistic when all attempts to achieve radical reforms of tax, social security and housing finance during the previous decade failed. Even the projected computerisation of the tax system offers limited opportunities for such integration.

Simply adopting the dialectic of rights and freedoms will not get Labour out of the impasse they have reached in their search for 'a coherent socialist theory of individual property ownership' (Saunders 1984: 223). It was no mean task when the Party set the NEC to produce a detailed alternative policy for the 1985 Conference.[2]

The Property Revolution: A Political Conundrum
The controversy over the allocation of housing costs between individuals and the state and the distribution of state property have been at the heart of political debate on housing since 1970. During this period 'fair rents' and the right to buy have towered above and overshadowed the three major reforms of the subsidy system, the introduction of rent rebates and housing benefits, housing association provision and housing investment programmes and the tenants' charter, all of which have been significant elements in promoting radical changes in residential property rights and entitlement to housing assistance. Although the property revolution has not solved the fundamental problems that faced the new Conservative administration in 1970 — there is still concern over the cost of housing support, the amount of council housing and the role of the state in the housing market — it will be difficult to break outside of the framework it has created in the search for solutions.

The 'new welfare state' is firmly established. While the state cannot secede in favour of a free market it can withdraw from direct provision to confine its role to housing finance. The principle that individuals should hold the maximum rights in residential property compatible with similar rights for others and that only those who choose home ownership should be guaranteed a minimum level of state support without a test of need has been firmly established. As systems of property can both induce as well as reflect values it is unlikely that this legal framework will be radically changed, despite the evidence of injustices and inequalities, with over 60 per cent of households owner-occupying and almost 80 per cent expressing a preference for the tenure (Building Societies Association 1983). Even with the outcry over the implementation of housing benefits, evidence of the illogicalities of the system of local government finance, growing unemployment and their evident failure to realise their economic goals the Conservatives were re-elected in 1983 with a massive majority, and the continuing political controversy over rate-capping and the abolition of the GLC and the Metropolitan Counties did not appear to be reflected in 1984 EEC and by-election results. The electorate are keeping faith with the new political order. Hence there appears to be little prospect for any significant increase in public spending and the balance between the public and private sectors is unlikely to be redressed. Rather:

> the further privatization extends, the greater becomes its momentum. The more council tenants who buy their houses, the greater will be the pressures on government to support and generalize the home ownership option and the stronger will be the desire on the part of the remaining tenants to escape the increasingly marginal and inadequate state sector. (Saunders 1984: 213).

Although there are difficulties in extending the right to buy because of the poverty of tenants, there is no prospect of its repeal. All the major political parties have had to come to terms with it, although both Labour and the SDP/Liberal Alliance have reached an uneasy compromise. Both are in favour of reviewing the discount levels but while Labour at least has recognised that for a 'right' to have any substance it must be capable of being enforced the Alliance wish to retain the right to buy but with an exceptional temporary waiver in areas of housing stress on application by the council in that area to the Secretary of State, a policy which will neither meet the aspirations of the electors or the Alliance's aim of allowing local authorities to decide for themselves. The Conservatives have given no clear indication of how far they would be prepared to extend the right to buy. There is clearly resistance within their own Party to sales of specially designed and adapted dwellings and they were defeated on this as well as on housing association sales in 1982 and 1983. In such circumstances they might regard it as unwise to pursue a more radical policy such as the Walker plan to transmute rents into mortgage repayments.

While the mechanism for selling public housing is firmly established there is uncertainty about how far governments can continue to promote home ownership in a society with an ageing population, an increasing rate of marital breakdown and growing inequalities in the distribution of incomes and wealth. As the potential problems of universal home ownership are not admitted by the Conservatives there has been no appraisal of possible solutions. However, the legal and practical problems in acquiring, maintaining, living in and disposing of flats in the private sector were better known. Occupiers suffered at the hands of freeholders who failed to maintain the structure and common parts, levied extortionate charges for inadequate services, failed to enforce covenants in reciprocal leases and refused requests for lease extensions or charged unfair prices. However, a more fundamental problem had been explored by the Wilberforce Committee (Cmnd 2719, 1965) some years earlier: leases were depreciating assets and could become unmortgageable and unsaleable with the consequent limitations on the occupier's mobility. Leasehold was perhaps an outmoded form of tenure. Despite these known difficulties the government made no provision to meet them when granting the right to buy apart from a 125-year lease rather than the more usual 99-year term. Nothing was done about the legal title although Wilberforce had recommended the adoption of the strata title system, one of a number of condominium systems developed in, for example, the United States, Australia, New Zealand, Finland, Norway and the Netherlands which provided for the freehold ownership of the dwelling and individual ownership of a corporate body which held the freehold of the common property. Neither was any provision made for a model lease although the Housing and Building Control Act 1984 did allow the Secretary of State to override inappropriate covenants but only when it appeared that onerous conditions were being imposed as a device to deter prospective purchasers. Even more surprising, considering the Conservative government's advocacy of freedom and independence, was their failure to consider any proposals for collective management, whether a residents' association, co-operative, company or condominium. Some arrangement could have been made to give leaseholders more effective control. Instead the government relied on regulations tucked away in Schedule 19 of the Housing Act 1980 (amended subsequently by the 1984 Act) to define the division of responsibility for repairs and to lay down a code of conduct for determining service charges. This code was not comprehensive and as the flat owner was dependent upon the freeholder for essential services any deficiency in the standard of management and maintenance previously experienced might be expected to continue.

The Law Commission (1984) reported on these issues during 1984 and recommended freehold flats, standardisation of leases and their extension to 999 years as a means of resolving the legal difficulties but the growing concern that leasehold tenure was incompatible with home ownership had already resulted in three Private Members' Bills on the subject since 1980: Allan Roberts' Private Tenants' Rights Bill, John Fraser's Leasehold Flats Enfranchisement Bill and Sir Brandon Rhys Williams' Co-ownership of Flats Bill. While differing in detail there was a common purpose: the provision of basic statutory covenants and a mechanism for corporate management by residents through tenant ownership schemes. A far smaller proportion of council flats have been sold than council houses (Forrest and Murie 1984b) partly for these reasons, so that any government which seriously wishes to maintain the rate of sales will have to contemplate fundamental legal reforms along these lines to enhance the rights of the leasehold occupiers and place them a little closer to their counterparts in the house sector whose capacity to exclude all comers they wish to emulate.[3]

Ball (1983) has detected a weakening of political support for home ownership which he attributes to the growing problems of disrepair and mortgage default in the sector and which he claims is opening up a space on the political agenda for new forms of housing provision. There is, however, little evidence to support this contention or of widespread interest in alternative tenures such as co-operatives or shared ownership. What seems more certain is that there is unlikely to be a revival of public rented housing, unless it is to cater specifically for minority groups such as the elderly or disabled who are unable to satisfy their needs in the market place. Labour's pious hopes of restoring a right to rent with equality of esteem belong to a mythology of public housing. There is no way in which social control can be maintained and tenants granted the rights of disposal that ensure both control and the accumulation of wealth. Neither do the precedents from other fields of social policy promise much hope of success: the Binary system failed to establish equality of esteem between the universities and the polytechnics and even in the unlikely event of Labour extending the tenants' charter and neutralising the housing finance system there is enough evidence to suggest people would prefer home ownership even if it were stripped of its financial advantages. The stage has been set for any future development to take place within the two main tenures but with owner-occupation playing the leading role.

With a quarter of households in council housing it would be naïve to suggest state housing will have an insignificant part to play in housing provision but its role will be constrained by the elaborate system of controls that have proliferated in the seventies and eighties as governments have fought to control local authority spending and their housing policies and practices. Although these controls have proved to be inexact instruments and have on occasions had unexpected and undesired consequences, they are capable of refinement. It would take a considerable strength of political will to relinquish a means of containing what could become surrogate socialist or capitalist governments in exile. Any government would be reluctant to forgo a means to control housing income and expenditure because this is one of the few ways to ensure savings for taxpayers and ratepayers. Therefore while it would be possible to untangle the nexus of housing and local government finance it is unlikely that any government would choose to do so.

Notwithstanding this it will be impossible to avoid further reform of housing finance. Rather than the hoped-for reduction in the state's contribution towards housing costs, subsidies to tenants and home owners have increased overall. Although the council sector is no longer generally subsidised the growth in means-tested benefits has maintained the overall level of the state's contribution although much of this is now debited to the social security rather than the housing budget. This has ensured that the costs are met out of general taxation rather than rents, as was envisaged in 1972, but has also created more susceptibility to cuts in public expenditure. The system of housing support for tenants has developed outside of both the taxation and main income maintenance systems, partly because of technical difficulties in designing a system of general assistance to take cognisance of different rent levels but also because administrative complexities and political constraints impede comprehensive reforms of tax, income maintenance and housing finance systems.[4]

While housing benefit has resolved some of the problems of overlap between rent rebates and supplementary benefits it has brought new difficulties of delivery and entitlement. The tenants' plight, the growing numbers of home owners in receipt of supplementary benefit and the rise in volume of tax relief has resurrected the debate about financial equity between the tenures and schemes for integrated forms of assistance such as universal housing allowances or tax credits have been dusted off and brought out for discussion. Yet the wealth of evidence submitted to the social security reviews shows there was no greater measure of agreement in 1984 than there had been ten years earlier when Crosland embarked on his ill-fated Housing Finance Review. With council housing self-financing there is no possibility of a return to direct subsidies, nor of significant changes in the housing benefit system.[5]

Labour's right to choose is built upon a neutral housing finance system yet it is difficult to believe that the Party which let two chances of achieving financial equity slip by will be more successful in the future. They could have incorporated housing subsidy into the tax system in 1967 and prevented the subsequent erosion of assistance to tenants. However, at this time the importance of tax relief was not so apparent. Their inaction in 1977 is less easy to excuse.

Although Labour's programme for the eighties would not be fully revealed until the NEC published its report in 1985 the possibilities were aired by the Housing Policy Review in the seventies and even in the debates over rents in the sixties. The Labour Housing Group (1984) have considered two sets of options: either an extension of tax reliefs to rents coupled with some restriction on reliefs on mortgage interest such as to a single annuity, or a package of measures in which rents were based on capital values and home owners were taxed on imputed rental income based on capital values in addition to national rent pooling, a capital gains tax and a universal housing allowance. This kind of programme would be difficult to achieve in the short term because of pressures on the legislative timetable. Equally the administrative difficulties should not be underestimated especially in the set of proposals where a property revaluation would be a prerequisite for their implementation. The last two such revaluations have been 'deferred' because of the costs involved and because of the sensitivity of a process that is intimately connected to the unresolved question of how to finance local government.[6]

The Alliance was in agreement with Labour in admitting that reform of housing finance was essential but they too have yet to find a convincing method of bringing it about without courting electoral disaster. Such caution also underlies the Conservatives' position. When it was disclosed during Mrs Thatcher's first administration that the government was examining the future of social security benefits, the National Health Service and their financing, the matter was promptly shelved on the express instructions of the Prime Minister (*Economist*, 18 September 1982). The terms of reference of the social security reviews all reflect this caution. And despite Chancellor Nigel Lawson's declared commitment to 'tax neutrality' including his personal desire for the reform of mortgage tax relief and the need for more radical policies if the government is 'to arrest and then reverse the long decline' as Sir Geoffrey Howe put it in his first budget speech, the Prime Minister made it clear that she would not countenance any tampering with what has become a sacred cow. However, the escalating cost of this 'tax spending' will make it difficult to suppress it from public debate and the contradictions within the Conservatives' economic policies cannot but fail to become more self-evident. If tax concessions are kept to the forefront of public debate the Chancellor may get the opportunity to effect the kind of marginal reductions the Danish government have made to tax benefits. The comparison is appropriate as owner-occupation in Denmark is also in excess of 60 per cent (Haywood 1984).[7]

The prospects for the eighties are for a greater degree of consensus between the major political parties on systems of property and the role of the state in housing. It will not be possible to redress the balance between public and private property in favour of state ownership but the state could rectify the distribution of 'new property' rights and thereby leaven what has been described as the 'new welfare state' by curbing its individualist tendencies. As Labour has accepted the right to buy so they would be wise to reflect on the credibility of a right to rent dependent upon large-scale building and municipalisation programmes. Electors favouring rate and tax cuts are unlikely to be swayed by prospects of further social expenditure and few council tenants appear to share their partiality for municipal landlords. The discontent and disaffection amongst local authority tenants has led the Alliance to adopt a more innovative proposal for public housing based on neighbourhood housing trusts, similar to the local co-operative societies being developed in West Germany (Kennedy 1984), which would offer locally controlled non-commercial housing to rent. Should Labour wish to reinstate the principles of equality and collectivism they will have to reform housing finance rather than rebuild the council sector.

There is no necessity for a socialist housing programme to be based on direct provision, as the same objectives can be achieved through indirect aid (Weale 1978). If Labour accepts it is inappropriate to infringe the individual's claim to the maximum residential property rights compatible with similar rights for others, they will need to supplement this with a right not to be excluded from a form of housing assistance that gives tenants and home owners equal access to resources provided by progressive taxation. The task of examining and equating benefits, grants, loans, subsidies, tax concessions and capital gains proved daunting in 1977 when Labour could call on the full resources of DOE. The resources of the Opposition are limited and in 1985 making comparisons would be more problematical because of the interrelationships between housing, income maintenance and the financing of local government. Nevertheless the kind of integrated approach which has been adopted by, for example, France, Germany and Denmark, whose governments have instituted a range of support covering all tenures by using taxation and subsidies, savings plans, loans and mortgage guarantees according to the needs of lower, middle and upper income groups (Donnison and Ungerson 1982), is the only way forward for a Party committed to public planning.

The Conservatives cannot claim to be non-interventionist while they continue to cling to tax reliefs on mortgage interest payments. Either they will have to reconcile themselves to the fact that the market cannot be freely competitive in market societies or they will have to accept the dictates of economic liberalism and reduce 'tax spending'. It is unlikely that they will consider fundamental reforms but there will have to be marginal changes to improve fairness in response to public concern over housing and social security or Party pressures for more radical initiatives.

Despite the striking contrasts in the philosophy and approach of the Labour and Conservative parties there is a growing convergence of views on the forms of residential property and housing assistance appropriate for the last quarter of the twentieth century, which originated with the need to promote a populist image in a society comprising predominantly of home owners. Both parties have accepted home ownership as the natural form of tenure and by endorsing the right to buy have ensured that the private sector will grow at the expense of the public sector. And although the Conservatives' favoured universal home ownership they, along with Labour, supported housing association provision. Throughout the seventies there was a surprising consistency in the parties' approach to public sector subsidies and the retention of tax reliefs for owner-occupiers. The degree of consensus is exemplified by the way in which governments found it possible to borrow ideas and even legislation already drafted from earlier administrations. Labour's Leasehold Reform Act 1967 provided the Conservatives with the rationale for their right to buy and they inverted 'fair rents' and rent rebates originally conceived of as means to protect poor tenants as a basis for rent increases. The Conservatives' 1980 Housing Act subsidy like that of 1972 was developed under Labour, who took the Conservatives' Housing and Planning Bill 1973 as the basis for their 1974 Act.

The complex nature of the relationship between housing subsidy, taxation and social security and the affinity between local authorities' current and capital programmes exacerbates the difficulty of devising a strategy for reform whose outcome can be predicted accurately. This unreliability compounds the problem of generating political support for proposals of dubious appeal especially where there is the danger of their being presented as undesirable by the political opposition. Not surprisingly, the detail of housing finance has been infrequently debated at party conferences because the specifications for benefit tapers, HCDs and LCDs, GRE and the mechanics of HRAs and so on do not lend themselves to public discussion. Therefore any popular programme of reform would have to overcome these obstacles as well as home owners' opposition to any erosion of their privileges and the sensitivity of building societies and the building industry to any reductions in mortgage interest tax relief. The seventies have shown how difficult it is to depart from the status quo and if Labour intended to win an election on a reforming platform they would have to be well prepared. The Conservatives had their plans: the reviews of social security and capital finance and the committee of inquiry set up in 1984 to examine the problems in privately owned blocks of flats were all due to report by the end of 1985, well in advance of the next election. In contrast Labour had a few committed members on an NEC working party.

There is therefore the prospect of the late 1980s and the 1990s being as dominated by Conservative Party policies as the period between 1970 and 1984 has been. During this time Labour achieved little of lasting importance, except indirectly to the extent that the Conservatives adopted some of their ideas. With the benefit of hindsight, the Labour Party let the best opportunity for achieving equity slip by in 1977. The likelihood of any significant revival of public interest in socialist values during the eighties are slim given the lack of widespread political support for even the principles of the middle ground as advocated by the SDP/Liberal Alliance. There is less uncertainty about the effect of the changes wrought in housing upon the structure of the welfare state. Greater personal freedom has been achieved but at the cost of less equality in income and wealth, widening social divisions, more discrimination and a diminution of political power with the demise of local democracy and the increase in central government's power.

These developments have paralleled a move to the Right along the political spectrum and have been part of a plan to wind down the welfare state and restore *laissez-faire* capitalism. However, it is clear from the foregoing discussion that such an objective cannot be achieved and that there will have to be some form of mixed system in which the state retains responsibility for housing and general welfare. Even if the post-war welfare state had ceased to exist in its fullest sense the 'new welfare state' is a 'hybrid of democratic-welfare-capitalism' (Mishra 1984: 175). The rejection of the welfare state is no more a possibility than the sale of council housing was the final solution to freeing the state of both its holdings and its financial commitments. Not only was the home owner not self-sufficient but there were more and more potential owners — elderly, disabled, single parents and unemployed — who needed help with mortgage repayments and repairs and a very large group of council tenants who were too poor to buy. Moreover with councils' investment programmes heavily dependent upon capital receipts from sales the logic of continuing to build only to dispose of the dwellings to better-off tenants at substantial discounts is intuitively and practically incapable of being sustained. Because the only expedient will be to direct local authorities to build specially designed dwellings for the elderly and disabled which will remain outside the right to buy provisions, there will no longer be any doubt about the welfare role of the public sector. As a 'right to rent' is irreconcilable with the right to buy, and the latter cannot be rescinded, the balance will shift even further towards private property and away from public housing. It will be difficult to justify continuing to discriminate against public tenants when the costs of private support are challenged and there may be the opportunity for Labour to reclaim the mantle of equity and claim the right to fair rents and fair reliefs.

Notes

Chapter 3

1   The provision of central government subsidies towards the cost of rent rebates is detailed in Chapter 4. Under the housing benefit scheme these contributions were 90 per cent of the cost of standard rebates, 100.06 per cent for certificated rebates and nearly all of the administrative costs of the scheme. The Housing Benefit Review Team maintained that assistance should be below 100 per cent of actual costs to discourage local authorities from adopting rent policies designed to capitalise upon housing benefits and the 1985 Green Paper further proposed that subsidy be cut to 80 per cent and administrative support be subsumed within the Block Grant. Yet while the DHSS were endeavouring to curb rent rises environment ministers were considering introducing additional penalties through the RSG for authorities failing to increase rents in line with government guidelines (*The Sunday Times* 5 May 1985). The DOE and the DHSS evidently had differing views of 'realistic rents' and of the mechanisms necessary to ensure prudent administration.

2   The Housing Benefit Review Team accepted the need to rationalise the division between housing benefit and supplementary benefit in providing help with housing costs. However their suggestion that housing benefit be extended to include mortgage interest for all on low incomes was rejected by the government who reversed their equity arguments by proposing to discontinue payments to supplementary benefit recipients (on the grounds that it acted as a disincentive to return to work), despite the problem of mortgage arrears and the conflict with their own policy of extending home ownership to lower income groups.

Chapter 5

1   The prescribed proportions of capital receipts which might be used to enhance an authority's HIP allocation were reduced from 1 April 1985 to 20 per cent for house sales, 30 per cent for land sales and shared ownership, and 30 per cent for non-housing receipts. The government conceded that receipts from building for sale could be applied at 100 per cent after a threat of a backbench revolt. Although the revisions were designed to encourage local authorites to lend rather than spend receipts and to adhere to cash limits, overspending in 1984/5 was exacerbated as authorities tried to spend accumulated receipts at the higher

rate before the end of the financial year and entered into prefunding arrangements with bankers and building contractors.

2   Norwich City Council regained full control over right to buy procedures in May 1985 after more than three years of DOE intervention.

Chapter 6

1   Although the scheme was initially restricted to properties within prescribed price limits, these limits were raised by £5000 to £45,000 in Greater London and £40,000 in the South East (the figure elsewhere in England and Wales remained at £30,000) from 1 April 1985 and purchases were permitted outside these limits providing individuals met the excess from their own resources (Parliamentary Debates (Commons) 1985, vol. 76, col. 440).

Chapter 7

1   There was no indication by June 1985 of when the government's review of local government finance was likely to be completed, despite the criticisms of the Audit Commission and the Comptroller and Auditor General in reports published earlier in the year on 'Capital Expenditure Controls in Local Government in England' and the 'Operation of the Rate Support Grant System'. Elements of the systems for controlling local authority expenditure were found to be ineffective, inequitable and detrimental to sound financial management.

2   The policy document produced by the joint committee of members of the Shadow Cabinet and the NEC is likely to be put to the 1985 Party Conference with a recommendation that the Party accept the right to buy. Levels of discount would be reviewed and limitations placed on sales in inner city areas, where tenants would be eligible for a transferable discount similar to that provided for housing association tenants. These proposals would be balanced by a relaxation of controls to enable councils to finance an enhanced council house building programme from the receipts from sales, a Housing Rights Act which would grant owners a right to sell to the local authority and remain as tenants and grant private tenants a right to buy, and the extension of the Leasehold Reform Act to flat-dwellers who would also be granted the right to purchase the freehold collectively. Local authority tenants would be given the right to manage their own housing through tenant management co-operatives (*The Sunday Times* 12 May 1985; *Guardian* 14 June 1985).

3   Despite reports of government plans for further legislation to increase sales of flats by higher discounts and reduced service charges (*The Sunday Times* 19 May 1985) there was no indication that the government were preparing to implement any of the more radical proposals for the reform of the leasehold system (Parliamentary Debates (Commons) 1985, vol. 75, cols 310–11). They were, however, considering increasing home ownership by providing grants to enable council tenants to buy in the private market and giving a legal right to private developers to acquire empty council properties for refurbishment and sale (*The Sunday Times* 16 June 1985; *Sunday Telegraph* 16 June 1985).

4   Notwithstanding Norman Fowler's reference to his review as the most substantial examination of the social security system since Beveridge, the 1985 Green Paper left the divisions between taxation, income maintenance and housing finance largely intact. Although there would be changes in the form of assistance

the structure of universal benefits and national insurance benefits would be mostly untouched (with the exception of the phased abolition of the State Earnings Related Pension Scheme which would be replaced by private pensions). The superstructure of means-tested benefits would be reformed to tackle the poverty trap and provide a common basis for assessment. A family credit paid through the wage packet (but still necessitating a claim to the DHSS) would replace FIS and there would be a new scheme of income support instead of supplementary benefit. Housing benefit would be tailored to complement these schemes. Since the Green Paper omitted all the figures on the level of future benefits it was difficult to identify the gainers and losers. However the prospects of harsher means testing suggest the government was trying to curb expenditure by reducing the entitlements of comparatively poor people. Conservatives' preferences for limiting the role of the state and targeting resources to those in greatest need might have led them to question the contribution of tax concessions and introduce wholesale means testing. Yet with implementation scheduled for 1987, a likely election year, prudence triumphed over ideological zeal and the more controversial proposals, such as the abolition of child benefit and limiting entitlement to unemployment benefit, were dropped. Furthermore the Green Paper only made passing reference to the integration of benefits and income taxation. The date of uprating benefits would be altered to coincide with the tax year but there was no suggestion of radical reform, such as the introduction of a tax credit system, even though a Green Paper on personal taxation was expected later in the year. The inability of the Treasury and the DHSS to coordinate their proposals and their disagreements over the primary objectives of the social security system and the cost of tax reliefs resulting from the privatisation of pensions are indicative of the government's failure to learn the lesson that the tax and benefit systems have to be viewed in conjunction (*Reform of Social Security* Cmnd 9517; *Reform of Social Security: Programme for Change* Cmnd 9518; *Reform of Social Security: Background Papers* Cmnd 9519; *Housing Benefit Review: Report of the Review Team* Cmnd 9520).

5   The Housing Benefit Review Team recommended that the scheme be unified to ensure the same level of support for those on supplementary benefit or equivalent levels of income whether in or out of work and simplified by the replacement of the array of tapers, which determined the rate at which assistance was withdrawn as income rose, by a single income-related taper. Local authorities would continue to administer the scheme. Although they did not specify benefit levels their proposals would have resulted in about 5 million gaining or having no change in benefit and 3 million losing on a cost-neutral basis. Assistance would be redistributed according to size of housing cost and to families with incomes close to supplementary benefit level. However the Green Paper proposals for all to contribute at least 20 per cent towards their rates bill (to encourage people to act more responsibly when voting for high spending authorities) and to steepen the taper would lead to about 7 million losers, a large proportion of whom would be occupational pensioners, the group whose interests had previously led to a government decision to defer planned reductions in housing benefits in 1984/5 (see page 47).

6   The Labour leadership evidently believed that even questioning the value of tax concessions, and in particular tax relief on mortgage interest payments, would be so electorally damaging that Neil Kinnock was prepared to disown Michael Meacher's 'Green Paper' on social security within days of publication (*Financial Times* 17 and 18 April 1985), although they offered an alternative policy which attempted to get back to socialist values. Tax reliefs would be abolished and national insurance contributions raised for the better-off to finance an income protection plan based on higher national insurance and child benefits

rather than means testing. A system of universal housing allowances would be paid as benefits to the unemployed or as tax allowances for those in work.

7   The growing pressure upon the government to release the figures showing the costs of reforming social security may have contributed to the decision to drop the proposed Rent Bill and other controversial measures from the legislative programme until after the next General Election (*Guardian* 10 and 11 June 1985; *Financial Times* 13 June 1985). The only alternative to a large number of cash losers which would result from the Green Paper proposals would be to maintain existing payments while changing the benefit system. However this would involve extra costs which could only be met either by raising taxes or reducing allowances. The government would have to decide before the publication of the White Paper which of these options would be most likely to guarantee the support of the electorate and such an exercise could present a further opportunity to appraise the current system of housing finance.

Bibliography

Arden, A. 1980, *The Housing Act 1980*, London, Sweet & Maxwell.

Arden, A. 1983, *Report on Housing Associations to the Greater London Council*, London, GLC.

Aspinall, P. 1978, *The Evolution of Urban Tenure Systems in 19th Century Cities*, Research Memorandum 63, Centre for Urban and Regional Studies, University of Birmingham.

Atkinson, A.B. 1983, 'Shall we ever reform taxes and benefits?', *New Society*, 16 June, pp. 423–5.

Baker, C.V. 1976, *Housing Associations*, London, Estates Gazette.

Ball, M. 1983, *Housing Policy and Economic Power*, London, Methuen.

Banting, K.G. 1979, *Poverty, Politics and Policy*, London, Macmillan.

Barker, D. 1971, 'Negative income tax' in D. Bull (ed.), *Family Poverty*, London, Gerald Duckworth.

Beirne, P. 1977, *Fair Rent and Legal Fiction*, London, Macmillan.

Bellairs, C. 1976, 'Home Ownership', *Politics Today*, no. 11, Conservative Research Department.

Beloff, M. and Plender, R. 1975, 'Varieties of amnesty', *New Society*, 22 May, pp. 463–4.

Best, R. 1973, *Housing Associations in London: 1972–73*, London, National Federation of Housing Societies.

Best, R. 1980, *A Guide for Housing Associations to the New Housing Bill*, London, National Federation of Housing Associations.

Bird, B.E.I. and Palmer, J.A.D. 1979, *Housing Association Tenants*, London, Housing Corporation.

Boddy, M. 1980, *The Building Societies*, London, Macmillan.

Boleat, M. 1982, *The Building Society Industry*, London, George Allen & Unwin.

Bradley, S. 1984, *Housing Benefit — the cost to the claimant*, London, National Association of Citizens Advice Bureaux and the Greater London Citizens Advice Bureaux Service.

Building Societies Association 1983, *Housing Tenure*, London.

Building Societies Association 1984, *Leaseholds — Time for a change?*, London.

Burgess, T. and Travers, T. 1980, *Ten Billion Pounds*, London, Grant McIntyre.

Cmnd 2650 1965, *Report of the Committee on Housing in Greater London*, (Milner Holland), London, HMSO.

Cmnd 2719 1965, *Positive Covenants Affecting Land* (Wilberforce), London, HMSO.

Cmnd 2838 1965, *The Housing Programme 1965 to 1970*, London, HMSO.

Cmnd 3604 1968, *Increases in Rents of Local Authority Housing*, National Board for Prices and Incomes, Report no. 62, London, HMSO.

Cmnd 4609 1971, *Report of the Committee on the Rent Acts* (Francis), London, HMSO.

Cmnd 4728 1971, *Fair Deal for Housing*, London, HMSO.

Cmnd 5116 1972, *Proposals for a Tax-Credit System*, London, HMSO.

Cmnd 5280 1973, *Widening the Choice: The Next Steps in Housing*, London, HMSO.

Cmnd 5539 1973, *Better Homes the Next Priorities*, London, HMSO.

Cmnd 5879 1975, *Public Expenditure to 1978—79*, London, HMSO.

Cmnd 6151 1975, *The Attack on Inflation*, London, HMSO.

Cmnd 6851 1977, *Housing Policy A Consultative Document*, London, HMSO.

Cmnd 6910 1977, *Supplementary Benefits Commission, Annual Report 1976*, London, HMSO.

Cmnd 7392 1978, *Supplementary Benefits Commission, Annual Report 1977*, London, HMSO.

Cmnd 7634 1979, *Central Government Controls over Local Authorities*, London, HMSO.

Cmnd 7746 1980, *The Government's Expenditure Plans 1980—81*, London, HMSO.

Cmnd 7841 1980, *The Government's Expenditure Plans 1980—81 to 1983—84*, London, HMSO.

Cmnd 8105 1980, *The Government's reply to the First Report from the Environment Committee*, Session 1979—80, HC 714, London, HMSO.

Cmnd 8175 1981, *The Government's Expenditure Plans 1981—82 to 1983—84*, London, HMSO.

Cmnd 8377 1981, *Council House Sales: The Government's reply to the Second Report from the Environment Committee*, Session 1980—81, HC 366, London, HMSO.

Cmnd 8435 1981, *The Government's reply to the Third Report from the Environment Committee*, Session 1980—81, HC 383, London, HMSO.

Cmnd 8494 1982, *The Government's Expenditure Plans 1982—83 to 1984—85*, London, HMSO.

Cmnd 8789 1983, *The Government's Expenditure Plans 1983—84 to 1985—86*, London, HMSO.

Cmnd 9008 1983, *Rates: proposals for rate limitation and reform of the rating system*, London, HMSO.

Cmnd 9063 1983, *Streamlining the Cities*, London, HMSO.

Cmnd 9143 1984, *The Government's Expenditure Plans 1984—85 to 1986—87*, London, HMSO.

Cmnd 9517 1985, *Reform of Social Security*, London, HMSO.

Cmnd 9518 1985, *Reform of Social Security: Programme for Change*, London, HMSO.

Cmnd 9519 1985, *Reform of Social Security: Background Papers*, London, HMSO.

Cmnd 9520 1985, *Housing Benefit Review: Report of the Review Team*, London, HMSO.

Clapham, C. and Maclennan, D. 1983, 'Residualization of public housing a non-issue', *Housing Review*, vol. 32, no. 1, pp. 9—10.

Coates, D. 1980, *Labour in Power? A Study of the Labour Government 1974—1979*, London, Longman.

Cohen, M. 1978, 'Property and sovereignty' in C.B. Macpherson (ed.), *Property*, Oxford, Basil Blackwell.

Conservative Party 1970, *A Better Tomorrow The Conservative Programme for the next 5 years*, London.

Conservative Party 1974a, *Firm Action for a Fair Britain. The Conservative Manifesto*, February, London.

Conservative Party 1974b, *Putting Britain First. A National Policy from the Conservatives*, October, London.
Conservative Party 1979, *The Conservative Manifesto*, London.
Conservative Party 1983, *The Conservative Manifesto*, London.
Cooper, P. 1983, 'Making the most of tenants' handbooks', *Housing*, vol. 19, no. 4, pp. 12–14.
Cooper, S. 1984, 'English Housing Policy 1972 to 1980', unpublished PhD thesis, University of London.
Court of Appeal 1982, *Regina v. Secretary of State for the Environment, Ex Parte Norwich City Council*, Transcript of the Shorthand Notes of the Association of Official Shorthandwriters Ltd, 9 February.
Craddock, J. 1975, *Council Tenant Participation in Housing Management*, London, Association of London Housing Estates.
Craven, E. 1975, 'Housing' in R. Klein (ed.), *Social Policy and Public Expenditure 1975: Inflation and Priorities*, London, Centre for Studies in Social Policy.
Crewe, I. 1983, 'The disturbing truth behind Labour's rout', *Guardian*, 13 June.
Crosland, A. 1975, 'The finance of housing', *Housing Review*, vol. 24, no. 5, pp. 128–30.
Cross, C. 1982, 'Law unto himself', *Local Government Chronicle*, 26 February, pp. 208–9.
Crossman, R. 1975, *The Diaries of a Cabinet Minister, Volume One, Minister of Housing, 1964–66*, London, Hamish Hamilton and Jonathan Cape.
Crown Estate Commissioners 1981, *The Crown Estate, Report of the Commissioners for the year ended 31 March 1981*, London, HMSO.
Cullingworth, J.B. 1966, *Housing and Local Government*, London, George Allen & Unwin.
Cullingworth, J.B. 1979, *Essays on Housing Policy*, London, George Allen & Unwin.
Cutting, M. 1977, *Landlord: Private or Public? A Study of the Rent Act 1974*, Occasional Paper no. 4, London, Catholic Housing Aid Society.
DOE 1971, *Housing Associations*, A Working Paper of the Central Housing Advisory Committee, London, HMSO.
DOE 1975, *Final Report of the Working Party on Housing Co-operatives* (Campbell), London, HMSO.
DOE 1977a, *Local Authorities and Building for Sale*, Housing Development Directorate Occasional Paper 1/77, London.
DOE 1977b, *Tenancy Agreements*, Housing Services Advisory Group, London.
DOE 1977c, *Access and Allocation*, A Consultation Paper, London.
DOE 1978a, *Housing Management: Eligibility*, A Consultation Paper, London.
DOE 1978b, *Housing Management: Tenants' Rights Involvement in Management*, A Consultation Paper, London.
DOE 1979a, *Housing Bill The Right to Buy*, A Consultation Paper, London.
DOE 1979b, *Legislation on Housing: Tenants' Charter Provisions*, A Consultation Paper, London.
DOE 1980a, *Appraisal of the Financial Effects of Council House Sales*, London.
DOE 1980b, *Consultation Paper: the New Local Authority Housing Subsidy System: Determination of Reckonable Income for 1980/81 and 1981/82*, London.
DOE 1980c, *Consultation Paper: The New Local Authority Housing Subsidy System: Proposals for Reckonable Expenditure and Reckonable Income*, London.
DOE 1980d, *Starter Homes*, Housing Development Directorate Occasional Paper 2/80, London.
DOE 1980e, *Model Scheme for Shared Ownership*, Ministerial Letter, 15 October, London.

DOE 1981a, *Sales of Council Houses and Flats and Disposal of Housing Land*, Ministerial Letter, 2 June, London.

DOE 1981b, *Assistance with Housing Costs*, London.

DOE 1981c, *New Housing Subsidy System: Matters Outstanding from Consultations to Date: Response by the Secretary of State*, London.

DOE 1981d, *The New Local Authority Housing Subsidy System: Outstanding Issues*, London.

DOE 1982a, *Housing Subsidies and Accounting Manual*, London, HMSO.

DOE 1982b, *Housing Act 1980: Housing Subsidy System: Determination of Reckonable Expenditure and Reckonable Income*, Ministerial Letter, 19 March, London.

DOE 1982c, *General Determination of Reckonable Income 1982/83*, Ministerial Letter, 19 March, London.

DOE 1983, *General Determination of Reckonable Income 1983/84*, Ministerial Letter, 17 January, London.

DOE 1984, *General Determination of Reckonable Income 1984/85*, Ministerial Letter, 13 January, London.

Dale, D. 1984, '"Community" and Conservatism', *New Statesman*, 27 January, pp. 13–14.

Denman, D.R. 1978, *The Place of Property*, Berkhampsted, Geographical Publications.

Donnison, D. 1967, *The Government of Housing*, Harmondsworth, Penguin Books.

Donnison, D. 1981, 'A rationalisation of housing benefits', *The Three Banks Review*, no. 131, pp. 3–13.

Donnison, D. 1982, *The Politics of Poverty*, Oxford, Martin Robertson.

Donnison, D. and Ungerson, C. 1982, *Housing Policy*, Harmondsworth, Penguin Books.

Downey, P., Matthews, A. and Mason, S. 1982, *Management Co-operatives: Tenants' Responsibility in Practice*, London, DOE.

Ermish, J. 1984, *Housing Finance: Who Gains?*, London, Policy Studies Institute.

Field, F. 1975, *Do we need Council Houses?*, Occasional Paper no. 2, London, Catholic Housing Aid Society.

Forrest, R. 1983, 'The meaning of homeownership?', *Environment and Planning D: Society and Space*, vol. 1, pp. 205–16.

Forrest, R. and Murie, A. 1983, 'Residualization and council housing: aspects of the changing social relations of housing tenure', *Journal of Social Policy*, vol. 12, no. 4, pp. 453–68.

Forrest, R. and Murie, A. 1984a, *Right to Buy? Issues of Need, Equity and Polarisation in the Sale of Council Houses*, Working Paper no. 39, Bristol, School for Advanced Urban Studies.

Forrest R. and Murie, A. 1984b, *Monitoring the Right to Buy 1980–1982*, Working Paper no. 40, Bristol, School for Advanced Urban Studies.

Forrest, R., Lansley, S. and Murie, A. 1984, *A Food on the Ladder? An evaluation of low cost home ownership initiatives*, Bristol, School for Advanced Urban Studies.

Fraser, D. 1973, *The Evolution of the British Welfare State*, London, Macmillan.

Gauldie, E. 1974, *Cruel Habitations*, London, George Allen & Unwin.

Gellner, E. 1979, *Spectacles and Predicaments*, Cambridge, Cambridge University Press.

George, V. and Wilding, P. 1976, *Ideology and Social Policy*, London, Routledge & Kegan Paul.

Gibson, J. 1981, *The New Housing Subsidy System and its Interaction with the Block Grant*, 2nd ed., Institute of Local Government Studies, University of Birmingham.

Ginsberg, M. 1965, *On Justice in Society*, London, Heinemann.

Glennerster, H. 1981, 'Social service spending in a hostile environment', in C. Hood and M. Wright (eds), *Big Government in Hard Times*, Oxford, Martin Robertson.

Glennerster, H. 1983, 'A new start for Labour' in J. Griffith (ed.), *Socialism in a Cold Climate*, London, Unwin Paperbacks.

Goodin, R.E. 1982, 'Freedom and the welfare state: theoretical foundations', *Journal of Social Policy*, vol. 11, no. 2, pp. 149–76.

Goodman Committee 1976, *Charity Law and Voluntary Organizations*, London, Bedford Square Press.

Goudie, J. 1972, *Councils and the Housing Finance Act*, Young Fabian Pamphlet no. 31, London, Fabian Society.

Gray, H. 1968, *The Cost of Council Housing*, London, Institute of Economic Affairs.

Greenwood, A. 1970, 'Housing achievements and prospects of the 1970s', *Housing Review*, vol. 19, no. 1, pp. 1–3.

Greenwood, R. 1981, 'Fiscal pressure and local government in England and Wales' in C. Hood and M. Wright (eds), *Big Government in Hard Times*, Oxford, Martin Robertson.

Greve, J. 1969, 'Housing policies and prospects', *Political Quarterly*, vol. 40, no. 1, pp. 23–34.

Griffin, Sir F. 1971, *Selling More Council Houses*, London, Conservative Political Centre.

Griffith, J.A.G. (ed.) 1983, *Socialism in a Cold Climate*, London, Unwin Paperbacks.

Griffiths, L.R.H. 1981, 'Premiums, service charges and leasehold reform' in College of Law, *The Housing Act 1980 – A Guide for the Practitioner*, London.

HC 473 1969, *Housing Subsidies*, Estimates Committee Session 1968–69, London, HMSO.

HC 600 1978, *Selected Public Expenditure Programmes*, Expenditure Committee Eighth Report Session 1977–78, Chapter III, 'Housing', London, HMSO.

HC 622 1978, *Capital Grants to Housing Associations*, Committee of Public Accounts Ninth Report Session 1977–78, London, HMSO.

HC 327 1979, *Housing Associations and the Housing Corporation*, Committee of Public Accounts Fifth Report Session 1978–79, London, HMSO.

HC 714 1980, *Enquiry into Implications of Government's Expenditure Plans 1980–81 to 1983–84 for the Housing Policies of the Department of the Environment*, Environment Committee Session 1979–80, London, HMSO.

HC 366 1981, *Council House Sales*, Environment Committee Session 1980–81, London, HMSO.

HC 383 1981, *DOE's Housing Policies: Enquiry into Government's Expenditure Plans 1981–82 to 1983–84 and the Updating of the Committee's First Report for the Session 1979–80*, Environment Committee Session 1980–81, London, HMSO.

HC 638 1984, *DHSS Housing Benefits Scheme*, Report by Comptroller and Auditor General Session 1983–84, London, HMSO.

Haines, J. 1977, *The Politics of Power*, Sevenoaks, Coronet Books.

Halsey, A.H. 1981, 'A sociologist's viewpoint' in OECD, *The Welfare State in Crisis*, Paris, Organisation for Economic Co-operation and Development.

Hamnett, C. 1983, 'The new geography of housing', *New Society*, 8 December, pp. 396–8.

Hands, J. 1975, *Housing Co-operatives*, London, Society for Co-operative Dwellings.

Harloe, M. 1977, 'Will the Green Paper mean better housing?', *Roof*, vol. 2, no. 5, pp. 143—8.

Harloe, M. and Martens, M. 1984, 'Comparative housing research', *Journal of Social Policy*, vol. 13, no. 3, pp. 255—77.

Harris, J. 1979, 'What happened after Beveridge?', *New Society*, 25 January, pp. 190—2.

Harris, R. and Seldon, A. 1979, *Over-ruled on Welfare*, London, Institute of Economic Affairs.

Harvey, A. 1968, 'What help for poor tenants?' in Fabian Society, *Social Services for All?*, London.

Harvey, A. 1982, 'Housing Benefit?', *New Law Journal*, 28 January, pp. 78—9.

Haywood, I. 1984, 'Denmark' in M. Wynn (ed.), *Housing in Europe*, London, Croom Helm.

Hepworth, N.P. 1975, 'Local government and housing finance' in Institute of Fiscal Studies, *Housing Finance*, IFS Publication no. 12, London.

Hepworth, N.P. 1976, *The Finance of Local Government*, London, George Allen & Unwin.

Hill, M. 1984a, *Housing Benefit Implementation: from Unified Ideal to Complex Reality*, Working Paper no. 36, Bristol, School for Advanced Urban Studies.

Hill, M. 1984b, 'The Implementation of housing benefit', *Journal of Social Policy*, vol. 13, no. 3, pp. 297—320.

Hoath, D.C. and Brown, A.A. 1981, *Main Changes in Housing Law*, London, Housing Centre Trust.

Hobhouse, L.T. 1966, *Sociology and Philosophy A Centenary Collection of Essays and Articles*, London, Bell.

Hood, C. and Wright, M. (eds) 1981, *Big Government in Hard Times*, Oxford, Martin Robertson.

Housing Centre Trust 1977a, *Response to Green Paper on Housing Policy No. 1 Memorandum on Housing Finance*, London.

Housing Centre Trust 1977b, *Response to Green Paper on Housing Policy No. 2 Memorandum on Access and Allocation*, London.

Housing Centre Trust 1978, *Response to Green Paper on Housing Policy No. 3 Housing Management: A Tenant's Charter*, London.

Housing Corporation 1984, *The Housing Corporation Report 1983/84*, London.

Housing Research Group, 1981 *Could Local Authorities Be Better Landlords?*, London, City University.

Howes, E. 1978, 'The new subsidy system: what it will mean for tenants, rate-payers and taxpayers', *CES Review* no. 4, pp. 6—12.

Jacobs, S. 1981, 'The sale of council houses: does it matter?', *Critical Social Policy*, vol. 1, no. 2, pp. 35—48.

Jeffries, J. 1982 'Is the new housing project control system better or worse?', *Housing*, vol. 18, no. 11, pp. 17—18.

Jones, P. 1982, 'Freedom and the redistribution of resources', *Journal of Social Policy*, vol. 11, no. 2, pp. 217—38.

Judge, K. 1982, 'The growth and decline of social expenditure' in A. Walker (ed.), *Public Expenditure and Social Policy*, London, Heinemann.

Karn, V. 1979, 'How can we liberate council tenants?', *New Society*, 29 March, pp. 738—40.

Karslake, H.H. 1967, *Leasehold Reform Act 1967*, London, Rating and Valuation Association.

Kaufman, G. (ed.) 1983, *Renewal: Labour's Britain in the 1980s*, Harmondsworth, Penguin Books.

Kemeny, J. 1981, *The Myth of Home Ownership*, London, Routledge & Kegan Paul.

Kennedy, D. 1984, 'Western Germany' in M. Wynn (ed.), *Housing in Europe*, London, Croom Helm.

Kilroy, B. 1978, *Housing Finance — Organic Reform?*, London, Labour Economic Finance and Taxation Association.

Kilroy, B. 1979, 'The cost of housing: subsidy implications of the Housing Bill', *Housing Review*, vol. 28, no. 4, pp. 110–13.

Kilroy, B. 1980, 'The financial implications of government policies on home ownership' in SHAC (London Housing Aid Centre), *Home Ownership in the 1980s*, 1980 Policy Paper 3, London.

Kilroy, B. 1981, 'Council house sales: was the government misled by DOE's evidence?', *Housing and Planning Review*, Summer, pp. 20–4.

Kilroy, B. 1982, 'Public expenditure on housing' in A. Walker (ed.), *Public Expenditure and Social Policy*, London, Heinemann.

Kilroy, B. 1984, 'Reforming housing finance' in Labour Housing Group, *Right to a Home*, Nottingham, Spokesman Books.

King, M. and Atkinson, A. 1980, 'Housing policy, taxation and reform', *Midland Bank Review*, Spring, pp. 7–15.

Klein, R. (ed.) 1975, *Social Policy and Public Expenditure 1975: Inflation and Priorities*, London, Centre for Studies in Social Policy.

Klein, R. with Barnes, J., Buxton, M. and Craven, E. 1974, *Social Policy and Public Expenditure 1974*, London, Centre for Studies in Social Policy.

Labour Housing Group 1984, *Right to a Home*, Nottingham, Spokesman Books.

Labour Party 1974a, *Labour's Way out of the Crisis. The Labour Party Manifesto*, January, London.

Labour Party 1974b, *Labour Party Manifesto*, October, London.

Labour Party 1979, *The Labour Way is the Better Way. The Labour Party Manifesto*, London.

Labour Party 1980, *The Tory Housing Act*, Information Paper no. 14, London.

Labour Party 1981a, *Re-Purchase of Council Houses Sold*, Statement by the National Executive Committee, February, London.

Labour Party 1981b, *A Future for Public Housing*, London.

Labour Party 1982, *Labour's Programme 1982*, London.

Labour Party 1983, *Labour's Plan. The New Hope for Britain. The Labour Party Manifesto*, London.

Lansley, S. 1979, *Housing and Public Policy*, London, Croom Helm.

Lansley, S. 1983, 'Private concern', *Roof*, vol. 8, no. 4, pp. 10–13.

Lansley, S. and Fiegehen, G. 1974, *One Nation? Housing and Conservative Policy*, Fabian Tract 432, London, Fabian Society.

Law Commission 1984, *Transfer of Land — The Law of Positive and Restrictive Covenants*, Report no. 127, London, HMSO.

Lawson, N. 1981, *Thatcherism in Practice. A Progress Report*, London, Conservative Political Centre.

Layton-Henry Z. (ed.) 1980, *Conservative Party Politics*, London, Macmillan.

Legg, C. and Brion, M. 1976, *The Administration of Rent Rebate and Rent Allowance Schemes*, London, DOE.

Longley, A.R., Dockray, M. and Sallon, J. 1979, *Charity Trustees' Guide*, London, Bedford Square Press.

MHLG 1969, *Council Housing, Purposes, Procedures and Priorities*, Central Housing Advisory Committee, London, HMSO.

McDonald, I.J. 1969, 'The leasehold system: towards a balanced land tenure for urban development', *Urban Studies*, vol. 6, no. 2, pp. 179–95.

McGurk, P. and Raynesford, N. 1982, *A Guide to Housing Benefits*, London, Institute of Housing and SHAC (London Housing Aid Centre).

McKay, D.H. and Cox, A.W. 1979, *The Politics of Urban Change*, London, Croom Helm.

Macpherson, C.B. 1962, *The Political Theory of Possessive Individualism*, Oxford, Oxford University Press.
Macpherson, C.B. (ed.) 1978, *Property: Mainstream and Critical Positions*, Oxford, Basil Blackwell.
Marshall, T.H. 1981, *The Right to Welfare and Other Essays*, London, Heinemann.
Massey, D. 1983, 'The shape of things to come', *Marxism Today*, April, pp. 18–27.
Massey, D. and Catalano, A. 1978, *Capital and Land: Landownership by Capital in Great Britain*, London, Edward Arnold.
Matthews, A. 1981, *Management Co-operatives: The Early Stages*, London, DOE.
Megarry, R.E. and Wade, H.W.R. 1975, *The Law of Real Property*, London, Stevens & Sons.
Merrett, S. 1979, *State Housing in Britain*, London, Routledge & Kegan Paul.
Merrett, S. 1982, *Owner Occupation in Britain*, London, Routledge & Kegan Paul.
Minns, R. 1974, 'The significance of Clay Cross: another look at District Audit', *Policy and Politics*, vol. 2, no. 4, pp. 309–29.
Mishra, R. 1984, *The Welfare State in Crisis*, Brighton, Wheatsheaf Books.
Mitchell, A. 1974, 'Clay Cross', *Political Quarterly*, vol. 45, no. 2, pp. 165–78.
Murie, A. 1975, *The Sale of Council Houses*, Occasional Paper no. 35, Centre for Urban and Regional Studies, University of Birmingham.
Murie, A. 1983, *Housing Inequality and Deprivation*, London, Heinemann.
Murie, A. and Forrest, R. 1976, *Social Segregation, Housing Need and the Sale of Council Houses*, Research Monograph no. 53, Centre for Urban and Regional Studies, University of Birmingham.
NALGO Housing Working Party (undated), *Housing: The Way Ahead*, London.
National Consumer Council 1976, *Tenancy Agreements*, London.
National Federation of Housing Associations 1977, *The Response of the National Federation of Housing Associations Council to the Government's Consultative Document on Housing Policy*, London.
National Federation of Housing Associations 1979, 'Housing associations and the government', *Federation News*, July.
Nevitt, A.A. 1966, *Housing, Taxation and Subsidies*, London, Nelson.
Nevitt, A.A. 1968a, 'A national housing allowance scheme' in Fabian Society, *Social Services for All?*, London.
Nevitt, A.A. 1968b, 'Conflicts in British housing policy', *Political Quarterly*, vol. 39, no. 4, pp. 439–50.
Nevitt, A.A. 1971, *Fair Deal for Householders*, Fabian Research Series no. 297, London, Fabian Society.
Nevitt, A.A. 1978, 'British housing policy', *Journal of Social Policy*, vol. 7, no. 3, pp. 329–34.
Nevitt, A.A. and Rhodes, G. 1972, 'Housing' in Gerald Rhodes (ed.), *The New Government of London: The First Five Years*, London, Weidenfeld & Nicolson.
Newby, H., Bull, C., Rose, D. and Saunders, P. 1978, *Property, Paternalism and Power*, London, Hutchinson.
Nightingale, B. 1973, *Charities*, London, Allen Lane.
Offer, A. 1981, *Property and Politics 1870–1914*, Cambridge, Cambridge University Press.
Orwell, G. 1954, *Nineteen Eighty-Four*, Harmondsworth, Penguin Books.
Page, D. 1979, *A Statutory Right of Purchase for Housing Association Tenants?*, London, National Federation of Housing Associations.
Parker, P.A. 1967, *The Rents of Council Houses*, Occasional Papers in Social Administration no. 22, London, Bell.

Bibliography 173

Parris, J. 1975, 'Standing by the Clay Cross', *New Law Journal*, 13 February, pp. 165–6.
Partington, M. 1980, *Landlord and Tenant*, 2nd edn, London, Weidenfeld & Nicolson.
Pawley, M. 1978, *Home Ownership*, London, Architectural Press.
Pearsall, J. 1984, 'France' in M. Wynn (ed.), *Housing in Europe*, London, Croom Helm.
Phillips, D.L. 1979, *Equality, Justice and Rectification*, London, Academic Press.
Phillips, D.R. and Williams, A.M. 1982, *Rural Housing and the Public Sector*, Aldershot, Gower.
Pinker, R. 1979, *The Idea of Welfare*, London, Heinemann.
Rawls, J. 1972, *A Theory of Justice*, Oxford, Oxford University Press.
Reich, C.A. 1978, 'The new property' in C.B. Macpherson (ed.), *Property*, Oxford, Basil Blackwell.
Richardson, A. 1977, *Tenant Participation in Council Housing Management*, Housing Development Directorate Occasional Paper 2/77, London, DOE.
Robinson, R. and O'Sullivan, T. 1983, 'Housing tenure polarization: some empirical evidence', *Housing Review*, vol. 32, no. 4, pp. 116–17.
Robson, W.A. 1966, *Local Government in Crisis*, London, George Allen & Unwin.
Robson, W.A. 1976, *Welfare State and Welfare Society*, London, George Allen & Unwin.
Rose, H. 1983, 'Property of the professionals', *New Statesman*, 30 September, pp. 12–13.
Saunders, P. 1984, 'Beyond housing classes: the sociological significance of private property rights in means of consumption', *International Journal of Urban and Regional Research*, vol. 8, no. 2, pp. 202–25.
Sharp, E. 1973, 'Baroness Sharp discusses Richard Crossman's homework', *The Listener*, vol. 15, no. 3, pp. 335–8.
Shelter 1982, *Housing and the Economy: A Priority for Reform*, London.
Shotton, T. 1983, 'Tenants' right to information', SNHAT News Bulletin, no. 25, pp. 15–16.
Skinner, D. and Langdon, J. 1974, *The Story of Clay Cross*, Nottingham, Spokesman Books.
Sklair, L. 1975, 'The struggle against the Housing Finance Act' in R. Miliband and J. Saville (eds), *The Socialist Register 1975*, London, Merlin Press.
Smith, M. 1977, 'Alternative approaches: unit costs versus deficit systems', *CES Review*, no. 2, pp. 68–77.
Smith, M. and Howes, E. 1978, 'Current trends in local authority housing finance', *CES Review*, no. 3, pp. 25–36.
Smith, P. 1983, 'How targets went wrong', *Public Finance and Accountancy*, December, pp. 28–31.
Spencer, K.M. 1973, 'The Housing Finance Act', *Social and Economic Administration*, vol. 7, no. 1, pp. 3–19.
Stafford, D.C. 1973, 'Housing: policy and administration' in M.H. Cooper (ed.), *Social Policy A Survey of Recent Developments*, Oxford, Basil Blackwell.
Stafford, D.C. 1978, *The Economics of Housing Policy*, London, Croom Helm.
Stanley, J. 1980, *Shared Purchase – a new route to home ownership*, Text of a speech to Chartered Institute of Public Finance and Accountancy, 15 October.
Steele, D. 1980, 'Labour in office: the post war experience' in C. Cook and I. Taylor (eds), *The Labour Party*, London, Longman.
Tarn, J.N. 1973, *Five Per Cent Philanthropy*, Cambridge, Cambridge University Press.
Tawney, R.H. 1978, 'Property and creative work' in C.B. Macpherson (ed.), *Property*, Oxford, Basil Blackwell.

Thoenes, P. 1966, *The Elite in the Welfare State*, J. Banks (ed.), London, Faber & Faber.

Thomas, D. 1983, 'Will the man who put Mrs Thatcher in do so again?', *New Society*, 26 May, pp. 291—3.

Timmins, N. and Walker, D. 1984, 'Anatomy of a bureaucratic bungle', *Times*, 20 January.

Titmuss, R.M. 1968, *Commitment to Welfare*, London, George Allen & Unwin.

Titmuss, R.M. 1973, *The Gift Relationship*, Harmondsworth, Penguin Books.

Townsend, P. 1972, *The Scope and Limitations of Means-Tested Social Services in Britain*, Manchester, Manchester Statistical Society.

Van Weesep, J. 1984, 'Intervention in the Netherlands: urban housing policy and market response', *Urban Affairs Quarterly*, vol. 19, no. 3, pp. 329—53.

Walker, A. (ed.) 1982, *Public Expenditure and Social Policy*, London, Heinemann.

Walsh, C.I. 1983, 'The housing subsidy and related financial implications of the 1980 Housing Act' in the CARAS Team, *A City Not Forsaken? Some political, economic and social implications of the 1980 Housing Act, with special reference to the London Borough of Wandsworth*, Occasional Papers in Sociology and Social Administration no. 1, London, Roehampton Institute.

Warburton, M. 1983, *Housing Finance: The Case for Reform*, London, Catholic Housing Aid Society.

Weale, A. 1978, *Equality and Social Policy*, London, Routledge & Kegan Paul.

Webster, D. 1977, 'New council and private housing: can the subsidy costs argument be settled?', *CES Review*, no. 3, pp. 38—44.

Webster, D. 1979, 'Rent structures: principles and practice', *CES Review*, no. 7, pp. 51—7.

Webster, D. 1980a, 'Housing' in N. Bosanquet and P. Townsend (eds), *Labour and Equality*, London, Heinemann.

Webster, D. 1980b, 'Why Labour failed on housing', *New Society*, 17 January, pp. 117—18.

Whitehead, C. 1977, 'Neutrality between tenures: a critique of the HPR comparisons', *CES Review*, no. 2, pp. 33—6.

Wicks, M. 1973, *Rented Housing and Social Ownership*, Fabian Tract 421, London, Fabian Society.

Williams, P. 1984, 'The politics of property: home ownership in Australia' in J. Halligan and C. Paris (eds) *Australian Urban Politics*, Melbourne, Longman Cheshire.

Wilson, H. 1979, *Final Term: The Labour Government 1974—1976*, London, Weidenfeld & Nicolson and Michael Joseph.

Wright, M. 1981, 'Big government in hard times: the restraint of public expenditure' in C. Hood and M. Wright (eds), *Big Government in Hard Times*, Oxford, Martin Robertson.

Yates, D. 1982, 'The English housing experience: an overview', *Urban Law and Policy*, vol. 5, pp. 203—33.

Index